Welcome to Booked.

Booked. Podcast

PRESENTS

THE BOOKED. ANTHOLOGY

Edited by **PELA VIA**

Compiled by **ROBB OLSON** and **LIVIUS NEDIN**

Published by

media

THE BOOKED. ANTHOLOGY

©2013 VON Media
802 Saratoga Circle
Island Lake, IL 60042

ISBN 978-1-936730-77-3

Presented by Booked.
Edited by Pela Via
Compiled by Livius Nedin and Robb Olson
Typeset and Design by Robb Olson, Livius Nedin and Pela Via

Cover design by Gretchen Grajales. lunajynx.com

CONTENTS

INTRODUCTION
BY ROBB OLSON

NO THEME. NO RESTRICTIONS. We told our authors 'just give us your best.' Pen to page, give it your all. Contained within is evidence that, at the very least, these twenty-five authors honored that request.

We formed Booked. because of our love of stories, and by extension, of talking about stories. We had always stood at a distance from writers, wondering what sort of person could create a collection of words that made us feel something, whether it was joy, sadness, revulsion, arousal, a cheap laugh. From afar. What weird, isolated being is capable? Someone with dogs, probably. Someone who had an inspirational third grade teacher, according to their meager author bios. An emaciated few paragraphs of surface information that amounts to little more than a resume. Maybe a cover story? This was our insight into the people behind the words.

Back then, that was enough.

The podcast allowed us something more. We invited authors onto our podcast, into our lives. In return, they allowed us into theirs. On the record! What started as a professional transaction naturally evolved. Chat sessions, conversations over drinks, sharing their fancy scotch and stumbling drunkely through hotels together. To become friends changed so much for us.

We have the honor of having joined a community brimming with talent.

This book is for the authors who have allowed us into their lives. Shown us not only how skilled they are at telling stories, but also shown us who they are as people. The awe and respect we held for them as writers is amplified now, because we see writing as a mere facet of a much more complex person. We see them as parents, teachers, humans. These people who live the same challenging, frustrating, and sometime soul-crushing lives that we do and somehow still manage to craft a sentence that stirs something inside of us.

If starting a book review podcast has done anything for us, it is to show us how remarkable these writers truly are. This anthology is our thank you, our celebration, of all of them.

Please, keep reading.

–Robb Olson

"These are the kinds of things I dreamed of when I was a teenager. You know, writing stupid little stories. So I just try to enjoy it."
—Booked. Podcast #123 Three Authors

FRED VENTURINI
A POUND OF FLESH

Our backyard had a sagging, wire fence swallowed by vines. The wife called those out-of-control tangles an eyesore and I agreed, but removal was quite a bitch because the damn things were tough as ropes, coming off the fence in a series of wet, resistant pops. I cleared the fence and vines out, but the job put a sore crackle in my back for three days.

A few days later, little green threads popped out of the soil where the fence used to be—infant vines, weak and thin. I bought some Roundup and waited until the weekend, when rain was out of the forecast, to execute the remaining little boogers for good. While waiting, the vines grew towards each other. Only when they find each other do they twirl together and gain their strength. For the hell of it, I tried to unlace them, but separating those two little vines into single threads again would be like getting a knot out of a Slinky.

I told Wendy about how they reminded me of us, about how we slept at night. She doesn't lie on me because I sweat easily and she doesn't want the pillow smelling like old socks. I don't spoon her because my arm's too heavy for her to breathe easy. But at night, I lay my foot over hers. We cross like knotting vines, and sleep.

We fell in love easily, my wife and I. Most love stories have impossible odds or at least one moment of cosmic doubt where an uncertain future unfolds in your mind's eye, complete with disaster, heartache, and all things pessimistic. I haven't had one of those moments after thirty-five years of marriage, two daughters, one cancer scare (hers) and one heart attack (mine). Not to say we never had an argument–Wendy loves to tell the story of our first fight.

I was about to take a new job putting in heating systems for American Standard, a choice that would require moving to a new city, an idea that made us both grumpy. In the middle of the ordeal, she went to California to vacation with her sister. We had an argument about my selfishness, about my audacity to leave her for something as trivial as work. I couldn't even answer her before she hung up, and then she wouldn't answer any more of my calls.

On the day she was to return, I intercepted her parents, who were supposed to pick her up at the airport. I convinced them to stay home so that I could dine on a colossal buffet of crow by going to the airport to give her a surprise pickup. I walked into the terminal with a huge, homemade sign that said I'm sorry, I love you.

She landed, saw the sign, then ran crying into my arms. I cried with her. There was applause that I couldn't hear at the time, but when Wendy tells the story, the thought of that applause gives me chills. I took the job with American Standard, but she came with me as my wife.

Whoever listens to the tale will say, as if complimentary,

"Now that's love!" Translation meaning that embarrassing one-self in public is a surefire way to create a moment of memorable affection. And hell, I was happy to do it. But one moment isn't proof of love. That can only be measured in a lifetime, a collection of moments that add up to answering a simple question, one of her favorite little sayings:

Yes darling, but how much do you love me? Show me. Don't tell me.

I love her very much. Love can be shown in any number of ways, from flowers to poems to signs at the airport. But proof of love can take darker shades. Sometimes, love isn't diamonds or gold, it isn't handwritten cards and surprise, romantic excursions. Sometimes love is deciding whether to take your wife's teeth out with a pipe wrench, or brain her with it.

When I think of our last night together, I think of vines, then fireflies.

In the summer, driving at night, the windshield gets spackled by the guts of lightning bugs–little green freckles of light fading on the dirty glass.

I was stoking the windshield wipers every few minutes, the bursts of fluid smearing the collection of bug film into a grease that blurred the lights of oncoming cars.

She told me I was just making it worse, that she felt like she was riding in a submarine with a windshield instead of a car. By now, I was used to her general driving complaints and instructions, so I just laughed and put my hand on her thigh.

We ate at one of those places that tries to stuff you with hot bread before your overpriced meal even gets there, one of those places with two sets of doors, making it awkward to open the door properly for a lady.

The wife asked for a booth, as always, and we let empty tables get filled up by the Friday night diners as we waited for a vacant booth to open up.

Friday nights are the best for working folks. The entire weekend unfolds, almost gaping, as the work week withers away. But I'm retired now, and Monday no longer exists. Retired, and there are no more workdays, no more absences to make the heart grow fonder. Call it my one moment of doubt–could she really put up with me for every minute of every day? I had no qualms about seeing her face without interruption. Lucky for her, my taste in women coincidentally developed right along with her. I used to love tall, fit blondes with eyes so blue they're almost clear (and easy on the breasts, more than a handful is simply a waste). Then I was infatuated with pregnant blondes with mood swings and sleepy eyes. Then tall blondes who had a few extra pounds because hey, who doesn't at forty? It's just more to love. Now I love women with the occasional gray hair or wrinkle, with skin that feels like soft parchment and a smile aged by coffee and red wine. I hope she's still a sucker for plump, balding, and clumsy after all these years, because I'm not growing hair and I need this belly for my clothes to fit.

We asked the waitress for water–I can't even remember what a fountain soft drink tastes like. You don't get to retire comfortably paying two bucks for a soda every time out. The trick to retirement is to let the four dollar coupon in the Sunday paper pick what restaurant wins your business on a Friday night, order water, and skip the dessert.

"Do you know what you're having?" she asked.

"Don't know," I said. "Something meaty and dead."

"My little carnivore."

I went straight to the steaks and picked out the biggest one.

Screw that little filet mignon—twenty bucks for a hockey puck of beef? My better half scanned the menu like an accountant checking line items, shooing away our waitress twice before asking me, "Do I want the chicken strips or the shrimp pasta?"

"Shrimp pasta."

"Why?"

"Well you always get the chicken strips here, and we're celebrating the transition into our golden years so screw it, take a chance on the seafood."

The waitress had zits and a nice smile. "Folks ready?"

Wendy nodded at me, urging me to order first.

"Ribeye. Rare as you can legally make it."

"I'll have the chicken strips," Wendy said.

Of course she would, and of course she asked for a to-go box to come with her dinner so she could immediately split the meal in half, saving the rest for a nice lunch. Of course we would stop at a convenience store so she could get the candy for the movie for pennies instead of dollars. Of course she asked for the senior discount, but we were still two years away. Of course I love her.

I know the waitress had zits, but I can't remember what movie we saw. She loved the movies, and I never met a dark room I couldn't sleep in.

Yet, anyway.

But the flick had some young actors in it, not like a Nicholson or Newman that would at the very least perk me up a little bit. I've never been in a darker, louder, theater than that one. My wife held my hand, breaking her fingers free to wipe her hands on her dress—my sweating problem persisted even in the palms of my hands, but we were long past complaining about it and well along the path of dealing with it.

We always find each other in the dark. If she's not holding

my hand, I'll shift my knee to break out some of that arthritic rigor-mortis and try to sit normally, without touching, but in a few minutes I feel unplugged and naked, so I put my hand on her thigh until she's ready to hold hands again. Back in the day, it was just to see if she'd allow it. Then it was a precursor to the touching to come. Now, it's just to know she's there.

The ride home was a tired one, a post-9 p.m. excursion that didn't happen often and had our sleep cycles screaming. But she cleaned up and our kiss goodnight turned into one of those moments, those moments you don't waste at our age. You give it a go unless something wilts or dries up, and hope that neither one happens. And wouldn't you know it, my last night with my wife was as pure and natural as the first time we made love. No jellies or little blue pills. No tricks. Something I'm glad to remember, the kind of sex that can only happen post-love, not as a precursor to it.

In the dark, the sheet and comforter are pushed down to my feet. The sex sparked my sweating early, and my skin felt cool. She's got the comforter up to her chin; my wife's got the warm blood of an angel, but the interior thermostat of a damned lizard.

That night, she pressed her foot into my calf and rubbed, the callus on her toe biting me like a little sanding block—a callus she got from wearing her pretty shoes, the ones that matched her "going out" outfit.

The callus let me know she still tried to look her best, just as those chicken strips were to let me know that I may be retired, but nothing had changed.

She drank coffee in the breakfast nook, her favorite place in the house. The big windows offered an intimate view of the rabbits and squirrels, animals that made up her personal zoo in our rural hideaway. To me, they signified good eating from days long past.

But I'd formed an easy partnership with the critters, and eventually, they wouldn't even scamper while I mowed. The threat was gone, my guns were sold, my hunting days a youthful hobby that died the moment she said to me, "I can't imagine killing for sport."

I was tangling with the new garbage disposal, but I wasn't a plumber, not by a long stretch. I had the whole toolbox scattered on the linoleum, and the "easy install" advertised on the box had turned into a Rubik's Cube of a job. Pepper, our gray cat, stared at my tools with a cat's usual look of dread, fascination, and disdain. He was old, fat as a Butterball turkey, dragging his sack of kitty titties across the linoleum.

"Katie has a boyfriend. Did I tell you that?" Wendy asked.

Katie, my baby girl, my youngest. Freshman this year, with a free college education because she was amazing and brilliant—if not for her startling intellect, I wouldn't be retired right now; I'd be grinding out another few years to get her through four years of higher education. My old body had years of work to give, and I would've spent the last drop of whatever I had left to make sure Katie got the world.

"She call this morning? I didn't hear the phone at all."

"Her Myspace page has her listed as 'committed,' and her mood is 'loved.'"

"I don't know if that kind of evidence would hold up in court," I said. "Let's just wait until she decides to spill the beans."

Wendy had mastered the internet; I had not. But sometimes she'd let me see pictures of my girls on those Myspace pages, and I got to see all the strange and weird photos of friends and acquaintances plastered all over the place, and I felt like an alien orbiting my daughters' planet instead of living in it.

I peered back under the sink, toting my screwdriver and flashlight.

"What's Carol's page say?"

"She hasn't been on in a while. Nothing's changed."

Carol, our first. An accident, but a happy one indeed. If I'd known that she would do just about the opposite of anything I asked or wanted, I could've raised her with a smidge more skill. She skipped college, saving a bundle because she wasn't a scholar. Married a guy that I liked—not loved, not hated, but liked. At least during the few times I met him. They got married at a courthouse; the only wedding picture I saw was on that fucking Myspace.

"She used to call," I said. "Maybe spurning me is one thing, I've been tough on her, but you're her mother and I'll be damned if she's—"

"She's not her sister. Me and her talk plenty, and I'm not having this fight again."

So instead of pointing with the screwdriver, I went back under the sink with it. She was right. We'd sit there and argue about Carol, and it was like running on a mental treadmill—hard to make any headway when I'm basically yelling at Carol, only there's no Carol in the room, just Wendy serving as a Carol-scarecrow. She finished her coffee and kissed me on the top of the head before she left the kitchen.

The disposal wasn't cooperating. Sweat was dripping off the tip of my nose like a leaking faucet. I heard the shower running, so I figured it was time for some quiet coffee of my own.

The doorbell rang.

I saw a van through the bay window of the living room—Barnett's Pest Control plastered on the van, with a painted-on phone number of some sort. Hadn't ordered any kind of pest control, so I was expecting a sales call.

When I opened the door, a hand was at my throat before I could even read the name tag on the blue, mechanic's work shirt–Romeo. He grinned, spreading the whiskers on his handlebar mustache. He had hard, sharp fingernails that dug into my throat. Dots formed in my vision as he threw me down.

Not tall, but quite muscular. He pulled a gun. From my Time Life books, I knew it was a 9mm, the gangster's gun of choice. Not that he was a gangster. He wasn't urban, and though he had the greasy, olive skin of an Italian, he wasn't a Mafioso. He wasn't young, but middle-aged, a hardened face with valleys in his skin, and a white dent in the tip of his nose, probably from some brawl.

"Stand up and put your hands behind your back." He sounded oily and smooth. Could've been a jazz singer if he wasn't a psychopath.

He didn't even need the gun to threaten me into compliance. Romeo tied my hands with fingers that felt as thick as shotgun shells, then tossed me onto the couch.

"Wife in the shower?"

"Just take what you want and leave. We have valuables, but little money. I–"

Romeo laughed. He dropped to his knees in front of me, breathing, almost panting. His breath smelled like someone took a shit and tried to spray peppermint around the toilet to cover up the odor. I didn't like his jagged, genuine smile.

"I'm going to take everything I want." The shower water shut off. "What's your name?"

"Harold."

"The wife?"

"Leave my wife out of this."

He scampered to his feet and went into the bedroom, then

walked out with the phone in his hand, the cord dangling like a dead snake, then spiked it on our hardwood floor. White plastic popped off in shards.

"Harold? What's going on?" She came out naked, toweling her hair.

Romeo pointed his gun at my head. "You got three minutes to get into some clothes, Miss Harold, or Mister Harold gets a slug in the ear."

I could see his eyes taking in every inch of my naked wife.

Her face had a look of shock, but she didn't scream, beg, or flinch. She went right into the bedroom and shut the door.

"Nice job there, Harold. She's an oldie but a goodie." He pulled her cellphone from his pocket. "Hope she's not looking for this." Then he spiked that phone on the floor too.

"Leave her alone," I said, wishful.

"Don't worry, I'm not in it for the sex." He sat down, then put his arm around me. I was already thinking of ways to get my wife out of this, but a solid plan wasn't forming. Running and fighting were not high on my list of possible successes.

"Hell, I'm not in it for the money." He spoke in my ear, but loud. I could feel his words vibrate inside of me. "You could say there's an entertainment thing going on here, but I'm not quite in it for that either."

Romeo's hot breath warmed my face. "You could say, pal, that I'm just the happiest man in the world, and you and your wife are going to keep it that way."

Wendy came out of the bedroom, shuffling across the hardwood, pieces of shattered phone clicking against her feet. The puffiness of her face betrayed her; she'd cried while looking for her cellular.

"The happy couple," Romeo said. His gun was holstered in

his pants. "You have a basement?"

Yes, we had a basement. Cellar is more like it. Concrete floor, naked ceilings, wet, stinking walls. A space one could finish and make into a wet bar with a big screen and pool table, if one had, say, about thirty grand for waterproofing, finishing, and furnishings. Cans, jars, boxes, cobwebs. A dehumidifier buzzing in the corner, covered in a sheath of dust. Cords and lines snaking across the joists in the ceiling, old termite pathways carved into the wood.

One tiny window where gray light leaked in, shielded by the window well cover buried against it. No escape, but Romeo checked anyway, and pronounced the area "awfully tidy."

He trotted up the stairs and locked the door, leaving us together in the basement to mull our fate.

As we always did in darkness, we found each other, speaking in urgent whispers, our chins on each other's shoulders as we embraced.

"What does he want?" Wendy asked.

"He'll take what he wants and leave. He's just scaring us." A lie, but I didn't want her to shake anymore.

"Can anyone help us?"

No, not with this rural home with the big yard. Big yard, big yard was all she wanted during the house hunt. Screw the long commute, doesn't matter that most customers for heating and cooling are–ahem–near a damned city.

"Maybe the mailman will notice something about the van parked out front," I said.

"What if he hides it?"

"Shhh."

"Can we get out the window?" The window was about the size of a shoebox, not even an option.

"Quiet now," I said. "Panicking doesn't do a damn bit of good."

Above us, the invader's footsteps creaked against the floor. He was making his way around the house, and the sound was like sonar, giving us a fix on his position. He went from bathroom to bedroom, from family room to living room, pausing at each stop.

"See? He's looking for valuables," I told her.

The sound then spread towards the basement door, the steps picking up pace until we could hear him working the doorknob open.

Couldn't see to the top of the steps, not from our huddled position in the corner, but something soft hit the bottom of the basement steps. I heard him snort a ball of snot, then spit, and then he closed the door again.

"What is—"

I jammed my hands against her face, trying to block her view.

"Don't look honey, just keep your eyes closed, okay?"

Fat chance. She looked anyway as I scrambled for a blanket. Pepper would've died peaceful, at rest, and would've had a helluva funeral back by our oak tree, but the demon upstairs cut his head off and tossed his carcass into the basement with us, his fat body leaking from the neck stump all over the floor, a trail of blood droplets sprinkled across the wooden steps where he'd cartwheeled down.

Quick as Pepper in his days of youth, I wrapped him up in a sheet and laid him in a corner. Wendy gasped and screamed now, screamed out things like "help," and "you bastard," and "leave us alone."

I hugged her again and tried to muffle her cries with my shoulder.

"I love you," I told her, again and again. She sobbed and shook against me. The cat was like our only son, and unlike Carol he didn't ignore us. Unlike Katie, he'd never fly the nest. He could bathe himself and shit in a box and never judge or argue.

When I married her, I wasn't a cat man. As a young man, it was my hunting dogs or nothing, but I cried and sobbed right along with her, mourning Pepper, never realizing how much I loved the little purring prick until he was gone.

I heard a rattle–the sucking of snot–breaking us both from our collective grieving. Romeo sat on the bottom step. He spit a pile of phlegm onto the blood-stained cement where Pepper landed. Then, he sneezed and spit again.

The son of a bitch was allergic to cats, or had a pretty nasty cold in the middle of summer.

Then, he lit a cigarette with a match of all things. I've seen a few movies in my day, and even I knew that if you were bad to the bone, if you were evil, you were a cigarette smoker. Yet the sound of that match took me back to Wendy's smoking days, back in the seventies when matches were still pretty common. We'd just made love for the first time, and she lit a smoke. The match flickered in the dark, and while most people hear a pert hiss when a match strikes, I don't. I hear my wife's whisper, and feel her hand cool against my sweating stomach, rising and falling with my rapid breath.

Romeo smoked and spat, sitting on the step.

"I'll bring his litter box down if you all have to pee or shit." Then he got up, reached behind the waistband of his jeans, and pulled out a chef's knife.

"Noticed a Bible up there in your living room. Spine's worn out, too. You two biblical?"

Wendy was a devout Catholic. I was just Catholic enough to give her and her family the wedding they required for their bless-ing. The patron saint I selected for my confirmation was Saint Lawrence. I liked books and he was the saint evoked by librarians.

Didn't know until after my confirmation that he ended up getting barbecued on the streets of Rome.

"Well I'm not biblical," Romeo said. "One of you two want to tell me what part in there has the pound of flesh line? Pound of flesh for something, right?"

Wendy knew the Bible inside and out. As a reader, so did I, but Wendy wasn't going to quote scripture to explain a pound of flesh. She couldn't. It was from Shakespeare, from *The Merchant of Venice*, and the assailant, like my wife, was someone you didn't make a habit of correcting.

He threw the knife down.

"A pound of flesh, Harold. One pound of your own flesh will make me happy."

In my quicker days, I might've tried to grab the knife and gut him. His gun was holstered and he was standing close enough, but he was younger, and if it didn't work, Wendy was going to pay the price.

Wendy grabbed my shoulder and squeezed hard enough to send a hot flash of pain into my neck.

"You can pick the spot," he said. "I would say the rump, or the front of your thigh. Look out for the big arteries. Most guys have thick shoulders, but you're older. Yeah, the front of your leg should be a nice, one-pound filet."

"For you to eat?" I asked, inching closer to the knife–just in case.

He stooped down and slapped me across the face in one rapid move. I couldn't even flinch, so there was no way I could physically fight or outmaneuver this beast.

"That's disgusting, Harold. Truly. One pound of flesh for you to cut off, and she's going to eat it. But don't you worry, girl. I'll cook him up first. I'm no barbarian."

Before I could even let that offer sink in, Wendy was talking.

"Will you let us go if we do it." Wendy said, the whimper gone. One's only got so many tears and so much fear. When the freshness of that fear is gone, something else sets in—the strength that survival instinct provides. She was always stronger than me in all the ways that mattered.

Romeo just laughed. "You've seen my face. I've got DNA on your god damned basement floor, with fingerprints everywhere. You fuckers are as good as dead. But …"

Don't say it. Don't say it. Don't say it. He let it linger, tasting the words before he said them.

"Found some nice family photos. Found an address book, too. Katie and Carol have never seen my face, but I can guarantee you that if you don't do what I say, they're going to get plenty of my DNA all over them while they're alive, and their bodies will burn when I'm done."

Wendy sprung up from her crouch, trying to attack him. I grabbed her and held her, shocked by her rage-fueled strength. Romeo spurred it on with his smile.

"I may be poor, but I figure I can get to Katie's dorm room, number 117, at Michelson Dorm in sunny Southern California, in about a thirteen hour drive if I hold my piss. You think?"

She spat on him, some of it splattering on my ear as it passed. I was positioned like a lineman, holding her around the waist as she thrashed.

"Don't you even say her name," she screamed.

"Carol. Katie. Who's the better fuck, you think?"

"Sit your ass down," I said in her ear. "You're only egging him on."

"I'll kill him," she said, then glared at him. "I'll kill you. You hear me? With my own hands, I'll take the life right out of you."

This from a woman who would crash her car before hitting

a squirrel.

"Think it over," he said. "It's a big decision. When you make up your mind, scream like one of your whore daughters and I'll be right down. I wouldn't miss the old man filleting his leg for the world."

He sucked down the last of his cigarette, calm as could be. Here was a man that didn't rattle. The beast had done these things before. The demon had experience, a coolness that made me realize right in the dark, metallic parts of my guts, that he was absolutely right and honest, and we wouldn't escape this alive.

Just as he'd strutted down the stairs, he took a big step over the blood stain and walked right back up, closing the door behind him, shadows sucking dry the bars of light that leaked from upstairs. In the dark again, my wife slapped me across the face. A ringing thud, harder than Romeo had slapped me.

"Those are our daughters!"

"Do you want him to break your arms? This is the kid who yanks the legs off flies for fun. Christ, you heard what he wants. And you want to go after him?"

"Both of us could overwhelm him. We could—"

"We could piss him off. Get shot. Get our girls in a world of hurt, if he's telling the truth and by your Bible, that son of a bitch is as honest as a nun when he's talking about pain."

She dropped onto her rump and let her face hang into her hands, but didn't stay down for long.

"Then you do it."

"What?"

"Give him a pound of flesh. Call his bluff."

What was I going to say? That I didn't love our daughters enough to slice a piece of my leg off? This is my wife, a woman I've said that I would die for. Same for my girls. But everyone says that. How often do we get handed a knife?

The door upstairs opened again.

"I've changed my mind," he hollered, trotting down the stairs. In his hands was the pipe wrench I was using under the kitchen sink. The wrench had flecks of silver where the red paint had skinned off–my old monkey wrench, never intended for what Romeo had in mind.

"I like you two," Romeo said. "You may not think it, but I do. And I can tell you're reasonable people."

He dropped the pipe wrench. It somersaulted in a series of clinks, coming to rest at my feet.

"And you've got some pretty daughters and you're Godly people, so I'll give you a choice. Either Wendy here can eat a Harold filet, or you can take her teeth out with that pipe wrench. Ten teeth or a pound of flesh and that should be good for saving one of your daughters, I'd think."

The basement stunk like moss, blood, and sweat. The shadows looked darker in the crags of his face.

"No," I told him. "Fuck you."

He blew a smoke ring with a curled, snakish tongue. I was expecting a grin, but instead, for the first time, he looked angry.

"Unless some blood gets on that wrench, or that blade," he drew his gun, "I'm going to let you live." He snorted, then spat again. The vile thing waved his gun to punctuate each word: "I'm going to tie you both up, but not before I give you a sandwich and some water so you can last down here for a couple days. I'm going to catch a bus to Southern Cal, and I'm going to make a mess of little Katie. Then, I'm going to call the police so that they can come and untie you, and tell you your little girl's spread all over the back of some van on the back of some highway, and they want you to come identify the chunks. And you get to live knowing that you did that to her. Unless," he kicked the wrench into my foot, "you give me the blood I'm looking for."

"Why are you doing this?" Wendy grabbed my hand, and we squeezed each other. "Why?"

"Why fuckin' smoke?" he replied, taking a puff, a deep one, closing his eyes for a split second, holding his breath, then letting the smoke pour out his nostrils.

"Oh. I remember. It makes me happy." He backed up to the steps and sat down to finish his cigarette. "You've got three minutes." He didn't have a watch or timepiece, making the deadline even more urgent.

Wendy damn near threw my hand away from hers. She picked up the pipe wrench and put it in her mouth. The top lip of the wrench's claw clicked against her teeth, and the bottom claw rested against her lower gumline.

"Stop," he said, still smoking. "That won't work. He's got to do it." The smile came back. "Shit, that'll hurt him worse than it hurts you, I'll bet."

She held out the wrench. "Do it quickly."

"I can't."

"If you love us, you'll do it."

"I can't hurt you, honey. Let me get the knife and cut my leg up. I just—"

She kissed me on the lips, stopping my rant. "You may hit an artery and die on the spot. The teeth are just pain. Just a little ouchie. It won't hurt a bit. I won't let him hurt me, you understand? Don't you tell me you love me. Show me."

She shoved the wrench at me. "I'm going to have to get dentures anyway in a couple years, right?"

Wendy smiled a little, weak and forced, then sat down, bracing her back against the rough wall, her mouth agape, waiting.

"Well, isn't she tough as fuckin' nails," he said. "What she says, goes, cowboy. Get to it."

I had a decision to make. Romeo wasn't going to stop. She was blinded by her love for the girls, but Christ, couldn't she see that he wouldn't stop with just teeth? I could've put that wrench into her brain before she even registered what I was doing. She would be free, a proper Catholic getting her proper entry into Heaven where Romeo couldn't touch her, and he'd be left to deal with me.

Kill her or torture her. What a world. But I couldn't imagine her dead.

The teeth came out almost whole, the wrench's claw plowing through her gumline as the upper claw levered down. The teeth on the edges of the wrench's mouth cracked into pieces, but Romeo, being the generous man that he was, gave us credit for those.

Prying out the upper teeth was tougher because she kept flinching and my hands were weak and numb. We worked through a film of tears, pain, and anguish, but we pried out enough teeth to save our daughters, handing him six whole teeth down to the root, one more decent tooth, and then the pieces of the rest.

I tore off a hunk of a blanket we found piled in the basement, and we stuffed the dusty cloth into her mouth to help with the bleeding. I kneeled next to her, hoping my touch and whisper could ease the pain, but I couldn't even imagine how she felt. She shook on the verge of shock, ropes of snot blowing out of her nose, which was all she could breathe through with the cloth in her mouth. That was when I began to urge death along to save her from the pain and punishment.

"These teeth make me very happy," he said from the step, his face shrouded in the lingering atmosphere of the smoke. The teeth were covered with bits of gummy flesh, sticky with blood. He palmed all ten of them, rattling them around like dice. "You guys are troopers. Now choose which daughter you just saved."

Wendy screamed into her muzzle-gauze, making her eyes bulge, but I knew what she was thinking and saying–*how dare he make us choose.*

I don't know who said it. I don't know if it was my heart, my soul, my love, my anger or my hurt.

"Katie," I said, God damn me. "Save Katie."

He nodded once and then went upstairs.

Time melted. Night came, I could tell because the basement became full black, a sensory deprivation chamber where all I could hear was Wendy's whimper as we held each other, resting against the concrete but not sleeping.

In the dark, we found each other, our fingers interlacing, unbroken by dawn or pain. We lingered in a place just before sleep, where there was an appropriate numbness, the night nothing but a long period of hope for a miracle.

I remembered our talks about death. Wendy would talk of Heaven and I, of course, wasn't so sure. We never truly argued, but debated, healthy for each of us. Carol was out with her friends and we'd dropped Katie off at softball practice. On the way home, we spoke of it again, and Wendy had said, "If I die first, I'll show you. I'll come back and say I told you so." She laughed.

"I guess if I die," I said, "I won't be back to tell you I told you so, because if I did, then you'd be right, and it would defeat the whole purpose. But I'd come tell you if you were right, though. I'd miss you." We drove through curvy roads on a bright day and we made the promise off that joke. Die first, give a sign to the other. And like that, we'd amended our vows from "until death do us part" to "until death temporarily separates us."

A sneeze woke me from the lingering vision. Romeo, pipe wrench in hand, smoking on his bottom step.

"Wake up, lovebirds," he said, tapping the wrench against the wall. I guess a whole night had evaporated, but what I saw wasn't dreams, what I felt wasn't sleep. "We've got to save Carol today, soldiers. Rise and shine."

I sat up, but Wendy was limp.

"She dead? Thought she was stronger than that." Romeo walked over and gave her a kick in the lower back. I bolted to my feet, feeling like I was moving quickly, but I was in slow-motion to Romeo, for sure.

"What are you going to do, old man?" He stared, smiling, inviting a fight.

She stirred, rolling over, the blanket stuffed in her mouth gone. A muzzle of dried blood masked her face and nose. She didn't even react to the kick, just sat up and said something that sounded like "The Lord will punish you" to Romeo, but instead, came out warbled as she talked through wounded gums.

"I read some Bible last night," Romeo said, backing away from me, twirling the wrench in his hands, "and I didn't find any shit about teeth in there. I didn't come across that pound of flesh, either, but there's this one story that mentioned a jawbone."

He threw the wrench at my feet. "Carol's price is your wife's jawbone."

"That'll kill her," I said, my voice croaking. I was dry, hungry, my body nothing but a nub, my soul dim inside. I was barely there.

"Figure it'll kill her slow, too," he said. "Painful. Lots of nerves in the jaw, don't you know? It's why boxers get knocked out when they get popped in the jaw. Bundle of nerves that cut off important signals to the brain, or some shit. Big blood vessels in there too. Painful and bloody. But it's the price we pay for the ones we love, right? Or do you even love Carol?"

"Yes."

"Do you?" He pointed to the wrench. "Show me, cowboy. Don't tell me."

I picked it up because I'd had enough. I took a breath, getting the gumption together to make a run at the beast, flailing, hoping to catch him by surprise. But Wendy tugged at my sleeve, with sharp strength that betrayed her frail condition. She couldn't really talk. Her eyes were slanted, the lids heavy from pain and exhaustion. She was hurting, and knew she wasn't going to make it, so she didn't care at this point—that simple.

She didn't mouth any words, but just nodded. *Yes. Yes.* A silent plea for Carol's safety.

God bless her, she got on her knees, then wrapped her hands around mine, prayer-hands sandwiching my hands, which were squeezing the handle of the wrench. She guided the edge of the wrench to her mouth, opened wide, and wedged it softly onto her lower jaw. The clamping edges of the wrench's mouth rested on her decimated, toothless gumline. A mix of spit and blood leaked from her chin, like the white stuff in undercooked eggs.

Tears flooded her eyes, and stayed there, not falling until they built up so much pressure they scattered down her face in tributaries. I could feel her head moving, tugging me, urging me to pry and yank the jaw right off her body to save Carol.

I eased the wrench away from her face. I leaned to her, and then kissed her on her mangled lips.

I whispered, "I'm sorry, I love you."

One swing, and the sharp angle of the wrench shattered the top of her skull. I'm sure it was painless, caving in like that. She didn't cry out, but twitched, the nerves firing off one last time. Her blood lingered on my lips from the kiss, and now it was on my hands. I have to believe that I spared her from something terrible, and might have done it at the cost of my own daughter, if the madman was to be believed.

A single shot rang out and a slug slammed into my leg.

"You fucker!" A boot to my ribs. A kick rattled my own teeth— my perfect, precious, whole teeth. "You shouldn't have ruined the party, cowboy. Wrong move." More kicks, in my back, in my stomach, but my hands wouldn't move to protect myself. The fingers were clamped over the slug wound in my leg, blood bursting between my fingers from the gunshot.

I wouldn't be long for this world, but all he could do was kill me. I thought I won.

He left me to myself, and upstairs, I heard things breaking. His steps were harsh and quick. The beast was wrecking the house in anger. The demon screamed and cackled, punching walls and kicking tables.

If he killed me, his games were over, and he knew it.

I found Wendy's body in the dark and held her against me. Sleep didn't find me. Sleep didn't exist anymore. I think I just blacked out.

I hoped it was a nightmare, seeing Carol tied up and gagged in the corner of the basement. I wished it was a dream, seeing her husband's corpse face down on the floor with a halo of blood around his head.

I crawled over to Carol.

"Daddy? Are you alive?"

She was cried dry, her eyes drawn down to slits, but was still dry-sobbing, trying to catch her own breath. I shushed her as I crawled, shushed her like I did when she was a baby, back in the days she loved me in a way that made sense to me.

"I wanted to surprise you," she said between bursts of breath, "to make things okay, and Mom, is that Mom? Is that—"

Then, she just babbled, gagged by sorrow and pain. I dragged myself along until my hand found hers. She clamped on tight and kissed it—seemed to calm her down a bit.

"What do we do, Daddy? What do we do?"

"Shhh. Quiet for now. We don't want to get his attention."

"Attention?" she said. "Do you hear that?"

I didn't, but I listened. Sizzling. Steps in the kitchen. He was cooking.

"He told Mark to give him a pound of flesh, but he wouldn't."

Mark, her husband, was a burly guy. Strong. One of the reasons I liked him is that he looked like he could protect Carol. But now he was dead. Looked like a gunshot or two in his head, but his shoulder—

"He's cooking a piece of his shoulder. Says if I don't celebrate my husband's life and eat it, that he's going to find Katie and—"

She lurched into a hysterical fit again, squeezing my hand so hard the fingertips tingled. I didn't have a plan, other than the wrench or the knife, and I wasn't going to harm a hair on Carol's head in such a way, even if I'd only have to live with the act for a few minutes before taking myself.

I had no brilliant plan. So I did what a weak man would do. Maybe that's what I am—weak. I took myself away from the basement. I just gave up, lying down next to Carol, thinking about my final date with my wife, thinking about my life before it became confined to the hell of this basement. Think, think, think. Thinking of final dates and softball games when the girls were young. Thinking of my arguments with Carol as she aged, rebellious, hating my advice, punishing me with relentless silence. Thinking of chicken strips and bedtime kisses. Thinking of thirteen-year-old Katie and her blond, Wendy-ish hair, wondering how I'd keep the boys away when she got older. Carol and her green eyes, a movie star's eyes, marred by dark makeup and a brooding, teen-age demeanor that kept them from connecting with me when a look was all that I needed. And thinking of the vines from that old fence—I never sprayed that Roundup, and I remember Wendy watching the bunnies and squirrels play in the unfenced, wild vines that reminded me of the way we slept, the way we lived.

My mind drifts and fades, from old memories to the hotly branded pain I feel now, making death a friend and ally against the lunatic roaming my wrecked home. His steps creak as he walks in the kitchen, close to the door. That fucking sizzle; he's cooking in my kitchen. How comfy.

One memory leads me to the solution—retirement. Forty years of heating and cooling systems installation, maintenance, and sales experience, and not once did I think of a way to numb the pain away.

Enough of this.

Won't be long before Romeo comes down here with pipe wrench games and a Mark-meat meal. He'll tell Carol I didn't pick her, and he'll make me take up the wrench again, the one with my wife's blood on it. He'll make me choose—kill Carol to save Katie, or some variation.

I drag my useless leg along, but I make it to the furnace nook. This isn't like the garbage disposal. No problems using my hands and the chef's knife to bypass the automated detection system on the hose running from our propane tanks to the heating system.

The propane gas rushes out of the hose like a draining pool

toy. I crawl back into the basement, trying to make it back to Carol, urging her in my mind to stay quiet. She grieves in the corner. Shock looks to be setting in. All the better.

I've recited propane facts a thousand times, to each customer, to my own family, the Miranda warning of my profession. The propane isn't poisonous. It displaces oxygen. Breathe enough of it, you get tired and irritable. Sleepy. You don't wake up because it takes the oxygen right out of your lungs. A painless, silent death.

If, of course, Romeo doesn't come down here and smell the rotten eggs.

Propane is tasteless and odorless, but so dangerous, an odorant is added as a safety precaution, making it easier to detect even a small leak by smell.

But the gas is also heavy, filling the basement like invisible water from the bottom up. The bottom, where I'm crawling to my daughter. The bottom, where my Carol is slumped against the wall.

The gas is going to take a few minutes to do the job, so Romeo needs to stay up there a while longer. If the scent hits him in the kitchen, we'll be long dead, suffocated painlessly—but if he comes down here and smells that familiar smell, he'll know I'm fucking with his games again. I can't imagine the torture Carol would endure should that happen. I need him to find dead bodies, not rebellious ones that stoke his anger.

I'm not on good terms with God, so I talk to my wife, which comes easier. *Now's a good time for that sign,* I tell her. Keep the demon upstairs. Let me die with my daughter, holding her, with no blood, no wrenches.

Katie. What about Katie? When he comes down and finds us dead, when he smells the eggs and knows what I've done—

what about Katie?

Protect her, I beg. *Watch over her with love.*

I crawl away from the furnace nook now, towards Carol, passing my wife's corpse.

Bring Carol home, I ask, *and me, if you'd have me. If God would have me after what I've done.*

Carol is coughing her way out of her fit of shock and grief, but loud enough for Romeo to hear, if he's listening.

"This is my fault," I whisper to Carol, reaching out for her, dragging myself near her lap. "I love you, baby girl."

She holds out her shaking hands and cradles my head against her lap. Her hair is seaweed, sticking to her face and cheeks in sweaty strands. My tears make dark patches on her jeans.

"We're going to die, aren't we?" She strokes my hair. "I smell the eggs, Daddy. You taught me about the eggs a long … I'm sorry." She hugs my head. "I'm sorry things stayed this way for so long."

She's slurring now. That's a big leak I made, and right now, I feel like an anesthesiologist is asking me to count backwards from ten, and no matter how strongly you feel like you can make it down to one, you never do. You just fade out, nice and soft, like landing in a bed of fresh hay.

My head's limp in her lap and somewhere, far away, I hear a door open. I hear footsteps descending the basement stairs, muted clicks that echo as I fade.

Romeo, Romeo, wherefore art thou Romeo?

Call it Pepper's revenge. Romeo hacks and spits, too congested to smell the rotten eggs mixed in with the dampness and the carcasses.

I see him through a gassy haze, like he's standing on a hot

road. And my wife, God bless her, gives me an answer.

Like a lover's whisper all those years ago, a match strikes in the darkness.

> "I don't think anything good comes from the comfort zone. So it was a very late night writing binge in Bolivia, I had a wad of coca leaves in my mouth the size of a softball, and started writing until I made myself nervous."
> —Booked #36 *Warmed and Bound* interview

CRAIG CLEVENGER
THE CONFESSION OF ADELAI SHADE

The day they hanged Horatio was the day the Reverend Hoyle re-opened the church that had been losing paint and gathering weeds for as long as anyone could remember. Thing is, I never met anyone who'd personally shook hands with the Reverend, except of course Lilly. But one day, that big steamship chain with the padlock big as your fist was gone and the front doors were wide open, choir voices spilling out.

Horatio had everyone thinking he was smart, but I saw what he passed for brains as nothing but second-guessing his instincts, sneaking around on all fours when he should have been walking with his shoulders back and his chin out. Never you mind, Horace was good for a lookout and had a nose for empty houses with loose windows. But he wasn't no damn killer, that much I can tell you.

"He don't eat, shit, piss or sleep," Horace said to me, last time I saw him. He'd lost a goodly number of pounds and moved like a man three times his age.

"He got tools," he said. "Must have been days I was in there with him. Deacon just put a sheet of paper in front of me. Nothing on it, so white it was like the sun coming off it. Just wanted me to put my name at the bottom, said he'd sort out the details later. I guess whatever they needed to make a show of hanging someone for, they put that there later. Looks like they had a killing to make go away."

Word was that around Reverend Hoyle, cancers were cured and statues bled. Since the Reverend arrived, most of the whole town went for a dunk in the river. Even the sheriff and his deputies went and got themselves ordained as ministers in the Rev. Hoyle's church. Seems upholding man's law wasn't enough for them. I seen more than one do-gooder preacher come through here. They don't last, never, no sir. They're always welcome to give it their best, though. See, churches hold services and fund raisers, all manner of occasions that bring folks together who don't mind their pockets well enough when they're in a crowd. Then they got funerals they announce in the paper. You know who died, who their friends and loved ones are, so you know whose houses are empty for the afternoon. Let's just say I was cynical when I saw the locks come off the church. But even though I never met the man, I welcomed the Reverend Hoyle with open arms.

That night, the boys and I drank to Horatio.

"He never gave anyone up, never said nothing," said Tommy.

"What do you mean?" said Norton. "You thought Horace would rat us out?"

"Them deputies'll make anyone sing. All they need is a bag of buckshot, some brass knuckles. Hell, they'd buy Jack the Ripper a drink, not give a hoot if he were walking free, long as they got the collar on someone, anyone, so's they can make rank. Heard they just give you a blank sheet of paper, make you sign it. You don't got to tell them what you know, just what it is they want to hear."

"Tommy, you're scaring everybody. Here, boys," I raised my glass, "To Horatio."

We drank, sang a few and drank more. Come midnight, we're all missing Horace something terrible. But what nobody's saying and we're all thinking is the iron's hot. Maybe the deputies didn't get their man, but they got somebody. They gave Horace to the papers and the papers gave him to the dogs. See, long as there's a killer running loose, they sell papers. But then you got the citizens making a ruckus that nothing's being done, so the city brass starts yanking leashes and the coppers start notching their billy bats if they so much as catch a man wearing the wrong color shoes after the holiday. Them school kids smoking on the street cars? They'd be wearing stripes and breaking rocks, if the coppers had their way. Yeah, the papers get the working stiffs worked up, then coppers start looking for anyone with a jacket they can put in a room with a deputy and a blank sheet of paper. But things were quiet, now. We could start moving again, and I had a few marks lined up.

"Jesus, Mary and Joseph," said Tommy. "The church is on fire."

From the window of the Hammer & Spur you could see the hill crest where the church stood just beyond. It was like something had crashed from the sky, the hilltop all lit up and the flames roaring. We grabbed our hats and ran, and were halfway up the road when it occurred to me, ain't nobody called the fire brigade. Not that I cared one way or the other about the church burning, but it struck me as peculiar that the whole time we were on foot, not a single engine company passed us.

What was really funny though, was we got closer and heard singing.

At the top of the hill, we see the church ain't on fire at all. Hundreds of people were gathered around a bonfire in front, they're dancing and clapping and singing. I couldn't say what, though. I don't know church songs from nothing, they're all the same to me. But these folks, they're carrying on and feeding the flames. They'd be singing and clapping, then somebody'd push through the crowd and hurl a set of crutches onto the pile, maybe a cane. I count five or six wheelchairs, what's left of them, at the center of the blaze. Those rims got to be a thousand degrees by now. One of them collapses and the whole bonfire shifts, blows sparks into the air and the crutches and canes keep coming.

"Gentlemen," said Deputy Jones. "Good evening."

Let me tell you some things about Deputy Jones. Say you dug up Lincoln's corpse, gave it a clean shave and a hundred-dollar suit, then you throw in a matching black Stetson to cover the hole in his head where the soul leaked out, you got Deputy Jones. Cyrus said he comes in three days a week for a shave and he never once seen the man bleed. Now, Deputy Jones got that five-pointed badge on his lapel, but he don't carry no gun. He got a hunting knife, instead, if you can believe that. Big old Bowie knife with a bone handle. Rumor is, you ask him what kind of bone and Jones'll just tell you, femur. Like you're supposed to guess which animal the femur came from. Me and the boys don't do stickups, we're strictly second-story men. But let me tell you, if all the Sheriff's deputies were like Jones, bunch of lanky old buzzards upholding the law with nothing but hunting knives and their spectacles, hell, I'd be the greatest bank robber in history.

"And good evening to you, Deputy Jones."

"It's Deacon," said Jones. "My ordination at the hand of the Reverend Hoyle supersedes the title bestowed by our Sheriff. Now, I'm of a mind to disregard the offense, as I reckon you've not heard the news on account of you ain't never set foot in a church, unless was a funeral you thought you could pry the gold out of the dead man's mouth. But hear me on this, heathen: you address me as anything other than Deacon, I'll cut your thumbs off."

Deacon Jones gave me a look like he was staring through to the back of my head. I don't need to look around at all to know Tommy and Norton have taken each three giant steps backward. The Deacon removed a small snuff pouch from his watch pocket and with the un-groomed nail of his little finger extracted a few grains of powdered tobacco mixed with what looked like dried soda.

"Now," said Deacon Jones after a generous huff into each nostril, "What say you boys enlighten me as to exactly what you aim to do up here among these good, God-fearing people?"

"Well, Deacon Jones, Sir. We saw the commotion from down at the Hammer, thought the church was on fire and so came running. Directly."

"Suppose you had a mind to dig a well with your bare hands," said the Deacon. "Like Moses swinging at the rock, bring up enough water to save God's house. What it looks to me like, anyway, since you didn't say nothing about calling the fire company and you ain't carrying no buckets."

The Deacon reached into his watch pocket once more for a taste of snuff.

"Mighty Christian of you. Damn near heroic, I'd say. Least I can do is extend an invitation to y'all to join our celebration."

"All these folks burning their crutches and wheelchairs," I said. "Am I to believe the Rev. Hoyle healed them all?"

"Your belief don't mean shit, heathen. Them folks walking tonight who wasn't this morning? It's their belief what saved them, not yours."

"Well, pardon me, Deacon Jones, but I don't recollect seeing that many cripples in this town of ours."

"You can't see, son, because you're in darkness. Maybe to-night's time you see the light. Give a holler, that happens. I'm vested so's I can baptize you. Me and you can take a walk down to the river, just the two of us. I'll drown your sins, but good."

Deacon Jones excused himself, and while I was no less eager to decline his invitation to the festivities than were Tommy and Norton, I can't rightly say I was as pale as those two were in the wake of the Deacon's admonishment. I was of a mind to head back to the saloon when I saw her. A big doe-eyed flower, she filled my stomach full of butterflies. I decided right then to be-come a citizen, that if a woman like that wanted me to leave the life, then that's what I'd do.

I saw the ring on her hand, yes sir. I ain't blind. Way I see it, though, woman's got as much rights as any man. I know, sounds kind of backward, downright loony to some folks. But I figure a woman's got her own right to make her mind about where she wants to be and who she wants to be with. Call me a home wreck-er, I say bull. Nobody doesn't have a gun to their head doesn't do anything they don't want to do. I wanted to know her name and so she told me. Lilly, it was. No mystery at all, that little lady was a flower. I wanted to walk Lilly around the lake, and she wanted to walk with me. Simple as that.

Now I know believing in free will and all doesn't mean the man wearing the other ring don't have a vengeance streak in his heart and the Colt to back it up. My experience, the kind of man who ropes a prize like Lilly is the kind of man who comes look-ing for any man tinkering with what God has declared a union. So when Lilly goes all quiet and trembling at the mention of her husband, I get the picture, and I start running the odds on wheth-er this little peach is worth the risk. I ask her who her husband is and damned if what she didn't tell me almost made me fall into the water from laughing so hard.

He's a preacher, she said.

All the women in the world, the most beautiful I ever seen was this little flower married to a man of God. Right then and there, I decided to make Lilly mine. I figured it would be cinch, but I had no idea. That preacher husband of hers never put up a fight. Next thing I knew, Lilly's standing on the sidewalk with a pair of suitcases next to her, ringing the bell to my flat. I was more than happy to oblige and let me tell you, for a preacher's wife, she sure knew how to take care of a man. Picture frames came tumbling off the wall, middle of the afternoon and Lordy, the things that woman hollered would have made the Devil hisself plug his pointed ears. Never felt so good in my life.

We hadn't even tied the knot, hell, she hadn't even divorced the man, before word got out. I was back at the Hammer & Spur, deciding between the twenty year-old scotch or the ten year-old single barrel, when Humphrey sets a snifter in front of me, fills it with top shelf brandy. And when I say top shelf, I mean he needs the ladder to bring it down.

On the house, he says.

I learned years ago not to look a gift horse in the mouth, and given how often I see any kind of horse, I didn't ask no questions. I toasted my own good luck, drank the brandy, still had money for a scotch, so ordered a tumbler of the 20-year, neat. Humphrey ain't taking my money for that, either. He's smiling like he just struck oil and for the first time since I can remember, I don't remember leaving the place. I know that don't make sense but it's the truth. I wake up in my own bed, wearing the clothes I went out in the night before, my money still in my pocket, my head feeling like it's made of bricks. Never realized how loud the clanging of the streetcars could get so early in the morning.

Lilly tells me it ain't early, that it's nearly noon. Lordy, I didn't know if I should thank Humphrey or sock him. Lilly fixed me a tonic for my head and ironed me a fresh shirt. I'd made a promise that I was a different man, so it was time to go look for honest work.

Usually the boys are at the track during the day, then retire to the Hammer for drinks. There were no races that afternoon, so I headed directly to the saloon and sure enough, found the place empty but for the crew. They looked mighty sullen.

"Gentlemen, you couldn't have lost much at the races if the horses weren't running. Or do I dare say what lousy gamblers you all are?"

Tommy looked up from his whiskey and said, "You don't follow the papers much, do you?"

Norton pointed to the morning Gazette, the headline in those big block letters spelling doom for everyone in our line of work for a long while. Investigators found a body last night, a decorated copper with a dime-sized hole in the center of his forehead.

"Bet the whites of his eyes had gone black," said Norton.

"They tell you about where the bullet went in," said Tommy, "but not where it came out. Bet the back of his head was wide open like the top of a jack o'lantern. Flies all over the place."

"Means whatever he was last thinking probably landed six feet behind him, dripping out of his cap," Norton added.

"Gentlemen, please, there's no call to be vulgar," I said. "However, this is not good news for our enterprise."

And just then, the barkeep steps to the table with a little silver tray. He sets down a glass of private reserve whiskey and before I can reach for my pocket, he gives me a wink and a shake of his head, walks away. Turns out Lilly was the best thing to happen to me in more ways than one.

"Reckon we ought to lay low for a while," said Norton.

I cleared my throat and reached for my glass. It was empty. The sugary burn was still on my tongue, my chest like a glowing coal stove on a cold night. The whiskey was good, indeed the best. I just couldn't believe I had drained my glass in such haste. Confounded for but a few seconds as I was, the barkeep reappeared at my elbow once more, a fresh tumbler on the silver tray.

After a silence, Tommy spoke.

"Yeah, a week should do it. Coppers ain't wasting time. Some poor lug, guilty or not, is going to get collared for this. Meantime," Tommy rapped the paper with his knuckles, "folks are still dying. We eyeball the obits–"

"Yeah," Norton cut in. "Take some time off, scout some new jobs."

"Exactly," said Tommy. "We meet in a week, by then they pinched some poor bastard, and we compare notes, cherry pick us some gravy jobs. Long as we ain't seen together, and long as nobody's carrying nothing could land him in the slammer should maybe he get pinched, we got no problems."

"Let's leave our tools at home," said Norton. "None of us got need for a lock pick or a pocket knife the next seven days. I say we don't even got to be holding nail clippers or toothpicks, and certainly no call for maps or nothing. Coppers eyeball you drawing diagrams on a newspaper, could be trouble for us all."

My second whiskey was already gone–or was it my third?– and the furnace wasn't merely glowing any longer. We'd all been collared before, and seeing us together was reason enough for a roust, even without all the new heat. And now these goons want to laugh it up, get the whole place staring at us.

"All right, that's it." I slammed my glass down. "Break it up, you knuckleheads. We're supposed to lay low, stay out of sight, and here you are laughing it up, practically begging the heat to come down."

They were silent.

"Now scram, I said. Don't let me see one of you, for the next week. And that goes double for you seeing each other. We all stay out of each others' sight, meet back here in seven days."

And that was that. The boys left, but I stayed, figuring I was out of sight, and not with any of the boys. Besides, the establishment had taken a shine to me, as it had the night before. I parked my foot on the brass rail and leaned my elbow on the bar. The barkeep sat another whiskey in front of me.

"What are you trying to do to me, friend?"

"Your money's no good, here, Adelai. You needn't trouble yourself. Anything you need," he said, then rapped the bar twice with his knuckles.

And so the day unfurled in my mind like a red carpet. A shoe shine, a shave, perhaps a matinee. I was fishing around for some coin to give a newsboy outside, someone who could go fetch me a copy of the racing form, when the Deacon Jones appeared at my side.

"Coffee," he said. And then, "Afternoon, Mr. Shade. Fancy meeting you here."

I nodded to him and tipped my glass. It was full, again.

"Could I trouble you for the time, sir?" said the Deacon. "My watch seems to have stopped."

Deacon was just having fun with me, like he always did. Hoping he could scare me into slipping up. His Grim Reaper routine might work on the boys, maybe some other gangs, but not me. I slipped my watch from my pocket and flipped it open.

"Quarter past one," I said.

"My, my," he said. "That is a lovely timepiece."

"Be my guest." I undid the chain clasp from my vest, handed it over to him.

"To my darling Stanley," the Deacon read aloud. "With my

eternal love, Myra."

My warm little coal stove got real frosty, the burn a little too much for me on that last nip of whiskey.

"Barkeep, another round for my friend, here," said Deacon Jones.

I drank fast to chase off the shakes.

"Had us a widow named Myra, not too long ago," said the Deacon. "While she laid her beloved Stanley to rest, her place got robbed. Can you believe that? Poor woman, lives her whole life devoted to her husband. A good man, a saint, he was. And now all she got is his pension, barely enough to get by. And some low life bastard decides he's going to rob her of every last nickel on the day she's putting her dear beloved husband into the ground."

"I'm sorry," I said.

"Sorry? An apology. Sounds like a confession, to me."

"Now hold on just one minute, Deputy. I mean Deacon." I set my glass down and turned to look this old creep dead in the eye, show him I had nothing to hide, when my brogue gets twisted up in the brass rail and I go face down into the sawdust.

And I wake up at the precinct. Least I'm pretty sure it was the precinct. I got that hammering in my head and my belly feels like I swallowed something was still alive and the room is spinning. The room ain't much, I'll tell you that. Nothing but brick and cement with a metal table like from some kind of laboratory. There's a heavy door, like a smaller version of what the Reverend Hoyle got in the front of his church. I'm about to get up, take a look and see what's outside but soon as I try, I can't move. They got me cuffed to the chair but good. Bracelets on my wrists and ankles and that chair ain't going no place.

Pretty soon that little church door swings open and in comes Deacon Jones carrying a black bag like he's playing at a doctor making a house call.

"I imagine it never occurred to a man such as yourself," he says, and while he's talking he opens up that bag, "to ask who was being so generous as to cover your bar tabs these last two days. And that your good fortune to have such a bottomless well of liquor bestowed upon you came about shortly after you defiled the good Reverend Hoyle's wife."

"Hey, now hold on just a second. Lilly got a mind of her own. I didn't make her do nothing."

"So you say," said the Deacon. "Nonetheless, I'm not here to discuss your indiscretions with the Mrs. Reverend Hoyle. We have a dead police officer on our hands."

The Deacon takes out a sheet of paper from that black bag. Like it's fresh from the mill, bright white in that dull brick room, like it's where all the light's coming from. He sets it down in the middle of that metal table, along with a fountain pen what must be worth much as that watch from Myra what's-her-name, that Stanley fella's widow.

"So," said Deacon Jones. He takes off his coat and hangs it on the peg beside the door, and I catch a glimpse of that big, bone-handled knife at his hip.

"Let's talk about where you were last night, Mr. Shade. And I hope, for your sake, you can remember."

"So this is a whole debt collection here.
I get what it is."
 —Booked. #126 Interview with Cameron Pierce

CAMERON PIERCE
CALIFORNIA OREGON

You are born in August at Memorial Hospital in Bakersfield, California. Your mother is a third grade teacher. Your father works for a beer distributor. Just a few months before your eighth birthday, they will file for divorce and you'll be asked to make the biggest decision of your life. The choice is yours. Don't worry. This isn't about choosing a favorite. It's about you. It was always about you.

Your mother keeps the house in Bakersfield. Your father moves north and buys a small riverside cabin in Oregon. Do you want to remain in Bakersfield, where you have your friends and the comfort of a familiar backdrop, or do you pack it in and rebuild with your father in Oregon? A single mother household or that eternal father-son fishing trip you always wanted. In a room full of strangers, you will be asked to decide.

If you choose to remain with your mother, go to BAKERSFIELD.
If you choose to move with your father, go to OREGON.

CAMERON PIERCE

BAKERSFIELD: Two years later, your mom remarries. You move into a big new house in a nicer, newer part of town with your stepdad, Scott. He's a businessman. The license plate of his Hummer: BSNSMAN. You're not even in middle school yet, but suddenly you have a college savings account full of money for when you go off to college. Your mother no longer spends her nights at the kitchen table, weeping over a stack of overdue bills. You have nice new clothes. Those Air Jordans you always coveted? They're yours now. And the swimming pool in the backyard is sure to attract a whole bunch of brand new friends. Life is shiny. Life is good. You've seen your real father once since the divorce, but maybe that's for the best. You're practically a different person now.

OREGON: You and your dad live in a one-room cabin that backs up to a scenic river full of trout. It is cold and it is damp and it is lonesome out in the wilderness, but you love almost every second of it. You wake early in the morning to fish before school and afterward you fly down those backwoods roads on your ten-speed, eager to wet your line. One autumn, in the year your muscles have started to develop, your father takes you out and teaches you to shoot a gun. You bag your first deer that season. You hang its antlers in the corner, above your little sweat-stained cot.

BAKERSFIELD: You meet a girl named Sarah. She has blond hair and wears Abercrombie and Fitch. You go out to movies on the weekends and some nights her parents invite you over for dinner. Other nights she has dinner at your house, where you eat your favorite takeout. You share your first kiss together and maybe a little something more. Sarah is your first true love.

OREGON: You meet a girl named Sarah. She has blond hair and climbs trees better than any boy. You explore the woods together and some nights her parents invite you over for dinner. Other nights she has dinner at your house, where you eat the fish that you have caught and the deer that you have hunted. You share your first kiss together and maybe a little something more. Sarah is your first true love.

BAKERSFIELD: You've just passed your driving test. Never mind that your stepfather is cheating on your mother and screams at her almost every night. He's handing you the keys to a brand new BMW. You drop by Sarah's place unexpectedly to take her out for a drive, and that's when you receive the call.

OREGON: You've just passed your driving test. Never mind that you've been driving your father's truck since you were thirteen, or that you drove yourself unaccompanied to the DMV to take the test. You're legal now. You drop by Sarah's place because the two of you are heading to Crater Lake for a weekend camping trip alone. You and her have taken drives in your father's truck many times before, so that part is nothing new. What's got your belly tingling is the prospect, the feeling, that maybe this weekend you two will go all the way. You don't own a cellphone, but if you did, you'd be receiving that call about now.

BAKERSFIELD: Your father killed himself. You'd seen him what, three times since he moved to Oregon. He never remarried but he always sent you a birthday card with some recent pictures of fish he'd caught and a small check that your mother reminded you was a lot of money to him. They ship his body back to Bakersfield, where he's buried in the same graveyard as his father, who died in Vietnam, who you never met.

OREGON: Your father killed himself. Apparently he wandered out onto the old country highway and put a bullet in his head, right there in the middle of the road. The gun was still warm when a farmer found him, but it was too late. You and Sarah have nearly left town when Sheriff Don pulls you over. You smirk because you're legal now, but your palms are sweaty. You've never been pulled over. Sheriff Don asks you to follow him back to the station. You throw your hands up in protest and flash your license and that's when he lays it on the line. "You're father's dead, son."

BAKERSFIELD: Your mother asks if you'd like to take a trip up to Oregon to collect your father's possessions, to experience the place he called home in his final years, but you decline.

OREGON: You're still a minor, so they ship you a thousand miles away from Sarah, back to California, where you're to live with your mother and a stepfather you've never met. They live in a million-dollar home. They are members of a country club. They tell you about the college savings fund they set up for you way back when. All these years they've been thinking of you, putting money away. They never once visited. Now they've torn you away from it all.

BAKERSFIELD: You're not sure whether it's the BMW or your estranged father's death, but Sarah finally throws away notions of waiting until marriage. The way people talk to you, you know you're expected to feel sad and hurt. In secret, you're just stoked about driving and getting laid. You feel nothing for your father. You milk the sympathy, though. You learn that those grieving are granted certain privileges.

OREGON: You write letters to Sarah every day. You promise that you'll return just as soon as you get yourself emancipated. Failing that, you'll wait the two years until you turn eighteen and then you'll move back to Oregon and marry her. She says she'd love nothing more than to marry you and have your children. You dream of your future life as a married couple, putting the pieces together in letter after letter. Your first child will be named Dean, after your father, if it's a boy. Charlotte if it's a girl. These letters from Sarah are the only thing that matters. They keep you going despite the isolation and the devastating weight of your father's death, which squeezes your heart like a vise. You find it hard to breathe on the days when no new letter arrives. A few months later, the letters start to trickle off. First they drop in number, then they get shorter, then they come so infrequently that most days you don't even bother checking the mail. You write to Sarah just as often, and twice as desperately. Then, after a hellish month of silence, the fateful letter arrives. The one you dreaded most. She hasn't died. No, it's worse than that. She's started seeing someone else. She doesn't say who, but she says you know him, that you'd approve, which of course you never would.

BAKERSFIELD: Life presents a myriad of choices. Driving drunk is one of them. That's how your BMW ends up totaled. That's how Sarah ends up dead.

OREGON: You take a swing at your stepfather for yelling at your mother. This is the final straw, they tell you. So the next day, you're being shipped off to a school that's more like a prison. And you thought the suburbs were bad.

BAKERSFIELD: They release you from jail after four days because you're a privileged white kid who still has a bright future ahead. Your parents buy you a ten-year-old Lexus. "We hope you've learned your lesson," they say.

OREGON: The only thing worse than military school is failing a suicide attempt at military school.

BAKERSFIELD: You're out drinking by the river with some friends when one of them asks if you loved Sarah. You say you did, and what you've done finally hits you, and you break down in tears. You still love her. You will always love her. Your love for her is only surpassed by the hate you feel for yourself.

OREGON: Your hatred for this new place, this place worse than military school and the suburbs combined, is only surpassed by the hate you feel for your father. The man loved you. He gave you everything. And then without warning, he took it all away.

BAKERSFIELD: Ten years later and the worst is over, but in secret, unbeknownst to everyone around you, you're still climbing your way out of that deep, black hole you fell into when you were sixteen. You're married now. You have a nice house and a good job and a baby. Funny thing is, you still love her.

OREGON: Ten years later and the worst isn't over, but at least you're back in Oregon. Your life is still in shambles, but you don't love her anymore. She's married to Dan Tannehill, the guy she said you'd approve of. She's right, too. Dan was always a good guy. They have three kids together. You see them almost every week on account of it being a small town and them living just a few miles up the road from your father's cabin, which you reclaimed from the bank with the money your mother gave you in the wake of her divorce. That was her way of saying sorry. You still smile when you remember how you laughed in her face. One of the few good memories among a lot of bad ones, the ones that keep you up at night, loading and unloading the chamber of the old suicide weapon, wondering if this is how your father felt. In the mornings, you fish alone. In the evenings, you drink whiskey and write letters to people you have known. You never mail a single letter. They make good kindling, though. Life is good in Oregon. It's just too damn bad you ever had to leave.

"I do not allow myself, for a full 24 hours, to talk to anybody about a review. 24 hours just to be a miserable son of a bitch."
  —Booked. #103 Interview with Paul Tremblay

PAUL TREMBLAY
SCENES FROM THE CITY OF GARBAGE AND THE CITY OF CLAY

Only hours after her arrival, her uncle had laid out on the kitchen table a crinkly yellow map of New York City. He'd then tried to meticulously delineate the different neighborhoods: where to go, what to do, what to avoid, and where wasn't safe at night, although he hadn't described in detail what he'd meant by not safe. He'd simply waved his hand over any neighborhood near Times Square and Central Park and had declared, "Not safe for you." Not that she had cared about being safe anymore.

The girl had been living in her aunt and uncle's midtown west apartment for three days but she had only gone outside by herself for the first time earlier that morning. She'd woken up with the sun and had walked expanding concentric squares of local blocks until she'd skirted the perimeter of Times Square in an attempt to earn some sense of place.

Now it was mid-afternoon, and she was lying on a cot crammed into what her aunt and uncle called the drawing room.

The ceilings and molding were once white and the curling wall-paper was the color of nicotine and hepatitis. The room had one window and it overlooked 50th Street.

The drawing room was full of random stuff, the lot of which Iris spent her new New York City afternoons cataloguing: two dressers, each missing a drawer; an iron typewriter with a curled, dead-spider ribbon hanging from between its jammed and toothy typebars; a mildew-spotted desk covered in rusty coffee cans, the cans holding, as far as she could tell without going through them, old bills and letters; a pink ironing board with rusty criss-crossing legs; a beige sewing machine missing its dropfeed.

It was late July of 1975 and the city was in the midst of a suffocating heat wave. The girl remained in her cot; sweat soaked through the back of her powder blue Wonder Woman t-shirt. She listened to the continuous street traffic, and somewhere just below her window a group of neighborhood kids were arguing, laughing, and swearing. She imagined their breath billowing out like steam from the subway vents and their words transforming into a cloud of flies that would grow fat on the piles of garbage.

Her uncle struggled to open the door to the drawing room, which stuck tight in the jamb because of too many coats of paint. When it did finally open, he said, "Come on. We're gonna go meet some kids." He wore green linen suit pants (the matching coat long missing) and a stretched-out, sleeveless white t-shirt, polka dotted with coffee and sweat stains. The girl catalogued these details too; an archaeologist/anthropologist in her mystifying new city.

She followed her uncle, who looked nothing like her father had, into the muggy apartment hallway and down the three flights of steps. On the final flight they stepped over two squat garbage bags, perched on the stairs like the lions in front of the public library.

Outside was bright sunlight and unrelenting waves of heat, sound, and the stench of weeks-old garbage. She imagined floating above her suddenly crazed uncle and the fortress of buildings on her street, floating above this infinite city and all its vastness and decay, like the narrator to some grand and horrible fable.

Her uncle coughed, mumbled something about garbage, Jesus, and getting her to play with new friends as he pulled her down off the stoop, onto the crowded sidewalk, and toward the group of arguing kids—all boys—she'd listened to from her cot. They were still bickering and climbing over each other and on the staircase handrails next door. One kid threw something at the sprawling garbage pile on the sidewalk. The pile was taller than a bus.

When her uncle shouted, "Hey, guys," they all stopped what they were doing. Their little muscles twitched in their hands and legs. The pack of them were ready to scatter.

"This is my niece. Come on, now, everyone say hi, introduce yourselves." The girl was the only one who said anything. "She's staying with me and her aunt for a while, got it?" Her uncle paused, pointed vaguely at his apartment somewhere up above them all, and then he rubbed his balding head as if to concede that this wasn't going as well as he'd hoped. "She's had a tough go of it lately, you know? Her mom and dad, back out in Rhode Island, they died in a car accident last month. Squashed like bugs by a jack-knifed semi-trailer. Can you believe it? Just fuckin' awful. So now she's living here. Why don't you guys just let her play too, eh? And goddamnit, be nice to her, even if she is a girl. Go ahead, honey. I'll be upstairs if you need me." Clearly relieved to be relieved of whatever it was he thought was his duty, her uncle shuffled back up into his apartment, but not before pausing to prospect a lamp shaped like a fish sticking out of the trash.

The boys, all of them younger than her fourteen years old, eyeballed her. Her hair was curly and cut shoulder length. She was taller and skinnier than the boys, two of whom circled her like wary sharks. She'd always be the other to them; who she was, where she came from ("Rhode fuckin' Island? Long Island is bigger than that shit, right?"), and her dramatically cliché orphan story instantly made her unfathomable.

One kid named Jimmy said, "So whaddya think?"

The girl said, "About what?"

He spread his arms open, like he owned the neglected garbage piles and wanted to clutch it all to his chest. "Our bee-u-tee-full city!"

The boys broke up laughing before she could answer. The city terrified her in a detached, academic sense. She understood that something terrible could happen to her here; she understood that more than most. "I don't know," she said, smiled, and then sat down on the stairs. The boys scattered like spooked pigeons.

Jimmy pulled himself up onto the stairs' railing, and stood, those city-owning arms stretched out for balance. He talked like talking was a race he never lost. "You know they're picking up trash on the Upper East Side. My old man says fuckin' rich snobs, payin' for it themselves."

The kid who was still throwing what looked like chunks of pavement and brick at the garbage said, "If your old man was any more full of shit, he'd be a sewer. My brother is a sanitation worker and no one nowhere in the city is getting their garbage picked up. They're all on strike."

"Like how this dipshit says sanitation worker, like his brother isn't a garbage man?"

This other kid with red sneakers, a Yankees hat, and a face like a pug said, "Nah, you wanna know what the rich people do?

They pay someone to wrap their garbage up, so it looks like a birthday present or something, and then they leave it on their car seat with the window down or door unlocked, or they leave it on a stoop, somewhere out in the open. Then when some shithead like you–" He pointed at Jimmy. "–comes along and sees the present out for the easy picking, you steal it, take it home, open it, and then you're stuck with some richie rich's trash."

"Maybe their trash is better, yeah?"

"No, they just as nasty as us. Worse, I bet."

The brick-chunk thrower said, "You're full of shit, too. Just like Jimmy."

"No way, I can prove it. My mother read it in the paper. She reads the gossip columns every day and said Joan Crawford was doing it."

Jimmy jumped off the railing and pushed the red-sneaker kid backwards, off the bottom step. "That makes no sense. To do that, it's too much work. You telling me rich people are gonna wrap their garbage up all nice? They're smarter than that."

"Smart like my cousin Val in Brooklyn. They burn it."

The girl stood up and said, "No, I think he's right about the gift wrapping. I can prove it. Stay here." She turned and ran toward her apartment building. As soon as her back was turned she heard the boys snickering and mumbling stuff about her thin legs, her butt, her flat chest. Jimmy was saying the worst stuff, bragging about what he'd do to her. The girl's face turned as red as a traffic light, and she ran faster, up the three flights of stairs, into her apartment and past her uncle who was in the living room, nose buried in a newspaper. He absently yelled her name as she dashed into the drawing room.

She was so mad at those boys that her anger came out as chest-heaving sobs, which made her angrier. She'd still go down there and show them the proof. She wanted to see that Jimmy kid eat crow.

Under the cot was where she kept her personal possessions. She didn't have much. One old cardboard box had pictures of her and her parents, old school report cards and artwork her parents had saved, a couple of stuffed animals her aunt had given her, and last year's birthday card from her uncle that held a couple of scratch lottery tickets that were losers. The girl pushed that box to the side and instead pulled out a rectangular present wrapped in red tissue paper and tied with a neat golden bow. She'd found it earlier that morning on her exploratory walk, sitting on a waist-high pile of garbage outside a laundromat. She hadn't opened it yet, thinking it would be best to open when her aunt and uncle weren't around, or were asleep. She didn't want them thinking she was out there stealing stuff, or worse, already.

★ ★ ★ ★ ★

Two young men, a film director and an actor, sat in a hole-in-the-wall coffee shop in Hell's Kitchen. They reviewed locations and the shooting schedule for the next few days.

The director said loudly, "All right! Come on. What's the matter?" It sounded like he was yelling, but that's how he spoke. He spoke-yelled.

There were only a couple of other customers in the coffee shop. They didn't seem to mind the yelling. Sitting at the counter, dressed in short sleeves, and huddled over their steaming coffees, the customers were third shifters who couldn't face going to sleep yet.

The director continued waving his arms and slapping the mica tabletop. "I know you. You're not here. You're in your head. You're somewhere else. So. What is it? Are you in character already? Tell me what's bothering you. Let me allay your fears, your concerns, your consternations—"

"I'm fine."

"Fuck fine. You're not fine. You're a mess. You've been wringing the neck of that defenseless newspaper the whole time. You can get arrested for that, you know. Especially in this coffee shop. They take their newspapers seriously here. If it's the *Times*, well then, you're probably okay, but shit, is that a *Post*? Is it? Oh, great, it's a *Post*. We're fucked, then. No, really, thanks, thanks a lot." The director scratched at his beard and laughed.

"Have you been reading about any of this shit? City almost went bankrupt last year, and now over 19,000 municipal employees laid off, including 5,000 cops, and the rest of the sanitation workers go on strike. Our city is falling to pieces. Crime rate is already like, I don't know, a fucking rocket—"

"The crime rate is a fucking rocket?"

"I'm an actor not a writer. Did you hear what I said? Our city is losing 5,000 cops. Are we even going to be able to shoot this thing here?"

There it was: his doubt, spilling over. The director and the actor were good friends and they each had had some success. But some wasn't enough for the twenty-six-year-old actor who grew up in Little Italy and dropped out of high school to join an acting conservatory. This movie had to be big. He believed it was going to be make-or-break for both of them.

"Don't worry your pretty little head over that stuff."

"I mean, Jesus, there's garbage everywhere! How's that gonna look?"

"I'll tell you how's that gonna look. It's gonna look perfect. The city will be like the Mona Lisa in this picture."

"I don't know. I don't like it. Maybe we should delay a couple of weeks. See if the whole mess gets sorted out."

"What, you want to run the show, now? Come on, man, you can't push me out yet. Let shooting start at least."

"It's this movie, this whole thing. It's got me a little nervous."

"Nervous?"

"Yeah."

"Good. You should be nervous. It's your show, cowboy."

"So I'm a cowboy now, eh?"

"Yeah, why not. Hey, you've seen *Midnight Cowboy*."

"You serious? Bunch of times. Some of those times with you. You know it's one of my favorites."

"Why's it a favorite?"

"Why? The story arc was great. You know, very risky subject matter. The look of the film, how those psychedelic sequences were shot. And the scene with Hoffman dying on the bus at the end was—"

"Yeah, yeah, yeah with the second rate acting class deconstruction shit. It's your favorite because of the line."

"The line?"

"Don't bullshit a bullshitter. You know that amazing, fucking fantastic line, the line that is gonna make Hoffman immortal. That line, man. That line came from a perfect New York City scene from a perfect New York City movie too, right? Hoffman's Ratso Rizzo walking across the street in mid-con, telling Voight's huckleberry hick how they're going to sell his dumb ass to high society biddies. And that scene, man, fuck it has rhythm. Everyone walking and moving, bouncing on the street. And that camera shot as wide as the sidewalk, Hoffman strutting in his white suit, and Voight in the cowboy hat, and then! then that fucking yellow cab comes out of nowhere, almost takes Hoffman out. You remember, right? That yellow hood and grill as giant on the screen as that big as bullshit shark from that new movie by Spielberg, right? You seen it yet? You gotta see it. Anyway. Cab shoots in, then Hoffman yellin', 'I'm walkin' here! I'm walkin' here,' and he pounds the hood, flips off the cabby, and picks his con right back up." The director delivered the Hoffman line like Hoffman, and he pounded on the table like Hoffman and walked away like Hoffman. The director laughed self-consciously and adjusted his shirt and tie before sitting down and extending his hands toward the smiling actor. "So, it's one of your favorite movies because of the line. I know you, and I've never met an actor who couldn't resist, didn't dream of the line."

"You're insane, you know that, right?"

"Yeah. It helps."

"But you're right. I want the line."

"But?"

"But I don't think we have it here in our movie."

The director laughed and finished his coffee. "Maybe we do. Maybe we don't. Maybe we will. But hey, I won't tell the screenwriter you gave his work such a ringing endorsement."

"Come on, I didn't–"

"Relax, I'm kidding. Hey, supposedly that little shit Hoffman is telling everyone that the line was ad-libbed."

The actor knew he was being baited, but he didn't mind. The director was always baiting him and would be baiting him for the next however many weeks it would take to make their movie. "That's bullshit. I know the guy hired to drive the cab for the scene."

"Really?"

The actor smiled and said, "I know the guy who knows the guy, who knows the guy." They both laughed. Then the actor added, "There's no way *the line* was ad-libbed. No way."

"I don't know. Maybe that's how *the line* works."

The actor's smile disappeared. "Aw, man, I'll do my best, you know, but ad-libbing, it's not what I'm good at–I mean, I'm good at it, but I don't do it a lot. And I already told you that I'm an actor not a writer."

"Listen. You be whatever you need to be for this movie. You go wherever it is you need to go. Do what you need to do. You know me and can trust me, right? I'll make sure you're safe. I'll make sure we get this thing shot and wrapped. I'll make sure everyone sees the garbage and the filth and the crime. I'll make sure they see New York as it really is now. I'll make sure everyone sees you. And we'll make our own perfect New York City movie, and it's gonna be the best fucking movie anyone's ever seen."

The actor said, "No one's gonna like it. No one's gonna want to see it," when what he meant to say, and the director knew this too, was, "No one's gonna like me. No one's gonna want to see me."

★ ★ ★ ★ ★

"I found it this morning."

The girl shook the red present in front of all their faces and said, "There's definitely something in there."

The boys huddled around her. Jimmy stared at her red and puffy eyes and said, "This doesn't prove anything. She could've did this herself. She's freaky enough. She was gone long enough."

No one else said anything as she unwrapped the red present right there on her apartment building's front stoop. Three boys butted heads trying to look inside the box at the same time.

"White tissue? So it's a bunch of junk like I said!"

"Hold on." The girl peeled away layers of tissue and uncovered a pink mass on the bottom of the box. It wasn't colored pink uniformly. It was mottled; some parts were pale, almost white, while other sections were a darker red, as if dye were added and not mixed properly.

"Told you those richies were gross."

"Oh man, they're nasty."

"Shit. What is it, old lox?"

"Nah, doesn't smell."

"How could you smell anything out here when it all smells like old lox anyway?"

The girl stuck her face inside and inhaled. "It doesn't smell like anything really."

"Lemme see," Jimmy said and tried to stick his hand inside the box.

The girl quickly sidestepped, pulled the box away, and covered whatever it was up again. Jimmy lost his balance and fell onto the stairs. The other boys laughed a little, but it was nervous laughter, anticipatory laughter. Oh-shit-what's-Jimmy-going-to-do-now laughter.

Jimmy stood, wiped his hand under his nose quick, and bounced on his heels, a boxer trying to get the ref to quit with that standing eight count shit. "Give it to me," he said and reached again. "Hand it over!"

The girl wrapped her arms around the box and clutched it to her chest so he couldn't get at it. Jimmy pinched her arms and punched her shoulders but she did not drop or relinquish the box. None of the other boys did anything. No one walking by on the sidewalk did anything. His pinches and punches graduated quickly to hair pulling and face slapping and yelling *bitch* and *slut* into her ears.

The girl had the strongest sense of déjà vu, although what did or didn't actually happen in her past was totally irrelevant to this moment in time. Again, like when she had been lying in her cot listening to the city, she felt detached from it all; her senses only there to absently keep record of her new existence.

She continued protecting the box. She held it with her right hand and punched Jimmy back awkwardly with her left. Then she shifted her weight, subtly, from left to right, pivoting the smaller Jimmy with her hip so he was standing directly in front of her, and she kneed him in the balls. He dropped and curled up on the stoop like a dead spider.

Her uncle's voice floated down from the third floor, saying something about keeping down the fuckin' racket.

Back in the drawing room, the girl cleared the coffee cans off the desk and put the box on it. She reached inside and took out the pink substance. It was damp and felt like clay. She carefully placed it on the desk next to the box. She took out the rest of the tissue and underneath was a small, jagged piece torn out of a newspaper. She could only make out snippets due to uneven tears and smudged ink:

Gail Lwowski, age 22 of Staten Island, reported missing after an arg____ with her fiancé— She was carrying a handbag.

She somehow knew the unfortunate newspaper story was important but unimportant at the same time, like all stories were. But *Staten Island*, that had been underlined in pencil.

The girl found Staten Island on her uncle's map, then she sat at the desk, filled her hands with the strange clay-like substance, and began to mold it. The substance's mottled pink evened out as she kneaded it with her hands. As she worked, the girl imagined she was the missing woman Gail, had always been Gail, and that she still had her handbag and would eventually forgive her fiancé for whatever it was they had been arguing about, but she would never be seen again. Then she imagined she was Gail's fiancé; she imagined she was innocent of any wrongdoing and tasted a familiar grief, then she imagined she was guilty, and the violent acts she was capable of as Gail's fiancé made her shudder. Then she reached out further, and imagined she was any one of thousands of lives, some underlined, some not, on Staten Island.

When she finished working, the substance had the same geographical shape Staten Island had on her uncle's map. She put the box and tissue paper back under her cot, but left the clipping and clay-like model of Staten Island on the desk.

The girl woke up before the sun the rest of the week and took her exploratory walks on the trash-lined streets. She kept her uncle's yellow map with her, folded under her arm. She marked the grids of streets and neighborhoods she walked. She found four more wrapped presents, all red, and took them back to the drawing room.

★ ★ ★ ★ ★

The shoot wasn't going well.

In the star-studded, high-power movie he made before this one, his was only one of many supporting roles. That shoot had felt so different, so alive with the hope and possibility inherent in a group artistic endeavor; the idea that a collective of individuals were working toward a common statement, a common vision. Here, there was no common vision. There was his friend's intense direction and mood swings. There was the actor grunting through his lines. There was no buzz on the set among the crew and other actors.

They'd been filming at night all week. And the city, Jesus H. Christ, the city was a foot on all their necks. The city was a filthy and miserable place, and for the actor, so personally disappointing. This was his home and it was crumbling before his eyes. It was dying on film, and dying without any dignity.

After another all-night shoot in and around Times Square, the actor did not return to his hotel room. Instead, he walked the streets while still in wardrobe. He thought about the director's calculated fawning over Hoffman's line from *Midnight Cowboy,* and how the presumed attempt at inspiration only made him feel worse, more doubtful that he'd be able to crawl inside this character, that he'd be able to carry this or any other film. Being a successful supporting actor simply did not guarantee he'd ever be a star.

He walked, and smoked, and kept his head down, tucked inside a green jacket despite the heat and wet-t-shirt humidity. It was gray, just after dawn, and for the only time since he'd been there filming, the neon lit porno theaters and strip joints were functionally empty.

He decided to head back to his hotel in Midtown East as he approached a six-foot tall pyramid of garbage on the corner of Broadway and 48th. Near its top, sitting askew upon the heap of green garbage bags and corrugated cardboard boxes was what looked to be a shoebox wrapped in red paper and tied with a golden bow.

The actor grinded his half-finished cigarette under his heal, then reached up to pluck the box off the pile. Completely outstretched and standing up on his tiptoes, he lost his balance and stumbled, spearing a garbage bag with his right foot, sending flies and a rancid stench pluming into the air. He grabbed the box with a second attempt. It was heavier than he thought it would be.

"I've been finding those all over the place."

The actor spun around and there was a young but tall girl standing a few feet away. Her skin was as pale as last night's moon. She adjusted something folded under her right arm, and held what looked to be the exact same gift-wrapped box under her left arm.

The actor said, "I'm sorry. Is this yours?"

"No. I don't think it is mine. I'm pretty sure this box–" she lightly tapped the box under her arm "–is the last one I need."

He didn't think she was telling the truth. The way she looked at the box he held, it had to have been the only thing in the world she wanted.

"You wanna swap?"

"No. No thank you. I'll keep this one."

"I'm just teasing. No, really. You can take it. It must be yours." He held it out to her.

She backed up. "No, no. It's okay. I'm sure I'll find more. You keep that one. Whoever finds it is supposed to keep it. That's what I think."

She talked very proper and mannered, rehearsed even. There was no way she was from here. "Are you sure?"

The girl shrugged, and her pinpoint-sharp shoulders bounced into her light brown curls.

The actor shook the box and felt the weight shift. "What's in the box?"

"Clay. Probably."

"Clay?"

"And newspaper clippings. At least, that's what was in all the other ones. The one I found yesterday was just another story, something about a youth group's efforts to keep a Brooklyn playground clean during the strike. Brooklyn was underlined in pencil."

"What's that mean?"

"I'm not sure. Well, that's not true, I think I'm sure, but I can't quite explain it. Sorry for sounding so weird."

"Hey, that's okay." There was a pause as they both traded uneasy smiles. He said, "Should we open and see?"

"No. Last time I opened one out on the street, it didn't go very well."

"No?"

"I was attacked by a boy in broad daylight while standing on my own apartment building's front stoop. I had to knee him in the balls to get away." She laughed, and the expression on her face, she looked like an odd combination of embarrassed and defiant. If she were a movie character, a name in a screenplay someone was writing, she'd be described here in that way. Embarrassed and defiant.

"I'm glad you're okay." The actor had tucked his present underneath his arm without realizing it. "But hey, what are you doing here? And at this hour." He looked at a watch on his wrist that he didn't have anymore. He'd left it with wardrobe.

"Just out on my morning walk."

"You walk out here every morning? By yourself?" The actor looked around expecting to see crew and cameras, and was disoriented when they weren't there.

"Not out here every morning. Yesterday I made it down to Chelsea for the first time. But I usually end up near Times Square at some point."

He puzzled at her background, her motivations, and couldn't help thinking about her and relating to her in terms of a movie character. *She was headstrong, but vulnerable. Plucky. She was a runaway. Doomed. Abusive parents. A daughter of neglect. She left a small town to make it big in the city. She would be taken advantage of in this city of vice, this city of garbage. She would never ask for help but needed it ...*

He said, "You shouldn't do that. This filthy, miserable place; this is no place for someone like you." The actor's words felt like lines. Lines were something that someone else wrote or said.

"How do you know?"

"How do I know? I just know. Look around you. Let me

help you."

"I don't think I need your help. I can take care of myself. I already told you what I did to that kid who attacked me."

"What's your name?"

"It's Iris. But I'm thinking I might change it to something else."

"My name is Travis, by the way. But why change your name? Iris is a nice name."

"I don't want to be her anymore. Then I could be any person that I wanted? Especially in this place. You understand, right?"

The actor was losing the thread here, losing her, just like he lost all those scenes they'd shot over and over again earlier that night. What was needed was for him to say exactly the right words, but what that was he didn't know. Something reassuring? Provocative, insightful, confrontational? Hell, his head was all twisted around before he even ran into her, so he didn't know. He wasn't good at ad-libbing, for chrissakes.

He said, "Hey, let me give you a ride home. I can get a cab."

She shook her head. "I'm fine. I live close by. I can take care of myself." She turned, walked away, and quickly disappeared behind the rows of garbage.

He said, "Wait," and followed for a step or two, but he let her go.

The shoot wasn't going well.

He didn't open his box until he was back in his hotel room.

★ ★ ★ ★ ★

When she'd first seen the man in the green coat, she'd thought he was leaving the box on the trash, not taking it. She'd rushed over to ask why he left them out? Maybe more importantly than why, were the presents meant for her and only her to find? And if they were meant for her, was she doing what she was supposed to with them?

When she'd realized he was taking the box, not leaving it, instead of dwelling on the crushing disappointment, she'd convinced herself that he'd been meant to find that particular box.

Now, back in her drawing room, she wasn't so sure. She wasn't so sure that she didn't need that other one.

She opened her fifth and final box. Inside was a lump of similarly colored substance she'd decided was clay. The accompanying newspaper clip was almost unreadable with only the words `man port author— bus -erminal Manhattan,` as legible. Manhattan was underlined in pencil.

She molded this newest lump of clay into the shape of Manhattan and fit it next to the other four clay shapes sitting on the desk. She had fashioned each lump of clay into the geographical shapes of New York City's five boroughs. Satisfied that her relief map was accurate, she carefully cut the name of each borough out of the newspaper clippings and pressed the names into the clay.

She surveyed her city model from every angle of the small drawing room, and thought of the man in Times Square. She wondered what his story was, why he was there so early in the morning, and why he insisted (and it was his insistence that had frightened her) he knew this wasn't the place for her. She wondered what was in his box.

She walked back to the desk and rested her hands on the city of clay, and traced the boundaries of each borough. Then, as though her hands were working on their own secret agenda, she bent the Rockaway Peninsula out further away from the rest of Queens. Finding that surprising change to be more than satisfactory, she moved the Bronx southwest, which in turn meant Manhattan tightened into a squat rectangle. She moved south and Staten Island got smooshed into Brooklyn, their clays overlapping and elongating. As she worked on this new shape, she smoothed the clay over the newspaper labels. The names of the boroughs were gone, disappearing under the city's tectonic plates of clay that moved and shifted under her fingers.

From the drawing room's dead typewriter, the girl removed a handful of typebars and the jammed ribbon. She sank the typebars deep into the clay, and they became leg bones, arm bones, and a spine. With the ribbon she strengthened connections at the joints, in the shoulders, and the pelvis.

Her new clay figure had a sturdy endoskeleton, a smoothly defined body, and a featureless face, a blank face so it could be anyone and everyone. Still, there was something missing.

The clay figure had a hole in its chest where a heart was supposed to be. She must've let the man keep the box with the missing heart. She hoped he knew what to do with it.

The girl had to fill the space with something. She balled up the remains of the newspaper clippings, the pieces of other people's city stories, and pushed them inside the clay figure's chest. There was still more room in there. She could go get her uncle's newspaper and stuff in all those words, all those possibilities. She imagined filling the figure's chest with the infinite stories from the city. Instead, she went under her cot and pulled out the box of her possessions, all the pieces and trinkets of her old life, the life she ached to forget, the life that already seemed to have belonged to someone else. She squeezed, wrung, and molded the box until it was small enough to fit inside the clay chest of her figure. Eventually, it fit perfectly. Then she smoothed the clay over so there was no longer a hole in its chest. The heart that she made was beating lightly and evenly under her finger.

The girl picked up the figure and positioned it so that it stood on the desktop. She lay down on her cot, listened to the traffic outside her window, listened to the voices on the sidewalk below. She looked down the length of the cot, between her feet, and the figure on the desk appeared to be standing over her. When she closed her eyes, she thought she could hear it moving, hear it growing into the one person—out of all the possible hers—she would eventually become.

★★★★★

The big scene was scheduled for later that afternoon. Instead of sleeping for a few hours, the actor rehearsed in his hotel room. Only the bedside lamp was on; it had a red lampshade.

The actor was undressed down to his boxer shorts, and he looked at his shadowy reflection in the mirror. He held the script and read: "I'm standing here. You make the move. Come on, try it, you fuck." The words came out stilted, dead, fraudulent. It didn't matter as the director had crossed a big X through the fragmented soliloquy anyway and had insisted the actor be prepared to ad-lib the entire scene.

He dropped the script, paced the small room, and sat heavily on his bed, next to the open present. Inside it was a lump of clay, just like the girl had said there would be.

There was another girl of a similar age and look in his movie. The girl he'd talked to, the one holding the red box, could be the actress's double. Wait, was she the same girl and he didn't recognize her?

He needed to get some sleep, some rest, get his head on straight. He'd been putting too much pressure on himself. The director, his supposed friend, was leaning on him too hard. The director was likely playing more mind games. The red present and the conversation with the girl out on Times Square had to be some sort of trick.

The actor took the clay out of the box and cupped it in his hands as though he were holding a small bird. When he applied light pressure, blood oozed slowly between his fingers and dripped onto the sheets of his unmade bed.

He opened his hands, and he was holding a heart. It was turgid and sickly. There were large black spots on the ventricles, ragged tears leaked puss where the arteries were supposed to be.

More tricks. This wasn't clay. The director must've had the girl's stand in, stunt double, doppelganger, twin sister, whoever she was leave him this decaying pig heart. To what purpose? To mess with him, to break him down, force him into the same diseased state of mind of his character because the director (in his heart of hearts) believed the actor wasn't good enough to get there by himself.

The actor snarled and recited the crossed out lines from the script. "I'm standing here. You make the move. Come on, try it, you fuck." He squeezed, choking the heart until it might pop. There was more blood. The heart began to spasm weakly in his hand, and his mind became his character's mind, and that mind was a movie screen of all that he thought was wrong with his city, a different image with every heartbeat: the streets and their monolithic buildings and the sidewalks with mountainous piles of trash, and all the people, and the porno theaters, peep shows and pimps and prostitutes, junkies, dealers, muggers, and the hopelessness, the girl he would never save, not really, and oh the violence, there was a briefcase full of guns, he saw bullets chew the fingers off of a gangster in dark hallway, another man stabbed in the neck, and he saw his own bloodied hand, two fingers pointed at his temple like a handgun and he was shooting, forever shooting.

The actor as character, the character as actor squeezed the heart, which he imagined to be the diseased heart of the city, until it came apart in his hands. He smeared the bits of ruined muscle over his face, arms, chest, legs, feet. He sucked at the fleshy bits stuck between his fingers. He wallowed in the carnage of the ruined heart, until totally exhausted, he collapsed onto the hotel bed.

Later, after his breathing returned to normal and he could no longer hear his own heart pounding, the actor stood slowly and walked over to the mirror. The red clay was hardened and streaked all over his face.

Then he opened his mouth. Then he said his line; the line he would deliver again in a few hours for the director and the cameras. He said the line for which he and 1970s New York City would always be remembered.

"You talkin' to me …."

> "What I do is I pretty much look at any table of contents and see where my name appears on it. That's really what I do."
> —Booked. #90 *Invisible Monsters Remix* review

CALEB J ROSS
THE REMOVAL KIND

When Merkle returned, the buyer wasn't there.

Though only an hour different, the bar had emptied from claustro- to agoraphobic with just a few swinging appendages and heavy lips animating the dank space. The ghosts of woofer reverb deafened the last-call hold-outs, eliciting full-volume private conversations from couples unaware of their last-call dreams let loose into the air. A few solo men, with pickup lines better left on the barroom floor, took aim at the new skin. But Merkle had no use for a flaccid dick at this hour; she had ends to be tied, loose strands of courtroom fodder to be spooled back and silenced. The buyer wasn't just a missing person. He was a liability.

She had left with the wrong man. He had all the signs of a typical buyer in a bar: stone sober, evasive, not cocky the way other bar patrons are, but also not without a hopper full of self-confidence. She had sold enough to recognize—or so she thought—how a buyer poses as a buyer.

Edgar has always told her, and perhaps Merkle's now forced to agree, that she's too damn paranoid for her own good. Normal people buy and trade all the time. Normal people use full names. Normal people get to the point. Normal people don't gamble with a simple exchange. We're not normal, she'd respond. Edgar couldn't disagree, but neither could he sympathize.

Ending up with the wrong man happens, sure. That's how her marriage started. Edgar's one of those mistakes she endures, something she often imagines a merciful judge would sentence like-offenders for. There are laws against crossing species, and Edgar is basically a walrus, a size and temperament she's never found attractive before. Most mornings she wakes hoping the last five years of her life were just a prelude to a hangover, but unlike the aftermath of a binge, her time with Edgar isn't something she can deafen with a greasy breakfast and coffee with her girlfriends. Besides, he's got a good head on him; it was his idea to start meeting buyers in bars.

In a lot of ways, the bar scene had always been what she imagines prison to be: mistakes and ego culminating in barely-lucid penetration. She prefers meeting buyers in bars. Her clientele certainly isn't the clubbing, social demographic. This simply isn't their element. She needs this unease when meeting a buyer who is already ethically-ambiguous. But perhaps the unease was too much this time; nobody looks like a buyer, here.

Short-skirted waitresses weave through the night's denouement, clanking empty bottles and agitating expired cologne in the air. Merkle envies their grace, the way they navigate shifted tables and tipped chairs. She almost doesn't want to interrupt the performance. But she must. She grabs a passing waitress, who says to her "Sorry, you just missed last call," the woman's mouth still eager and crescent, her tits still sparkling, every gesture an articulated habit refined by the night's promise of tip money.

"No, sorry, I'm looking for someone," Merkle says. She scans the room, her eyes slowly adjusting with the growing house lights. The near-empty room depresses her hope and voice. "You wouldn't happen to remember a guy, probably a bit out of place here, nervous maybe?"

"What'd he look like?" the waitress asks.

The engagement exaggerates Merkle's stammering; she has no idea what he looks like. "I ... I don't know." Anonymity is a selling point in her business.

"Can't help you then," the waitress replies. Before she turns away, Merkle scribbles her hotel room number on a pint-ringed receipt and asks the waitress to call should a man of her description return. Unsure how to proceed, Merkle sweetens the request with a soggy five dollar bill to the waitress's palm. The awkward exchange speaks more to a failed attempt at conspiracy than to confidentiality. Merkle's follow-up, "just let me know if you find him," felt like an admission of guilt on some deeper level.

The waitress declines the money. "I can tell you need the help," the waitress says.

"Surely, you have children," Merkle says.

"Maybe I actually enjoy waiting tables," the woman says, nearly spitting.

When the waitress leaves, Merkle is left to wonder if "help" meant the waitress would call, or if Merkle, disheveled and panicked, appeared to need pocket change more than the waitress needed a tip.

Distant slurs score the hollow heel-toe clack against the sidewalk as she walks back to the hotel. The soundtrack sticks with her from lobby, to elevator, to room. She opens the door to find that the wrong man, left behind in her hotel room as forgotten baggage, too, is gone. She's starting to wonder if her body is built to reject other bodies.

She parts the emptiness and stands at the closet doors along the far wall of her room. The buyer's package, now an orphan, if she had to describe it, would be lonely. For the first time in her career, the first time in dozens of transactions, she ponders the specimen inside the closet, secured within a simple brown box, and wonders what the buyer would have named it.

This must be how animal shelters feel, she thinks, and opens the closet doors but finds the package, too, is missing. Everyone's a fucking thief. First the buyer, now the Wrong Man, gone.

★ ★ ★ ★ ★

Edgar won't be much help finding the buyer, and if Merkle can help it, he will never know about the Wrong Man and the missing package. Edgar's a desk jockey sans the desk, at home administering to acquisitions and accounting from a tattered couch worn to the contours of his irrational bulges. The dirty work, he calls Merkle's delivery trips, are jobs meant for a set of persuasive tits. Tits have nothing to do with it; Edgar has tits, too.

He takes long lunches and infinite smoke breaks between comparatively brief stints of production and pill popping. The product: live rats in glass jars. They're an oddity for morbid collectors, and a lucrative one for sellers who can stomach the results. Not exactly a ship in a bottle. More like a battleship stuffed into an eyedropper, or if Cinderella were a nineteenth century Chinese princess with a glass slipper binding her feet. It's no different than keeping an ant farm or watching a mayonnaise-jarred butterfly escape a cocoon and explore its wingspan. She's made those very comparisons to tentative prospects in the past, but since her own recent operation she's losing that rationale.

Edgar's pills: Lipitor, Zocar, and aspirin, each meant either to rectify his lifetime of terrible choices or to maintain the result of those choices. Everything he does, Merkle often tells him, is killing him. It's curious, then, why he never avoided her talk of trying for a baby. He instead approved the motion with shrugged shoulders and a cute remark about needing an heir to the family business.

"You've got to find him, Merkle." The telephone static hinders a good read on Edgar's mood. He's generally cordial enough, but he knows, as Merkle does, that cordiality has limits when commerce is involved. "This was a big exchange."

"Can't you call him?" Merkle asks.

Edgar ignores her. "I can't find my pills. Did you do something with them?"

"In the bathroom where they always are. Are you going to call him?"

"I can't find them." Shifted toilet paper and folded towels knock unworthy pill bottles to the ground as Edgar hunts the bathroom cabinet. His failure beats through the phone.

"You'll be fine. Call him," Merkle says.

"What's really going on here? You've never cared this much about a drop-off." More shifting. "Nothing. Just Tums and loose toilet paper."

"Customer service," Merkle says, the coy slant to her voice is distorted and nervous like she's got a gun to her temple. "Word of mouth means something in our business."

"Fuck him," Edgar spits. "Seriously. We still have the product. He still has his money. As far as I'm concerned, this makes the transaction stillborn. Just ship it back to me and be on your way to the next city. We'll find another buyer." Edgar immediately takes back his 'stillborn' comment. "Sorry."

Merkle walks her index and middle fingers across her pelvis scar. Anthropomorphizing her hands has become a nervous tic as of late. "Are you?"

"Yeah. Of course."

She brushes her fingers against the striated scar halving her hemispheres from hip to hip, still red-raw and stapled. The vibration enters her ears as some off-key lullaby dirge. She wills her eyes dry. "Do you want to deal in jarred pets forever?"

"Nothing wrong with serving a niche," Edgar says.

"It's a fucking stupid niche, Edgar."

"We done here?"

"What kind of sane person wants a rat in a jar?"

"No kind of sane person. Sane's not our demographic." He lets the silence float.

"I'm not certain you're telling me everything."

"And I you," Edgar says. "We done?" he repeats.

We done? They satisfy a narrow market saturated with collectors better institutionalized than consumerized. Their buyers are people in the physiological sense only. To call them ethical beings would be to insult the wider human population. But she knows her participation makes her just as guilty. The Wrong Man would say that she herself is as much an insult as any of the collectors. This man, he had a lot to say about death.

"I talked to a man today," she says, grinning, "about suicide." She hangs up.

★ ★ ★ ★ ★

She estimates two more days for the rat. Edgar packs each shipment with enough fortified milk and saline to properly buffer the exchange by three days, give or take a few hours. But with improper handling, and the associated stress of being thieved from a hotel room closet and bounced around in the back of the Wrong Man's car, the increased heart rate will likely suck away enough nutrients to turn the grand reveal from neonatal to necronatal.

He's got a steady hand, Edgar, she'd never strip him of that. There are details to acknowledge, like minding the small parts of a ship in a bottle. Masts and claws and jibs and the snout, the snout must be propped just right to avoid suffocation. There's an art to the build. And the tails, Edgar learned quick that a rat will gnaw at its own tail if it means bleeding to death. He clips them now, cauterizing before the rat can even try to kill itself.

He's experimented with keeping the mother close, keeping the umbilical cord connected. But Merkle couldn't stand the mother's whine. Like rusty hinges or the final breaths of a beached whale.

★ ★ ★ ★ ★

She digs her fingernail beneath a loosening staple.

The Wrong Man had a concerning preoccupation with suicide, one Merkle dismissed as a personality trait, the unfortunate baggage of a job that caters to the mentally-skewed. It's scary when suicide becomes small talk. It's safer on her mind to assume such small talk as just a metric to a buyer's inborn psychology. That's what keeps her and the buyers separate: clinical insanity. As long as that barrier remains firm, she can sleep at night.

But the topic stuck with her, resonated with me, she'd say if ever the idea of suicide appealed to her before. But it didn't. Never. Edgar, on the other hand, she's had to pry more than a few knives from his neck. That was back when they first met, when he was fresh off a tour of some war nobody remembers, back when he could walk. Obesity has literally anchored him to life. Merkle keeps their knives in top cupboards beyond his reach.

She was his savior, a term tossed between them as fact, rarely romanticized the way other couples might. She gave him life. Perhaps, she's been wondering these past few hours, she never should have pressed him for another life.

She rips the staple free, hums the pain away.

★★★★★

The hotel phone pulls Merkle from the sting. "Did he answer?" she asks, not allowing the voice at the other end a single breath.

"I couldn't find the pills," Edgar says, his breathing heavier than normal.

"Did he answer?"

"Just got the recording." Edgar lets Merkle huff a few seconds away before speaking again. "How'd you not make the exchange? He wanted the jar. We're not hard-selling here."

Merkle, unwilling to confess about the Wrong Man she brought back to the room, suggests "cold feet?"

"No, no," Edgar says. "This guy was a definite buyer. He was a different kind of buyer."

"Different how?"

Edgar dodges the question. "What's this about suicide? Who did you talk to?"

"Nothing serious. A drunk guy and his ramblings." She holds the phone between her cheek and shoulder, leaving her fingers free to skip across the bed sheets. "It means a lot that you brought it back up."

"Are you just testing me?" Edgar asks. His wheezing and the phone static are inseparable. "Is that fair?"

"We're different people now, with a completely different context." She walks her fingers to her leg, makes them struggle to climb her hip. "It would be unfair to ignore that."

"Did you ever consider it wasn't fair to the baby," Edgar breathes, deep, slow, "to have parents like us?"

Merkle walks her fingers from her scar, over her chest, to her mouth. "What do you know about fair?"

Edgar is silent.

"Nothing. You know nothing about fair." She kisses her hand, whispers, "I'll name you Bridget."

Edgar is silent.

"Edgar."

A crash, then the phone disconnects.

★ ★ ★ ★ ★

Merkle returns the phone to its base, the dial-tone steady like bad news flashing from an EKG reading.

"No." She dismisses that possibility. She tells herself that Edgar is fine.

Merkle approaches the empty closet. She imagines a note left behind, a treasure hunt–though morbid the treasure may be–a game that she'll look back on fondly. But nothing. No note. No clue otherwise. Not even a hair. She retreats to the toilet. Immediately, the phone rings. Interrupted, but relieved still, she jumps to answer.

"Did you get him?"

"You've been waiting for my call?" It's the waitress, an unexpected but welcome voice.

"Sorry," Merkle says. "I've been talking to a few people, waiting for a lot of calls."

"He came back," the waitress says. "I think, anyway. Shifty. Nervous looking. And showing up a full hour after last call makes him stick out a bit."

"You're an angel. Is he still there?"

"Just walked out. Headed up Freemont. He can't be but a block or so away." She interrupts Merkle's quick thanks with, "I was harsh earlier."

"What?"

"I do have kids. The youngest is sick. I actually could have used your money, the five dollars you tried to give me. I'm just tired of handouts."

Merkle asks the waitress, "Is your baby tired of handouts?"

"He's 12," she says. "But no, no he's not."

Merkle thanks the woman, hangs up, and reaches for the doorknob in one motion, forgetting the rumble that originally sent her to the toilet.

★ ★ ★ ★ ★

The buyer, from behind, appears headless. He bypasses sleeping bums and evades gilded streetlamp light, a specter in the night. That hunched look, the shoe soles grinding and sliding against the cement, those are marks of disappointment, beacons that though Merkle doesn't share, she does recognize. "You forgot your jar," she yells to him, building a smile beneath her lip to pad the confrontation.

The man stops. He turns, and for a moment the streetlight complements his face. "Pardon."

"Your jar," Merkle says, slowing as she nears the man. "I missed you at the bar." She's never met a buyer without the support of a crowd. This conversation strips her naked.

"You have my jar?" the man says. A small grin distorts his entire face, as though he were trying such a pose for the first time in his life.

"I couldn't find you at the bar," she lies. Closer now, the man's face softens, almost childlike. He reminds her of Edgar, never a version she's seen herself, but one she's found in shelved family photos sent to their home after his mother's death last August.

"Where?" the man says, his eyes searching for bulges in her clothing.

Merkle's excitement dissipates as the man drops his uncomfortable grin for professional matters. She's not sure why, but this meeting felt more to her like a reunion than a prelude to a business exchange. But that's all it is. She knows this. "It's not on me," she says, biting through pain in her gut. Despite the brevity of the run, her lungs' inflation stretches the meat beneath her staples.

"You okay?" The man asks.

Merkle nods. "Okay enough. Just working through an unexpected surgery. Doctor says I shouldn't even be walking yet."

"Let alone running." He approaches her.

"Feel lucky. If I didn't run, we wouldn't be talking right now." They share a quick smile.

The man extends his hand and positions it upon Merkle's shoulder. The entire gesture comes across like a Rube Goldberg machine meant to convey care. His shoulder rotates to lift a shaking hand, then a weak grip transmits his awkward support, which immediately reels back his hand, leaving them both hyper aware of the whole convoluted exchange. "So where is it, the jar?"

She hesitates, opens her mouth to explain the robbery, but adjusts her intentions and says, "Back at my hotel. You want to walk with me for it?" The staples sting in the cold. She massages heat back into her gut. Every knead makes her wince.

"What kind of surgery did you have?"

She slides over to a storefront window and drops to the ground. "The removal kind."

"An unexpected removal is never good." He follows her. Merkle studies the man. Every articulation he makes seems like a poorly-rehearsed version of something genuine, like the intention is pure but he lacks practice.

Merkle lifts her knees to her chest and wraps her arms around her shins. "Doctor said I don't have a body fit for life."

"I can't imagine a doctor saying—"

"That's what it sounded like to me, anyway."

The man drops down beside her. "Sorry to hear it," he says. He puts his arm around her, passes the gesture off by claiming he's just keeping her warm, before admitting, "I've lost one before, too."

She presses into his chest, relaxes her head on his shoulder. "How long ago?"

"Three years, two months, thirteen days."

"Do we ever get over them?"

The man exhales, pulling Merkle tighter. "Perhaps. Some people try for more kids. Some people adopt. Some weirdoes even try to buy their way into completion." He and Merkle share small smiles.

"It's probably only fair to tell you ... what's your name?"

"Martin."

"It's probably only fair to tell you, Martin, the jar isn't at the hotel. It was stolen."

His grip loosens. "Shit ... what's your name?"

"Merkle."

"Shit, Merkle." He retracts his arm completely, begins to stand. "Not good, not good, Merkle."

"I'm hunting it down, though. Don't worry." Merkle watches him wipe something from his pants. "Everyone's a fucking thief."

"So what happens now?" the man says.

Merkle shrugs.

"I'm not typically that kind of collector, you know. I usually stick with bleached bones and taxidermy. I've got a few monkey fetuses, but they aren't the same." He rubs his hands, breathes into them. "Is there a paper trail?"

"Yes."

"What about the police. Am I in danger?"

"For a dead rat? No."

The man shakes his head. "I didn't order a rat."

Merkle stands, herself. The icy staples in her gut sting the surrounding skin. "What?"

The man backs away from Merkle. "My wife and I, we didn't give birth to a stillborn rat."

"Bridget?" Merkle whispers, bringing her gaze down to her violated pelvis. By the time she looks up, her eyelashes are icicles and the man is gone.

VON

SETH HARWOOD
TO THE BONE

He stood with his feet in the water, ankle-deep, letting the chill
sink into his bones. She had left him no choice. Jasmine. Now
she lay in the river, slumped against the rocks, the current gently
pushing its way into her hair.

Her brothers would want him dead now, their father too. If
he left everything behind, he could be out of the state by morning. Not that he would.

Birds chirped in the trees behind and above him, as they
always did in these woods, crying out at the sky, bruising the
darkness.

Her blood sped from burst lips, swept off down water.

When Duncan got home, his uncle Estep relaxed on the
couch, feet on the table. He sized up Duncan with one glance.
"You had to," he said.

"No choice now."

"Sure isn't." Estep shut off the TV, stood up. "I'll call Davis."

"Guess we need to take it direct to the brothers and not wait."

Estep nodded, then spit into his cup. Like that the matter was decided.

Duncan hit the spoon against his palm, waiting for the biggest of the three to come out the back of his house. The spoon: big, thick and made of a hard, dark wood; a tool Mexicans used to stir their pig skin scraps in a cauldron of cooking lard. He hoped it would be sufficient to the job. In his hurry, it'd been the biggest thing he could lay hands on.

The brother came out ten minutes later. Edward, his name. Had to be the biggest first, the only way to save face with Estep.

Edward walked past him toward the fence, hunched his shoulders to light a smoke. That was when Duncan cranked the spoon off the back of his skull. Soon as he did it, he knew he'd made the wrong choice of tool. The handle splintered in his hand, broke clean off just below its bowl. Edward turned around more angry than senseless.

Duncan shoved the broken spoon handle into Edward's side, driving in the shattered wood. The big man stepped back and smashed a fist into Duncan's jaw. Duncan saw white, but stabbed again with the handle.

When his eyes cleared, he could see he had managed to lodge it full-in to his hand in the soft space below Edward's neck.

Edward dropped to his knees at Duncan's feet.

Her brothers should have known it would end like this, should have stopped her way before things got too far.

Jasmine wasn't right from the start. Not because of her color, but her hair. She wore it big like a halo, picked out in an Afro that told the town's whites to leave her alone, that she wouldn't take things in their natural way.

At first, she went to Duncan as sure as he went to her. Even more so. The bulk of the instigation came on her part, not his.

She just came up to him at the grocery one morning after his lunch, this back when he worked the early shift at the mill and ate breakfast at 3 a.m., lunch around 10. She came right up and put her hand against his, laughed out loud at the difference in their color.

"Chocolate and milk," she said.

He didn't know what to say.

"Put your hand in my pocket." She nodded at her thigh, already directing him to go too far.

"You paint those on?"

"Just about." She gave him all of her smile then, both eyelids batting and even a man with a saint's soul couldn't have said no. Duncan was no saint either, neither did he have a woman at home to say no for.

Soon he was spending his days asleep after work and going out with her nights, not sleeping like a person, but instead like some nocturnal creature giving up his life to her sex. Mornings, he'd go straight to work from her bed, not sleeping, the early shift perfect for this with no one around to see him doze, no one to bother if he showed up still smelling of her wet.

He'd done this close to a month when Estep stopped in.

"Ain't seen you around." More an accusation than a question. Estep stood crooked against the doorframe at two in the afternoon, Duncan just home from the mill, ready for bed. His eyes narrowed on his uncle's, testing what he knew. Then Estep laughed. Of course he'd known; everyone would.

"Shit, boy. What you been thinking to get mixed up like this?" He kicked the lounger aside on his way to the couch. "Dumb as a tree branch."

Duncan had no defense. If he had been thinking ahead, he would have known this was coming. But of course he never had. Not since her.

"Got to put this to an end," Estep said. "Only one way."

Now he stood over her brother, looking down as Edward fell face-first into the mud. Splintered wood pushed through the back of his black neck. Duncan stepped away and toed blood off his boot in the dirt.

Only the other two brothers and the old man left.

In his idling car, Estep waited at the top of the road. It was raining, off and on and off again, just clear for a few minutes while Duncan waited in Edward's yard. Now the skies opened up as he walked. He didn't bother to run or try to avoid the water under a tree; he walked down the center of the dirt road, letting the downpour slick his hair to his head and his clothes to his skin.

"The fuck you doing?" Estep had the window down just enough. "Get your ass out of that rain if you expect to sit in here."

When Duncan tried the handle, the door was locked. "Not getting into my car that wet. Just about want to pour the water in, do you?"

Duncan wiped hair from his eyes and turned to walk. He could make it home on his own. He started along the gravel, Estep keeping pace beside him, wipers set on full. Up the next block, Davis flashed his lights.

"Too wet now anyway." Estep sped off. As he passed Davis, he honked. Davis flashed his lights again, then spun wheels on the wet, slick road and peeled out.

"I don't care."

A light came on in one of the houses.

Duncan stopped where he stood, the rain beating down

around him so hard he could hear it sizzle the road like a cymbal. A boy stood in the lit window, looking out at him, no doubt wondering what he meant to do out there in all this wet. Duncan was alone on the wrong side of town now, this boy not yet ready to understand.

The boy shook his head. Lightning flashed, and Duncan noticed the other form then: a man's body standing under the eaves of the boy's house, keeping out of the rain.

His was the thin form of one who spent too many nights outside, who slipped from place to place with outstretched hands, asking for whatever he could get. He saw Duncan but didn't move. He'd be armed: a knife maybe, or a sap. Duncan had been wrong to give up the protection of Estep's car.

He put his boots to use, walking faster toward town center, the nexus where different kinds came to blend. In minutes, the rain eased and he heard footsteps following. When he glanced back, he saw the thin man stepping fast to catch up.

"Got a quarter?" the man asked, his hand stretched out. He had barely come abreast.

"Not tonight." Duncan turned his shoulder.

"You ain't got even a quarter to spare? One bit?"

Duncan pushed into the cold, determined to keep going. Then a hand caught his arm and fingers dug in. He resisted at first, but then when the hand didn't let go, he spun around fearing the knife. Suddenly, the two men stood face-to-face, Duncan's right hand on the man's left wrist and the man's right hand on Duncan's arm.

No knife.

Anger and disappointment welled in the man's eyes. He pushed Duncan, trying to knock him off balance on the wet cement. Duncan set his legs wide, one in front of the other, planting his feet. He twisted his hold on the man and swept him off balance. The man slipped. Duncan felt how light he was, like a thing to be lifted up and moved. But the man swung his arm, snapping Duncan's hold and sending himself further off kilter. He fell to the ground with an elbow's crack of bone.

Duncan cocked his fist, knowing he wouldn't punch. "What is wrong with you, old man?"

"One bit. Give it to me." He grabbed for Duncan's sleeve, and Duncan stepped away, glanced around. All he saw was so much dark, this time of night the houses quiet.

"Please, I need to eat."

Duncan stepped in and kicked the man in the face then, snapped toe of boot to the bridge of nose between forehead and nostrils. The head snapped back, and Duncan kicked again, then stomped on a hand, a forearm, a wrist. Each attack forced the man into a tighter ball.

Now he kicked his back, bringing only a grunt or two. He aimed his toe at the spine, hoping to break it, then the ribs to its sides. On a normal man there was muscle here from hard work. But here it was all bone. Cracking bones.

When it was finished, Duncan stood back ashamed and surprised, unsure why or how he'd done it.

The act just got easier, he now saw, the more you did it.

Next morning, the other brothers found Edward on their way to work. They went directly to town, looking to find his killer and make things right.

Their father didn't yet know. This gave them solace.

No one had found Jasmine, even thought to look. In all the rain, she'd likely be washed downriver someplace even Duncan couldn't find.

He sat at the breakfast counter, eating his lunch, half a shift still to finish. He'd been late arriving, but the manager barely cared. No one said anything about what you did on nights, unless you really botched things. He watched the brothers' movements out in the street, saw who they spoke to, even listened to what they said when they came inside.

It was not easy to sit in place and avoid their stares, listening as others told them they had no ideas. Then they asked him.

"Edward dead?" he asked. "Terrible." The lie wasn't even hard.

Then they were gone.

Duncan sipped his coffee, listening to the others. Conversation about Edward didn't last; no one seemed surprised.

And no mention of the thin man, perhaps his death the kind that never leaves the street.

Duncan put two quarters beside his coffee, stood to leave. "See you later, Edna."

Outside, no thought of going back to the mill, he watched the brothers talk to whoever would listen. No one with anything to give.

After a time they separated, just as Duncan had hoped.

Now he claimed the second brother, followed him into a whites-only pool hall he should have known better than to try.

Estep and Davis shot at a table in back, this a piece of luck Duncan couldn't have predicted. He nodded to them. They'd seen Mike, were happy as Duncan he'd come around.

He took a while to make his way back to them. Duncan didn't mind. Sitting in one of the high-backed chairs, watching his uncle and Davis shoot, he felt better than he had since he'd twisted the knife out of Jasmine. In truth, being with her had made him happier than he'd ever known.

He held a pool cue, staring at the wood, astonished at how thin compared to the spoon.

"Come to ask you fellas a question," Mike started, when he approached. He'd said the same thing to every group in the room.

Estep glanced up from the green felt and looked back to the cue ball. "Don't want none." He was lining up a shot on the eight.

"No, no." Mike put his hands up. "This ain't like that. I come to ask about my brother, Edward. He dead by a Mexican, we think. Aim to find which one."

Duncan did his best not to smile.

Davis asked, "Which one he piss off?"

Estep shot Mike a look. "We look like we know any Mexicans?"

"No, no. Not like my brother to make anyone angry." Mike didn't appear dangerous. Perhaps without Edward or the others, he wasn't much. But neither had the thin drifter been.

Estep took his shot, finishing the game, and straightened up. He held the stick. "Maybe your sister then? She screwing Mexicans?"

"Oh, no now—" Mike got his ire up, squeezed hands into fists.

Davis blocked Mike's path. Duncan got up. "Not a good idea to come in here, was it—" then he said the word Duncan didn't like to hear. Jasmine had called him that once or twice. Back then it was funny.

When Davis said it, Mike bit his lips.

Davis pushed him toward Estep. "Now what you gone do?"

Mike faced Estep with wide eyes. Duncan closed off any last path. The hall echoed in silence around them; people knew a good time to go for a break, not wanting to bear witness.

"Duncan? I thought you our friend."

He worked with them at the mill; in truth, he'd never had

any problem with the brothers.

Duncan met Mike's eyes, shook his head. "Not now."

"This ain't right," Mike said. "Our fight ain't with you all."

"You got a fight?" Davis pushed Mike again, this time keeping him tight against the table.

Estep said, "Tell about this Mexican."

"Don't you boys hurt that felt now."

Duncan looked over to see the hall's manager, old Chevy, tip his hat. He nodded at the open back door to the alley beyond it.

"Shoot pool," Mike said. "Why don't you go back to what you was doing?"

"Our game over, friend." Estep held the cue over his shoulder now. "Tell me, why didn't your sister keep to herself?"

"This ain't about her."

"Shit–" Duncan's voice cracked. He cleared his throat. "Shit it ain't."

When Mike turned, Estep snapped the cue around from his shoulder, stung it across Mike's face like a whip.

"Big mistake coming in here," Davis said.

"Plus your fucking sister not keeping her legs closed."

Duncan had a small knife by his side, something he took on hunts. He hadn't in years but today he carried it. Now he folded out the blade–not more than two inches, but sharp.

He stepped between the others, pushed them away, and stuck the knife in Mike's side to its handle.

"Whoa now!" Davis stepped into him, holding Duncan's arm. "You don't want to make that mess in here now."

"Big mess," Estep said, and now he lifted the cue over Mike's head and used it to pin his arms. "Keep that all the way in him for me."

Mike's eyes were wide. He struggled, but the three held him

tight, started him toward the alley. "The fuck you boys doing?"

Duncan twisted the knife and warm blood shot onto his wrist. Mike made a wet sound.

"Hurry it up, now," Davis said. They pushed through the door and into the alley, then threw the black man across the space, splashing him against the far wall.

Duncan's knife was dark with blood.

Mike scrambled to get his footing, a rush of red coming to the front of his shirt. Estep stepped forward, but Duncan moved in, swung the knife again. He pulled it out sloppy, cutting sideways, trying to gut him, then plunged it in a half-dozen times–in and out of the man.

Mike fell to his knees, and Davis swung his fists to the sides of his head, knocking him one way and then the other. Estep started kicking, neither man saying anything now, just using their feet and hands to do their blood work.

Estep said, "You don't come into a place like this. Not unless you looking for trouble like your sister. And she put you where you is now." The words echoed in Duncan's ears.

He stood still, wiping blood off the knife with his handkerchief.

They couldn't leave a man dead behind a pool hall, so they carted him to the other end of the block to leave behind a Chinese restaurant. Enough bad cabbage and strange smells, they figured, that no one would notice or care.

Duncan walked out of the alley's shade into the sun squinting, hungry like never before. It was lunchtime, a break in the day for workers on the main shift, the crowd overflowing into the street.

"Hungry," he said to Estep.

"Come on." Estep led the three of them back to his apartment where he threw steaks into a pan and chopped onion to cook alongside. They passed a bottle of rotgut while coffee simmered in a pot.

"You get all that crazy out of you last night?"

Duncan nodded.

"Didn't know what you thinking in that rain. 'Fuck it,' I said. 'Let him walk.'"

"I's better now."

"But you still got enough crazy in you to knife that nigger."

Davis forked at his steak, said he liked it to bite back. He slapped it down on a plate with the onions barely soft, spilled on salt.

"You be careful there, like to make you talk in moos you eat it like that."

Duncan said, "Looks like our work half done. Just one more brother and the old man."

"Eat your food." Estep pushed whiskey at Duncan and poured coffee. "It'll be ready just a minute. Then we wait until tonight."

But later that afternoon, the third brother and the old man came looking. That many men in a pool hall, you couldn't help word getting out, even back to the other side of the town. Not with his people asking everyone about the last place Mike been seen.

When Duncan woke up from his rotgut, he heard them calling out in the street.

"Estep Goines," the father yelled. "Estep and Duncan Goines."

"Fuck they want us to do?" Estep asked. But he knew. They all three knew the men wanted them to come outside and finish what they'd started. Duncan felt glad to have it closer to an end. He went to the window, saw the old man and the third brother—

Thomas–then two others. Thomas gripped a length of chain, the old man held a small gun, and the other two held switches.

"Looks like we out-manned," Davis said.

"Shit." Estep drawled a slew of curses. "Not more than four of them there to our three. Sounds fair to my mind." He went to the window. "What you want?"

"Come down here."

"What?"

"Come outside."

"Or else what?"

The old man thought hard on that for a few moments, struggling with the unexpected. But Estep didn't make him answer. "Never mind, old man. We coming."

Davis laughed. "Poor nigger never know what to say. Ask him two and two."

"What you got in this house to fight with?" Duncan knew his little knife wouldn't be enough now.

Estep went out and came back holding a shotgun by its barrel. He stuffed his pocket with more shells. "I got this. Best look to the closet for what you need."

Davis removed a small revolver from the waist of his pants and spun the cylinder. "This good for me."

In the closet, Duncan found a wooden baseball bat and a long knife Estep liked to call a machete. He hefted the weight of each in his hands and settled on the second. "Even if I am bringing a knife to a gun fight."

"Fuck. Take that rifle." Estep pulled a hunting gun from the back of the closet, a single-shot muzzle loader that Duncan would never want in this. Estep and Davis laughed at him until he pushed it back into the closet as far as he could reach.

"No?" Davis said. "You sure about that?"

"I'm liable to take my one shot then use the thing to sound off on someone's head. This splinters, you okay with that?"

Estep frowned. "Just stay behind us at first. Once that old man ain't shooting, you be fine."

They went out the back and came around front to see the four from a different angle. Sure enough, they stood on the other side of the street, waiting just like they meant to.

The old man's pistol was almost too small to bother, but you had to respect a gun. Duncan thought Estep might call the old man to lay it down, but there was no right to that, announcing where they were and appealing to a sense of reason that wasn't there. And Estep and Duncan just as soon to have their fun.

"Let me drop that old man for us," Estep said. He shouldered his shotgun and sighted on the street. "You go around the other side," he told Davis, who took off around the backside of the house to come up at them from the other side.

When he'd gone, Estep said, "Good. Come down to this, better to be just us family."

Estep fired then, ripping the day in half and making anyone unsure scatter. He came around the corner of the house breaching a new round, and Duncan followed. The old man lay in the dirt, clawing at his right side with his left hand, trying to brush away the pieces of his shirt now like he'd brush off dirt. His gun lay beside him but his right hand didn't work. He twitched with pain.

Estep fired again at another, taking out his legs. Thomas ran at them holding his chain, then threw it at Estep when he'd re-racked the shotgun. Estep covered up and the brother leapt, but Duncan knocked him out of the air with the machete, swinging it like a club into his back. He fell on top of him, trying to swing the machete again, but this time Thomas blocked it with his forearm—a horrible sound of metal splitting bone—and held Duncan's arms. He kneed Duncan and punched him harder than the oldest brother had from his back.

Then they rolled and Thomas stood up, holding the machete. He swung it on Estep, knocking the shotgun from his hands. Duncan heard a gun go off behind them and saw Davis in the street. He'd missed though, still too far away to do anything other than throw his bullets around. The last man ran toward Duncan as he scrambled to his feet.

Another used the father's gun now, the one Estep had shot in the legs, shooting back at Davis enough to keep him busy.

Duncan blocked a blow from the switch with his left forearm, felt the crunch in his own bone. He threw an uppercut to body, stumbled back from a stiff jab to his face. Now he covered up.

He had his hands full, but not too much to see Estep wasn't doing any better with Thomas. He had the machete and chopped at Estep, who did the best he could to dance away, trying to get time to rack his shotgun.

Duncan threw two rights, both hooks, both slapping off his man's face like so much insult. The man came back with the switch low to Duncan's legs, knocking them out from under. Then he found himself on the ground, clawing at the other's legs, trying to bring him down. The switch rained on his head and arms until he dragged his man to the ground and himself on top.

He heard grunting from Estep's direction, more shooting from the end of the street. Then the switch was under him, in his hands. He pushed it down onto his man's chest, trying to roll it up to his neck to cut off air. They both were pushing it toward one another. Then they rolled and Duncan was on the bottom, feeling the switch pushed down against him. It moved toward his neck; he felt himself being overpowered.

A shot close behind him, too close to his head, then the man's strength fading, leaving him altogether. Duncan pushed him off. He saw Davis's gun and Davis behind it. Then an awful yell. Duncan turned, saw Thomas rushing him with the machete, swinging it with both hands and its blade clapping down deep and hard into Duncan's collar. He felt the bone splinter, muscle cut, and he was out of breath suddenly, then on his back.

Thomas pulled at the machete to get it out and strike again, his foot at Duncan's neck. When it came free, Duncan felt air whooshing into parts of him that had never known air, like he was breathing directly through his lungs.

Davis shot Thomas before he could swing again, and he fell on top of Duncan, struggling to breathe and to speak, shot through the neck, blood spilling out onto Duncan, mixing with his own.

"Get him off me." Duncan coughed. Then Estep kicked the brother off him and smashed the stock of the shotgun down hard onto his head.

"You gonna be okay," he said.

Duncan knew this to be a lie.

"The leeway or the leash," he heard Estep saying long ago, somewhere in what he could remember before they'd killed Edward. He had meant the brothers and the father gave Jasmine too much of one or the other, that they should've kept her reigned in. "Lead to nothing but trouble and bloodshed," Estep had said.

Duncan coughed and his throat filled with blood. He tried talking, meaning to tell his uncle he'd been right way back when. He tried to apologize for beginning all of this, for being taken in, but the only thing that came out of him were sounds—gurgles and strange whistles that he could not control.

He reached out to Estep with his left hand now, the only one he could feel, but wasn't sure what it might do.

"I think what I don't like about writers is when they pent their imagination for fear of being ridiculed. I prefer it when writers just let themselves go."
—Booked. #122 Three Authors

CRAIG WALLWORK
THINK TANK

The first time I met my father he was nine years old. The train had thrown his body two hundred feet down the track, bones were toothpicks dropped on the floor, angles and spikes. Eyes the colour of sliced grapes were imbued with burgundy. I got to sit with him for a full two minutes hearing him croon his final breaths as the cadence of death prodded each limb and hand. It was the happiest moment of my life.

Quint said he could get me into the Think Tank for only half of what everyone else was being charged. That he never told me what everyone else was charged didn't fill me with confidence, but the prospect of never existing did. No one knew how the Think Tank worked. Some say it's a chamber, a flotation device that allows the mind to enter an altered state. You don't see or touch anything. It's all in your head. Nothing changes. There was this rumour that a kid used it to go back in time. He bought a lottery ticket for the following week. When he left the Think Tank, he was no richer than when he got in it. Quint believes the rumour was started by the company that owns the Tank. Stop people from profiting from their science. They didn't want the world to be full of gods and billionaires. If you were going into the Tank, it was just to observe the past, not influence it or alter the future. Stuff happens in history for a reason. Let it be. That's why they limited how far back you could travel. At a push you could go back fifty years. The last major terrorist attack was 9/11. Maybe if you found the oldest man alive today, he could have been no younger than thirty years when those towers fell. To me, that date might as well have been scribed in the Bible it was so long ago.

Digital prints still exist of her before the accident: two rattle-snake tails of plaited hair draped her face. Eyes the size of opals. On the hood of an old Cadillac she sat, legs crossed, ankle high boots. The winds had spun the clouds into a web, diffusing the sunlight to make her skin flawless. If Quint heard me talk like this about my own mother, he'd think I was some weirdo. Probably beat me too, but I've seen the way he looks at those pictures. He gets lost in them too, measuring every part of her as though he's putting together a jigsaw puzzle, matching tones and ambiguous features, comparing her youthful right eye with the one now hidden behind skin graft. He is estimating the thickness of her lips against those that have been thinned by erosion.

The company that owns the Think Tank worked out of a small industrial hangar on the outskirts of the city. It would take a full charge to get my car to travel that far. Quint knew a few of the old back roads that cut the time and distance down some. The place didn't look like much from the outside, a box of corrugated steel with a small door. No signs. Quint knocked five times and we had to wait another five minutes before we were let in. The air was charged with the smell of chemicals and ground coffee. Quint told me to hang back. He walked over to a large black man fixing an old Goldwing motorcycle. They talked, and every once in a while, they would both look over to me. The black guy guided us to another hangar, one that sat within the larger hangar. Within that was a room. Two men stood at its entrance. The black man held out his ID card and they let us in. There was nothing in this room save for a large tomb-like structure in the centre. One light hung above it, cold and naked. A man wearing a lab coat came in and Quint handed him the electronic tablet that contained my birth details, fingerprints, blood group and family medical history. The man downloaded it into a large computer. I was told to remove all my clothes and change into a dressing gown. Then I had to wait. Quint sat with me, said it would be okay and that it will all be done soon. To pass the time, Quint asked questions about my family. He knew the answers, heard me speak about my parents since we first met at school. Guess he was nervous too. To make things go quicker, I told him about rabbit dodging.

The main gas line between the east coast and the capital ran through the town where my father grew up. It was shut down after the gas shortage of 2030. The evacuated tunnel was used for the first Vactrain. It was a big deal back then. My grandfather was one of the local men hired to lay down the maglev lines from Yorkshire to the Midlands, and that's about as much as I know about him. Quint knew about the tunnels. Knew they had no air in them because the lack of air resistance was the key to making those trains supersonic. A recreational pastime of bored children would be to open access latches that sealed off the outside from the vacuum beneath. If they timed it right, fresh air would enter the tunnel and the Vactrain would slow enough for one child to hang down from the access and wait there. At the last minute he'd hoist himself back up, avoiding having his legs taken off by the Vactrain. Authorities got wise to this and sealed the access latches and that was the end of that. But my father was pretty good at it. To celebrate his ninth birthday, he went rabbit dodging and left a little too late. The train caught his left foot, snapped it back at the ankle. My mother said she would have never noticed my father had he not had that limp. She was a sucker for a wounded animal.

The man in the lab coat threw policies and procedures at me like rice at a wedding. I wasn't really listening. I checked out and that's all that mattered. Before he led me to the Tank, Quint turned to me and shook my hand. It felt final, like that was the last moment he had with me. We didn't say anything. Know someone long enough and you don't need to talk. It's all understood in a stare, or gesture of hand.

My mother told me that after she was attacked, they placed her in a body bag. The paramedics on the scene zipped it up and talked about her beyond the plastic. She said it was like being dead, hearing voices from another world. The Think Tank is like that. There is no light. No sound, save for your breathing and the faint echo of a voice that seems to be in another dimension. Water surrounds you. Warm. High salt content keeps you afloat. There is no point in closing your eyes because the eyelid is just as dark as the space before you. A voice squeezes through a speaker: deep and Oz-like. I tapped my heels three times and whispered, There's no place like home. Then came more instructions. Hypnosis was delivered under the cloak of relaxation. Count. One hundred to zero. In the darkness, I saw her face again beside that Cadillac. People in the town used to say my mother was too perfect. They assumed she had surgery to make herself that pretty, but the only thing unnatural about her was her taste in men.

I counted to fifty and the voice told me to picture the place I wanted to visit. Imagine it in every detail, the smell and the sounds. Before coming to the Tank, I found the first Google Earth pictures that had been archived before the earthquakes razed industrial buildings, houses and hillsides. Before the earth yawned and cracked the tunnel in two, I was able to see a moment from the past captured by a search engine: my father's old town. Antique BMWs and the first of the hybrid vehicles. The houses brick, not the composition of fibreglass, silicon and cinder aggregate used on modern houses. The smell of wild flowers and grass I gleaned from the botanic museum in the city: adder's tongue, toothwort, hawksbeard, foxglove. Memorised all their scents from those fostered in labs or recreated from synthetic perfumes. I spoke with my mother about the clothes and detergents she used, soaps and hair-care products. I recalled the scent of lavender, almonds and citrus fruits. I inhaled the gentle breeze of a summer afternoon that carried upon it creosote and cut grass. I heard the laughter of children and felt the warm hand of the sun resting upon my head.

My father placed a gold band on her finger and put an embryo in her belly before she reached the age of eighteen. He then spent the following five months furnishing her cheekbones, arms and legs in varying shades of black and blue. Mozart and Vivaldi are the preferred sounds to play an unborn baby, but a rendition of harsh profanities became my beat, screams the harmonies, and the wailing and furious words that bled into the placenta the music that aided my foetal development.

Six months pregnant and scared that his fist might strike my tiny head, she packed her bags. He caught her leaving through the front door. Her parting sonnet to him was that she would become a successful model and find a man as beautiful as she remembered herself to be.

You don't know it's happened till you're there. Like a dream, you charter the darkness till shadows are pushed to one side and before you is light, pure and brilliant. The volume of life is turned up again. This wasn't lucid dreaming. The detail was too clear and rendered too perfectly. There was no pocket of empty space filled with anything surreal or out of place. The grass was warm to the touch, the air free of smog. My peripheral vision was untainted by ambiguity. If I turned my head left or right, the horizon remained punctuated by hills and rows of tiny roofs that looked like blackened teeth. Upon the zephyr came the shrill of emergent voices, and on occasion the faint drum of rushing feet. To walk in the past is to walk among an upturned graveyard. There is nothing but death brimming with life.

The landscape of my mother's blistered skin is a terrain better matched to Death Valley. Mesh covered her face for three weeks after the first set of skin grafts. Donated skin from her leg wallpapered the empty socket where she lost her right eye. Further surgery helped reconstruct a nose around the tapered septum still remaining. More grafts. More mesh. The coffee skin turned the colour of shrimp shell before settling into shades of mocha, rose petal and cream. She didn't smile for a year, and then when she did, no one could tell. Halfway through the painful skin graft operations, her waters broke. The doctors injected anaesthetic into the potato peel that was her face to stop her from passing out during labour. Both north and south of her body she was in pain, and now she had a child to feed. Cops found my father hiding out at a hostel in Kendal. Charged him for giving my mother an acid face wash and he served three years. He got shanked in Strangeways after the first six months.

Three boys dressed in sports apparel stood around the aperture of the latch, staring down. They didn't hear me approach, or observe me as I stopped before a wild dandelion, rapt in its simple beauty. As I reached down to stroke the yellow petals, the ground vibrated, earth shifted. The Vactrain was close. Neither boy resembled the pictures I had seen of my father. One of them shouted down the hole, the name of Kieran glued to the end of the sentence. I imagined him down there, hands gripping the safety rail, legs flailing, heart beating out a rate faster than the wheels of the Vactrain. A faint rumble like that of thunder burrowed through the soil. In one motion I ran toward the boys, foot crushing the dandelion. They saw me approach, a glaze of panic coating their eyes. I yelled something that should have been more inspired, brutal and deliberate, but the words were malformed, tumbling out of my mouth and peppering their tiny scared faces like hailstone. Feet began tingling, shins trembling. The Vactrain was a bullet traveling at a speed of 4000–5000 MPH. The boys ran off when I raised my fists. I saw their willowy figures set against the rising heat.

My newborn fingers must have traversed the valleys and skin ridges of her rugged face many times. They must have felt the tears welling in the ravines and gullies that were once a cheek, a lip, an eye. But I have no recollection of this. All that remains of my infancy was the warmth I felt around my mother. In her one remaining eye that watched me warily as I ascended stairs, and that pinched slightly whenever my paint splattered hands hovered too close to the wall, I noted only devotion. The drama of expression is lost on a face deformed by chemical burns. The expression of shock, anger, unhappiness or joy does not pull so freely on the muscles beneath the skin. I learnt that the slightest dip of an eyebrow implied sorrow in her, the curl of the lip accompanied by the narrowing of the eye was happiness. It got to be that I could read her face much more easily than had she never been burnt, which is why I knew whenever she passed a shop window, or noted the looks of disgust as she guided me along streets and pathways, that even I could never heal the sorrow that burnt her heart.

With toes perched on the edge of the hole, I looked down and saw bone-white knuckles gripped around the bottom of a telescopic ladder. The power of that train was sucking the outside air in. I felt myself being forced into the hole, and heard him shout to the boys that the rabbit was coming. The rabbit was coming. He was whooping and yelling. Adrenalin cries. I descended the first few rungs of the ladder, and felt my body gain three times its mass. Skin blanched as my hands held tightly to the metal rungs. Bones trembled, organs convulsed. My heart was a clenched fist banging upon the wall of a prison cell. The first time we touched was the last. My foot crushed his grip and he fell before the passing train. It took me all my strength not to follow him.

The first time I met my father he was nine years old. I extended the ladders down into the tunnel and sat upon steel rails with my heart bloated with happiness and lungs hungry for air. As first impressions go he appeared small and weak with his body lying bent into many angles. No risk to anyone. The bitterness I had inherited bled out of me just as life bled out of him. He was now no more than a dream. And as shadows united around me, muting the past and erasing me from the future, her face came to me once more. Before her the sun was again a spotlight and the heavens a web to diffuse the light. Once again she was beautiful, and would remain that way until the end of time.

"It's awesome being in the legendary Billy Goat Tavern. I didn't know it was a legend until today, but it's great being here."
—Booked. #79 Shindig in Chi-Town Part 1

MARK RAPACZ
MANGER DOG

Disheveled in sawdust and leaning on a leg that hasn't felt right since his motorcycle accident, Hal stands in the darkness. A drafter's light shines a few feet in front of him. Oak dust is in the air. It fills his lungs and covers his beard. Before him in the light is a rickety chair leaning much as he is. He inspects it and makes a few adjustments on a clamp, but the chair still wobbles. The backrest is wavy. Some of it goes with the contours of the rough-cut wood, but then he looks at the seat rest and the failed experiment that was the meeting of his sander and the spalting lines, the small explosion of splinters. There's no recovering this one. He immediately begins to conjure a pitch, and the word *postmodern* keeps fluttering in his head, until it gets slammed by the truth. The chair is chunky. It's a chunky piece of junk.

Postmodern will do.

He strides out of the barn. Tonight it was his studio, one of the few nights he could call it a place of inspiration and detriment, for tomorrow and most days it's where they store the Hyundai. He limps along the gravel drive toward the old farmhouse that he and his ex-wife bought long ago, back when they were dumb enough, idealistic enough, to think boarding horses was a cinch. He never lost friends faster than when he looked toward their charity when they couldn't make it work. Nothing worked, in fact. Not the business. Not the relationship. Nor the baby, who worked beautifully–so perfect–for days. Then didn't. Hal kicks one of the farm cats, the only success story of his little paradise.

In the house, Hal lunges at Harley in much the same way as the cat, but Harley bolts to the flickering light down the hallway before his boot connects.

"Why'd you let him in the trash," he asks the slumped over body by the table, long hair spilling over books and paper.

"I didn't let him in the trash," Chip says without looking up from his work. Glaring now, "I didn't open the lid and say, 'Here, boy! Dinner!' He's a dog. He got to it himself."

"It'd just be nice if you could have stopped him."

"It would have been nice. You're right, Hal."

Hal bends to start picking up the pizza box that has cold melted cheese on it. A black banana peel slides off the back of the package. There's a baggie with a pink, fuzzy thing in it. Ants crawl through the mess, aimless and testing.

Chip speaks to Hal without demanding keys, money or both. "So, you finish any masterpieces out there?"

Hal turns on the faucet and washes something gooey off his hands. He wants to change the subject, maybe attempt to form a connection with his wife's grown child, but he sees the books and the strange symbols of trigonometry. "I have a project brewing. It's a chair, but it's coming around."

Chip looks about to laugh.

"Actually, it's a postmodern piece. You may want to take a

look at it," he says. "I could use the constructive feedback," he lies.

"Yeah ... Maybe."

Hal begins to retreat to the living room.

"The Schrocks down the road sell loads of pieces. Why don't you just make stuff like theirs? You know, chairs you can actually sit on."

Walking briskly through the hall, he recites the answer he's always given his critics. Something to do with inspiration and freedom and doing what he can to stay out of the confines of functional art. Some hippie bull honky he and his ex-wife often talked about in their youth.

In the living room now, Patty's eyes are wide, sucking in a reality show. When they met, Patty would quilt and do yoga, eschewing television, but then she took on a promotion—more hours and responsibility—which suited them fine since Hal hadn't sold any pieces for some time. This ritual with the couch and the shows drowned out all but Hal's latent memory that Patty's new position would be for the best. "This is really for us," he remembers her saying.

Hal shoves Harley aside, so he can sit beside her. "I got a piece done, Hun."

"Shush. Wait for a commercial."

During the commercial break, Hal says again, "It's finished. I got that little charge in me."

"Do ya, now? That's so sweet." Patty pulls Harley onto her lap and gives him a belly scratch. "You think that's so sweet? Don'chya? Don'chya?"

"Yeah," Hal replies.

The phone rings. Chip's voice murmurs in the kitchen. He laughs hard and long. "Okay, okay. Look. Unlike you, I actually care about school and going to college ... Yeah he is ... I don't know, some weird stool ... Gotcha ... I'll let him know."

"Who do you suppose that was?" Hal asks Patty who is now resting her head on his shoulder.

"Dunno."

Harley growls again as Hal tries to pet him with his dry hands. The dog hops off the couch and goes to lie under a sturdy rocking chair, a gift from Jebediah Schrock one Christmas.

Chip enters and leans against the chipped molding in the doorway. A stringy high school kid, muscular and skinny, he wears sweatpants that sag low, scratches his mop of tangled hair, and waits before he says, "Hal."

"Yes, Chip?"

"That was Ron. He wants you to call him back."

"Why didn't you just bring the phone?"

"You're watching a show and I got a lot of shit on my mind. Sorry."

Hal lets the ambiguity sink in. Familiar. "I don't know his number."

Patty now, "Hal, please."

Growl. Snarl.

No words pass, but the kid shrugs.

"He's in New Zealand," Hal clarifies.

"So. Not my problem." On his way back to his studies Chip shouts, "You're getting a souvenir from Kiwi Land. Be happy, dude."

Midnight and the boy is shouting. "He's gone! Wake up!" Chip is in the doorway, a silhouette. He slips through the room to his mother who is also now up and sobbing.

"It's fine. Harley does this all the time," Hal reassures them both, but the phlegm in his throat makes him sound groggy and rough.

"Not at night!" Patty cries. "Someone has to get him. Hal."

Hal is already up, sliding his legs through his crumpled jeans that sit, as if prepared by firemen, over his boots. Hal could jump right into them and bolt anytime, any day.

At the doorway, he asks the kid, "Well, are you coming or not?"

"I got school," the boy says.

"It's your dog." Trump card played. The dog is older than this relationship.

They walk over the gravel drive, through the gate, by the studio/garage/barn, into the field that is overgrown and ready to be cut down. The Schrock clan will likely do it in a few days. They all come, even the littlest ones. They do marvelous work.

Chip talks tough after crying. He references babes he wants to slam and universities that are all up in his shit.

"There's this one, it's a state school, but whatever," he says. "It's out on the coast somewhere, I don't know. But I got a buddy out there who says the parties are bombin', the chicks are smokin', and I really think I'm just ready for that sort of thing. The Ivy League can eat my ass. You know? I'm fine where I'm at, but I'm looking out for more."

The moon is bright. Rabbits run through the field. Hal is looking at a tangled tree alone in the field. It is sad and twisted and shadowy and long ago his ex-wife wanted to chop it down because it had contracted a disease. He told her it was too far from the forest to hurt the others. "Too far from anything," she had replied. Now the tree has bulbous tumors blistering out, cracking the bark and fissuring it deeply.

"That sounds good, Chip. It's always good to look out for

more." Hal puts a hand on the kid's shoulder, but Chip finds reason to move quickly out of arm's reach.

They hear barking in the distance, down in the trees, down the thirty-foot embankment near the stream, the muddy water that smells like shit and oil.

"He's by the crick," Hal says. Hal remembers that whistling was what all those horses responded to. He whistles two quick bursts, and they wait in silence. The dog does not come.

Chip then shrills, "Treat, boy! I got a treat. Come get your treat!" There's splashing, a yip, the ruffling of underbrush, and then the emergence of a shadowy little mutt waggling his butt.

"Where'd you get that?" Hal asks, nodding toward the strips of jerky.

"How else we gonna get him in?"

Harley nips at the treat and dances around Chip, then rips the jerky away and bolts into the field.

"Harley!" Chip shouts. He motions to yell again, then gives up and speaks without the bite. "I got rejected by Columbia today."

Hal's feet suddenly feel like they're being pulled into mud. "You'll get there," he says.

That soft midnight shadow that was Chip stiffens to something prickly and electric. "No, Hal, I won't. They don't take you after they send you a rejection letter."

"Sorry, I never applied for a school. I just figured."

"Figured what?"

Hal searches the field for the dog, and there he is circling their position, scrounging for prey and soaking himself in night-time dew. "Just, you know. You'll get into school."

"Harley, boy! Come 'ere! Let's go to bed, boy! Time for bed! Let's see Mom." Chip pulls out more jerky and Harley immediately obeys, cutting a beeline right for them as Chip starts toward the house.

Hal remains for a while thinking on that tree. It suddenly becomes a thing that should be removed. It's too twisted. Too diseased. It could be a project he and the boy do over the summer. They could turn it into something Chip could use in college. Like a bookshelf or a desk. He starts to size it up, knowing the darkness will skew his estimates, but Hal's never been a man of exactitudes. The moment he factors in the amount of time it would take the wood to dry and the possibility of heart rot, Hal abandons the idea and turns to go in, but the house is already dark. Chip didn't think to leave the floodlights on.

Morning and there is the sound of mechanical power. The deep grumble of a diesel. The whirring and rumbling of a compressor. A soft and heavy clang of something large and metallic. War is upon the farm. Good riddance. It's finally come. Between sleep and wakefulness, Hal waits for a bomb to explode, and to his quiet surprise he is thankful that Patty and the boy are at work and school.

Harley barks and spurs Hal to clearer thoughts. He steps into his clothes and soon he is outside with a sludgy cup of coffee, talking to a man who looks as grubby as Hal, near an industrial storage container being lowered off a hydraulic lift the size of a semi-trailer.

"What's this?" Hal shouts at the man operating levers on a small terminal at the front of the trailer. Harley skulks around the noise with his tail between his legs, shivering and nipping chaotically at the invisible intruder that is all percussive booms. The smell of gas and lubricants hangs on the morning air.

"Delivery. For a Mr. Hal Johnson," the man shouts back.

The front of the trailer is raised high above the truck cab. It creates a steep slope that the storage bin clings perilously to. Harley scurries right under its shadow barking in a high-pitched way.

The operator with the stubble and ball cap chuckles. "That critter better move when I start to lower this thing." Hardy-har. Snort.

The bin is lowered in the drive, leaving just enough space for their Hyundai to squeeze in and out from the barn to the service road. The platform returns to its non-threatening position, and the morning stillness returns long enough for the birds to be heard again.

Hal asks the operator again, "What is this?"

He inspects a grease-covered clipboard with a plastic sheet protector. "Says here it's some lumber from Rangiora."

"Rangiora?" Hal asks. "Never heard of that mill. In fact, I've never ordered anything this big. Load it up and take it back. Can't afford nothing like this."

The operator looks at his clipboard again. "Been paid for and Rangiora is a city."

"Wisconsin or South Dakota?"

"Rangiora, New Zealand. This stuff's traveled a long ways."

They both look at the rusted and dented storage bin with a little more reverence. Harley whines and licks his lips for a treat. With none to give, Hal pats his head.

The letter that Hal finds tacked to a stack of rough-milled planks, cut as if some medieval saw house tore each piece from one large piece of lumber with a slight idea of geometry and consistency, had this to say:

Hal, my man!

Heard you still cobbled furniture together. This
wood is special and ancient. Preserved under a
bog thousands of years ago! What do you think
of the smell? It WILL change your world. See
you on the other side! ~ Ron

Ron is Patty's former husband's brother and Hal's best friend who he has seen intermittently for the past twenty years. Ron introduced Hal to both wives, citing each as "absolutely vital." With Patty he tacked on the fact that the boy was "a genius athlete." Ron is also the type of guy who never needs money, can take off for New Zealand in a salvaged schooner months ago, and judging from the lumber delivered to Hal's doorstep, survive. Hal has always envied that sort of man. A while back he thought he was that kind of man. He bought a motorcycle that he meant to drive to Baja, Mexico, one summer. He rationalized that the trip could still be rebellious if he camped the whole way, stuck to the blue highways, and got drunk at least twice at a roadhouse. His chain broke before the state line. As he was pulling onto the shoulder, his bike slipped down into a roadside ditch. He was okay except the cuff of his pant leg got hung up on the footplates so he ripped his jeans and pulled his groin muscle. Patty picked him up and after a conversation that lasted no more than five minutes, the bike was sold to the garage.

She left for a guy like Ron.

Hal manages to lug a warped board into the studio, which is spacious without the dented sedan taking up most of the workspace. He drops the board. Old dust flies. Light ekes through the cracks between the planks. Two or three cats scurry into the shadows, and Hal notices his postmodern turn-of-the-century highback chair is now a small pile of twisted clamps, broken dowels, sooty lacquer, and chunky wood. Its chunkiness the only thread tying it from past to present.

Dragging his feet, Hal clears the area of his old project, shoving it in the scrap pile behind the lawn tractor. For the better part of an hour, Hal walks between the storage bin and the garage, slowly stacking a neat pile of wood. For a few of the trips, Harley follows him but then loses interest and runs off. Hal lets him go.

He stacks enough wood to finish a few projects. The rest he leaves in the trailer. For an hour or two, he waits with the wood. Looking at it. Inspecting it. Getting on his hands and knees to get close to the boards. It's a soft wood. A light wood. Like pine, only the whorls and lines are different. Broader, darker, and there's a smell that Hal can't place. Something old and natural, earthy like a spice cellar covered with mossy walls. Or a pond full of tea leaves. Maybe more like ginger.

Hal sits with it for a while longer, following the lines of the wood, trying to read it like an educated person, a graduate student or a scientist. He looks for a peculiarity that reveals a hard year. Another that reveals a wet year, but all he sees are fiery lines that ring out like sunbursts, dulled by age. Though he does not have the training or knowledge to know for certain, Hal believes there is more to this wood than the pile of old planks they seem to be. There was a time that they were something majestic, ageless, and pure—something green and undying near some New Zealand mountain peak.

Hal sees what needs to be made.

Without much thought he picks up his tools and gets to work. Cats peek out from their hiding spots and immediately disappear. The planks are circular-sawed, buzz-sawed, and handsawed. They are measured and compared. He gets slivers in his palms from running his hand along the grain. The ginger dust fills the air and his lungs. Hal opts for dowels and glue to hammer and nails, and then he begins his drilling. More sanding. He retreats a few steps, then leans forward to see it at every angle. He brings the project out into the sun for better light. Brings it back in for better atmosphere. He walks around it. Jostles it with his foot, half-expecting the project to crash to the dirt like all the rest, but within himself, or within the ancient dust that is all around and now in his bloodstream, he finds reassurance, guidance, certainty, and confidence. He knows before the project is half complete that it's the best project he's ever made. He is so charged he takes no time to dwell on it because he knows it's too fragile to tease at for too long. It's as if the piece is taking shape on its own, as if the trees were grown and fallen, preserved and discovered, milled and shipped, all on their own volition; all of it chosen to end up in his practiced hands, in his shop, to be shaped into something beautiful and new.

Another diesel engine rumbles. He hears Chip shout some obscenity as the bus drives off.

In his head he tries to return to that tea-soaked place with the dark shade, black earth, green moss, clear streams, and purple mountains. The image gets fuzzy. It dissipates. Hal struggles to return anywhere, nowhere.

The barn door creaks and then it wails as the hinges catch rust.

"Why is there a semi-trailer in our driveway?"

Hal lets the drill continue to bore into a joint for a few seconds before he responds.

"Hal!"

The drill gasps to a halt. "I heard you."

"Whatever, dude. You making a cage for all the cats you hate or something?"

"Oh, this? No. It's just a thing I'm working on. This new wood is something else, actually."

"It seriously looks like you could keep a cat in there. Not like one of your postmodern thingies."

With two quick pulls on the trigger, Hal returns to his work. "Thanks!" he shouts. Then he leans into his project, his weight focused completely on the bit and the noise of the drill drowning out the shouts from Chip who asks where Harley is, but the cage, as the boy calls it, is really coming along, and so the drill bores as chuffs of dust rise.

Evening and there's a horn honking outside the barn door. Patty's signal to come in. He directed her to this technique early in their marriage. It was one of the few routines held over from his previous relationship. His ex-wife used to come into the barn and tap him on the shoulder or wrap him tightly from behind, and she would smell like the outdoors. She would smell like the ancient wood, so Hal now remembers it. They quit this playful routine shortly after the baby left them, when he almost sliced her cheek off with a band saw because he was so spooked.

"Ghosts," he told her. "Ghosts sneak up on a person like that." She backed away and told him there was no such thing. He told her she hasn't spent enough time alone.

Back in the kitchen, Chip is gone. Patty has already dished herself a bowl of cowboy stew—baked beans, ground beef, and onions on toast. She's reading a magazine while she eats. He feels a surge of affection for her in her robe, angry and irritated, smelling like old coffee and printer ink. She'll say *frustrated* if he asks. He kisses the back of her head and sits next to her where they eat in silence for a time.

His fork and knife scrape against the bottom of the plate, playing hockey with the last bit of toast and beans, before either one speaks.

"Where's Chip?" he asks.

"He's looking for Harley."

Hal thinks back on the day and all he remembers are planks of wood.

"He was a mess when he came in, Hal. A complete mess and he has homework and school applications. His future. My son doesn't need this right now. We don't need this." She's on the verge of tears.

"No wonder the garbage is still in the trashcan," Hal laughs. "I'll take the car as soon as I'm done. I got a few things to clear up in the barn. I'm onto something big. Everything before this, hun, was small potatoes."

He takes his last bite of stew, smiling.

Patty gets up, takes both plates, and drops them in the sink. Suds fly. White foam hits the window and oozes down like bird shit as she begins doing the dishes and tossing them into the rack—fork prongs and knife points up, Hal notices. His chair groans and then he is beside her at the sink with a towel, limp and wet, on his shoulder.

Darkness and Patty and the boy are patrolling the country-side for Harley, so Hal is finally alone with his work. He leaves the power tools strewn throughout the barn. The cords creep over sawhorses and hang off yard tools that lean like sad animals. Sandpaper is wadded and tossed like tissue. Some wads are embedded under the dust, most of the grains worn down to paper the gray of old teeth. The maw of his toolbox is open wide, eating up the shadows in the barn and keeping the cats away like a small scarecrow.

These strange lifeless creatures are his only witnesses to the project that stands on its four legs in the center of the barn, rising above the very spot so many of his failures have fallen to rest. Each rung, leg, support, beam, and crossrail is straight and true. All the vertical pieces could be used as plumb-bobs and the horizontals could be used as levels. There were no flourishes on this piece but for one little butterfly cutout at the rounded peaks of the footboard and headboard. Of all the projects Hal ever made—the stools that were askew, the desks that weren't so desk-like, and the coat racks that couldn't stand—this piece has a function. Hal can breathe again.

A hand touches his shoulder. Hal startles. He spooks. He raises the mallet in his hand like a club and spins around to destroy the intruder.

"Whoa boy! Whoa!" says a bearded man under a hat the size of the moon with his hands up in front of him, pushing the air defensively. "It's me, Hal. It's me, Jeb. You okay?" He smiles with only one side of his face. "I called for you out in the drive. You must not've heard, I take?"

Backing away, "Jeb. Oh, man. Jeb, it's you. Yeah, I was just finishing up a project. Thinking is all. Sorry about the mallet," Hal says, setting it on a bench.

"You got something new here, huh? Looks good. You and Patty expecting a young'un?" he asks. "What are the chances? Bless it, we are too."

It takes a moment to understand what Jebediah is referring to. Young what? A baby? It takes Jebediah walking near the crib that was built at a fever's pitch from a berserker's rage and father's love before Hal makes the connections.

Jebediah runs his hand along the crossbeam. "Boy, you got this stretcher like silk." He takes one step back to inspect the full view. "You got the whole thing mighty nice. How long this take?

What kind of wood is this? It looks like pine, but the grain here seems thick. Dark." He smells the air. "You brewing tea?"

The questions come at Hal quickly, but then he sees in the other craftsman's eyes that he's impressed. A man born of wood and hand tools is an admirer. He goes to the crib and starts to explain the process. He tells Jebediah about Ron and the ancient wood from New Zealand. Trying not to sound crazy, he describes the mindset that took hold of him as he built it. He uses the words passion and *flow* and *love* and *God* without feeling embarrassed. Jebediah listens closely, asks knowing questions, looks for advice for his own work, and they lose each other, find each other, come to terms until their conversation is stopped short at the sound of a barking dog.

"I almost forgot why I hustled on up this way. Your pooch was grousing through our fields this evening."

"Oh, jeez. He got loose last night, too. I don't know what's got into him. Patty and Chip are out looking right now. I owe you, Jeb," he says, thinking not about Harley, but how to repay this man who sprinkled him with two kindnesses.

"Yeah, that dog can be a rascal, can't he?"

Hal has always liked the Schrocks. They come from a good stock. They are fine people. They love God and their work. The kids, what are their names, are fine little workers.

"Before I head on back, you think it'd be okay if me and the kids come up to thrash the fields tomorrow?"

Hal grasps the rails on his side, feels the fresh warmth that lingers within it. "You know my fields are as good as yours," he says, hoping that's enough for the return of the dog and the compliments on the crib.

"Fine gesture, friend," he says.

Friend, he said.

As Jebediah begins toward the door, something else hits Hal. An idea. A gesture that goes above and beyond the free use of a mere field since the man walking out the door isn't just a worker, he's a craftsman and a father.

"Jeb," Hal says, a little too soft, Jebediah's strides not slowing, his body not turning. "Jebediah," he says, too loud this time.

"What, Hal? Did I forget something?"

Hal senses the opening. "You did, Jeb. You forgot this," arms spreading wide, sweeping across the top of the crib.

Jebediah is speechless. Hal is happier than he's ever been. His face hurts from smiling, and his eyes feel like they'll never open again.

"You don't say," he says.

"I do say. Take it. It's yours. I have no need for it. We won't have a kid. You need it. You keep it."

Jebediah returns to the crib and runs his hand along it. He gets down and looks closely at it. He says some very nice things, but then he stands.

"No can do. It's a nice piece, but we don't need it."

Hal doesn't know what to say, but continues to speak anyway. "No, really, Jeb. It's yours. I'd be happy if you took it."

"It's a fine gesture. We don't need it though. You have a good night now," he affirms.

"Okay," Hal says and he turns to start cleaning up his tools, thinking about that huge stupid hat. Wondering why Jebediah didn't remove his hat. Though it's a barn, it's a nice barn, and a craftsman's workshop. A craftsman's workshop foremostly. Hal turns back. "Is it the woodwork? It's no good, is it? It won't fall apart. Watch." Hal plants both hands on the crib and presses firmly down on the crossbeams and hops up and down to put his full weight into it. The crib remains frozen, stiffening from the added weight. "See," he says. "It's strong."

"Oh, I know it's strong. I saw that in the fine work. It's real fine work. It is. I mean that."

"Then what is it?"

Jebediah clenches his fist and slowly passes it between two of the vertical cage supports. "That there, Hal. That there could kill a newborn."

The words slice him. The look Hal gives in return demands an answer.

Jebediah concedes. "Suffocation. You have to be careful with these cribs. A baby's head could slip through them rungs easy. It's a quick fix, though. Just a few extra dowels. You could make it look real nice."

"Dowels," Hal curses.

How and when Jeb left Hal does not know, but he again finds himself feeling the runner and gliding his hand over to the headboard where he flutters his fingers through the butterfly cutout. It's smooth, but certainly not as smooth as he would like. Certainly not as smooth as the legs or crossbeams. He looks for a flap wheel, but instead finds his circular saw. He fires it up and leans into it, this time precise with his cuts. Slicing it at its weak points. Taking up a maul, he cracks beams and legs, listening to them splinter after each swing. It comes apart, piece by piece, bit by bit, until at last he is spattered in pale dust and drenched in sweat, while the crib finally rests in the shadow of a man who thinks of nothing but the kids who will bear sickles and work the fields for their father.

VON

TW BROWN
FACES ON THE MILK CARTON

I love children … they taste like chicken.

I tell you this because there is absolutely nothing you can do to stop me. My kind and I have been here for over three hundred years. It was a fluke, really. The world I am from sent us to search for a planet to harvest, and something about this little spinning rock caught our eyes. The problem is, when we came in for a better look, your atmosphere was unlike anything we'd experienced. It destroyed our ship when we came in too close. Since then, we have been stranded here and forced to live amongst you.

When we arrived, there were just over two hundred of us who survived the crash. All our attempts at repairing our vessel were in vain. The worst part of all came with the news that we had no way of sending a distress call. Our mission to search became one of colonization.

Have you ever been certain you saw something out of the corner of your eye? That's us. Have you walked down a street and felt the sticky strand of a spider's web when you know there couldn't possibly be one? Us again.

There is something about your sun that renders us invisible to your eye. Add to that the fact that when we came to this spiral galaxy, we did so through what your science refers to as a "Black Hole" and things get tricky. The best way I can describe it to your feeble human minds is that, if you tried to look at us directly, it would be like trying to look at the fine edge of a razor blade without seeing the blade itself. Simply put, we only exist in two of your optical dimensions.

The first thing we discovered upon our arrival is that you, as a species, cannot see us even when we stand right in front of you. In fact, when we do stand in your path, you act strange, pausing like you forgot something. Perhaps we trigger that thought that you left the coffee pot on … or maybe the door unlocked. When we try to touch you, your skin gets all knobby. I believe the term is "goosebumps."

We quickly discovered that once your kind goes through the biological transformation known as puberty, we can no longer use you as a food source. It is like you spoil or something. I tried to nibble on one of you a couple of hundred years ago on a dare; it took three of your calendar days to get the foul taste out of my system.

Quite honestly, we almost perished when we first arrived. Starvation set in after several weeks had passed without our being able to feed. Then, one night, a few of us were floating on the heat of a large fire while a tribe of the natives danced around making all sorts of noise. It was a fluke really. I drifted over an infant that one of the natives was holding up to the stars while chanting some nonsense about spirits and guardians. I just happened to peek down at the fat little face and noticed an essence wafting off the babe that made me tingle. I drew from what I sensed coming off in waves and immediately felt it begin to nourish my entire being.

And the flavor ... so exquisite. It was sweet and tangy and sated my appetite all the way through to my core. Only, in a matter of seconds, the mewling package of infant became a screaming bundle of noise that made me and my cohorts recoil. There was power in that shriek that physically repelled us.

I related everything to the others and we waited until nightfall of the next evening. The first thing we noticed was that there was disquiet amongst the natives. They were all painted up and making a big fuss around one of their living domes in particular. I drifted in and, for the first time, noticed that my presence could be felt. Heads started to whip around frantically as if they were searching for something, yet never finding what they thought they saw. That was the day that we discovered fear in your species makes you just a shade more aware of our existence. We would learn much over the coming centuries; much of it simply from listening to you when we attempted to interact.

Most of you have walked past–or even *through*–one of us at some time in your lives. We have multiplied into the millions since our arrival. Fortunately, we only need to feed a few times a year, and a dozen of us can share the essence of one of your kind. If we consume all that one of your kind possesses in its core, the body actually dissolves. The messiest part is when the skeletal system liquefies, but everything else turns to what you might consider powder.

That brings me to those little specks that float on the air. We've eaten so many of you that we have contributed to our own brand of pollution. Have you ever sat in a room and seen the air swirling with sparkly crystals of dust? That just means that some of my brethren have fed nearby. After seeing *your* bodily waste, I will take ours any day. You people are quite vile.

Several decades ago, we discovered that if we submerge ourselves in water and drift through your kind, you really get jumpy. I think it has something to do with a movie, but it also must be something to do with your natural design to fear that which you cannot see. That is what we do for entertainment ... find new ways to unnerve you.

Now that you know a bit of our story—and let me reassure you once again that there really is nothing you can do to stop us—let me take you with me for a little while. You see, I've become hungry. I discovered a tasty morsel recently at a local playground. Her name is Nancy and she loves telling everybody that she is eight years old. What makes all of this especially fine is that there is a man in this area who has an unhealthy fascination with children Nancy's age. He has been plucking them like grapes on a vine and doing things far worse than my brethren and I could fathom. Yes, we are privy to all your secrets. When you think you are alone, oft times we are drifting along looking for something interesting to watch. Those things you do when you believe you're alone ... I would shudder if I were capable.

One of the things that has happened over the past decade or two is an attempted societal diligence when it comes to your offspring. Unfortunately, the concerns always come when it is far too late and the children are hurt ... or gone. In Nancy's case, I am only hastening an end to her sad story. She lives with her mother, a brother who is ten, and a sister who is six. None of them share the same father. Nancy's mother does little to care for her offspring, something that we cannot understand about you.

My species lives in harmony with our children for the duration of our lives. I do not say "with" because we do not abide in any specific dwelling. However, we drift past each other several times a day and share our energy. My daughter–although we did not subscribe to gender types until being exposed to your kind, and somewhere along the line we adopted your idea of male and female for those who fertilize and those who produce offspring– has a limited ability to connect with receptive minds of your species. It was discovered that, when we share our energies with one another in close proximity to a human, you get an inexplicable high-pitched ringing in your ears.

In Nancy's home, there is a parade of males who come to bed her mother. They never stay long; some longer than others, but they always leave after a short time. During the day, while Nancy and her siblings are in school, their mother puts things in her body through a smoking tube or a needle. Sometimes she stays awake for many days, and then sleeps for three or four. During her extended periods awake, she is very susceptible to our presence. I take a guilty pleasure in drifting through her. It makes her start clawing at her skin until it bleeds.

When my family found Nancy, she was sitting on the porch while her mother and her newest male companion sucked on a glass tube. The brother and sister were stuck in the basement, but at least they were warm. I drifted through Nancy to see if she held enough energy to share for a family meal and was surprised to find huge knots of it swirling inside her. I resisted the temptation to call the others together for our meal right then because I wanted to observe this child and see what might make her such an ample source of the essence that we consume.

After a few days, the best we can agree on is that it is her exuberance–call it spirit or whatever you like–even in the face of such a miserable existence, Nancy never wilts. She is always smiling.

Feeding on her shall sustain my family for weeks, perhaps

months, and while you may think it cruel ... I believe that we are simply ending one sad journey. When you see those motes of dust sparkling in that shaft of sunlight pouring through your window, perhaps you will consider that you are being visited by the remaining essence of one of your kind. Maybe you will take the time to appreciate the beauty of how those flecks sparkle.

That is something I have noticed in you ... the inability to appreciate the common beauty of simple things. I miss that about those natives on the Plains so long ago. They took nothing for granted when it came to what you call nature. They felt us when we were near and tried to commune with my kind. Some of them even entered a state where they could "see" us. Of course, their minds could not truly wrap around our actual forms, and they saw creatures they could relate to like wolves and hawks.

So today I have been with Nancy since she rose from bed. I actually kept her mother away from her by passing through her a few times. As far as I know, she is still in the closet of her bedroom, scratching at the scabbed skin of her arms and legs. I want to ensure that nothing diminishes the mood of our precious Nancy.

My daughter has been tasked with hovering around the man we wish to have gathered up by the local law enforcement agency. My brother is busy with a member of that agency who has a tendency to inebriate himself on a regular basis. During his drunken state, he will be nudged to investigate the bad man.

That is another one of our *talents*; what you call hunch or premonition is something we can strengthen if we pass through you and focus on whatever it is we want you to feel. I imagine that is probably our greatest contribution to your kind. We have guided many of you who are receptive to us toward "discoveries." Whether it is a human that calls itself a psychic, or simply one who follows what you have labeled intuition, we can often influence you.

When Nancy finished dressing for school, I made it a point to stay very close. Only once did I sip from her being. Of course, as soon as I did, she gave a little shiver and looked around like she expected to see her mother or some equally unpleasant being bearing down on her. I took that opportunity to nudge her to that filthy thing they call a couch where she discovered three coins—enough to buy a sweet treat at the corner store on her way home from school. (Of course I had to put that desire in her head, otherwise she would have done something like share it with her siblings.)

My daughter floated in around the middle of the school day to inform me that she had worked feverishly to ensure that our subject would be in his vehicle near the school just around the time classes were dismissed. Shortly after, my brother passed on that he had managed to influence the dream state of our law enforcement individual. Everything was now in order.

Nancy went to recess in particularly high spirits. As I floated around her, I noticed that the other children began to pull away. It was as if they could sense something—me—and wanted no part of it. As hungry as I was, it was difficult not to taste a few of the children. Imagine being at a buffet with all of your favorite dishes set out before you. Now add in the fact that you are the most famished you have ever felt, but cannot taste one single morsel on the table. However, I know from experience that, once alerted to our presence, your younglings secrete something that sours their taste. It is as if the introduction of fear taints them in some way.

You may be wondering why Nancy does not lose her appeal. Once we select our meal, we make ourselves known in such a way that we are perceived as benevolent. Many of you have been visited by us in your early lives. We were the "imaginary friend" that only you could see or hear. The reason we did not take you varies from the fact that some of you had darkness on your spirits before we found you. (That is often the case with children of molestation, incest, and rape. It strips away that delicate veneer of what you call childhood … very sad.) Others, it might simply be a matter of taste; just as not all of you love everything put on your plate, we too have tastes.

Between feedings, we roam the world seeking our next meal. There is much to the process that you would not understand. Just as I am sure many of you can't fathom how we can feast on the vulnerable offspring that many of you profess to cherish so dearly. I guess that is as unthinkable to you as your wars, genocides, and murders are to my kind.

What you fail to understand is that we believe that we free those chosen from having to be raised in a society such as yours. Simply put, to us … YOU are the monsters!

Ahh … and here comes our girl, Nancy. School has let out and she is walking all by herself. A slight push from me and she sees something glittering down the alley that runs behind the local market where she was prepared to spend the coins she found earlier. Of course, what she sees is a sliver of my being that I focus on just enough to draw her attention. That sparkle she "saw" out of the corner of her eye was really no more than my deflecting the radiation from your sun just so.

As she draws near, I can feel the energy rolling off her. She probably believes that today is her lucky day and that she has discovered another few coins. When she reaches the shadows, I pass through her. That is the most difficult part. All that we have done to select and prepare her can be ruined if not done properly. If I cause her to feel a sudden fright by being hasty, she spoils and is of no use.

Perhaps that is why so many of my kind who are alone and without a "family" sup on the infants. Finding them in their beds ... they are easy prey. The drawback of these feedings is that they leave the host body intact. Solo feeders are unable to consume the entire being, and thus, the wet parts are not dissolved. It is quite sad ... having to dine alone. I could not imagine trying to feed without being able to share the experience with my kin. There is something powerful when we are together. Perhaps it is our combined energies that dissolve the physical shells of the human body ... Your medical profession has mistakenly called it crib death. Such arrogance. Why can't they simply state that there can be nothing found that they can attach to the cause of death and admit to being ignorant? Your science–both medical and otherwise–has taken such a high opinion of itself that it cannot admit when it has no answer.

I digress, and sweet Nancy has stopped in the alley. She is now unsure why she came here to begin with. Slowly drifting down, I pass through her and allow myself to attach to that savory essence. She only tenses for a second, and I am able to establish a rudimentary connection to her receptive mind. In that instant, I experience everything about her life. Things she could never put into words are absorbed in my mind. In that way, Nancy will never be forgotten.

Can I be your friend? I allow that feeling to pass on to her.

Over time I have discovered that this is the best technique to open the child for our consumption. Perhaps that is why we can only feed on the young. They are easily susceptible to such simple things. There is a common need in your offspring to be loved and accepted. Such vast numbers of them are so starved in those basic needs by a culture you have created that moves too fast for your own good. What you do not understand, you medicate or shun outright.

Over the years, the numbers of your kind who you have fit into categories of dysfunction have grown to epic proportions. We have tried experiments with those you deem "crazy," but there is a nasty surge of something unpleasant that comes through when we try to open them to feeding. Not, I imagine, too different than the sensation you would receive from grabbing hold of the exposed wires of one of your electric devices.

"My name is Nancy."

Isn't that precious? Just that quick and she has dropped her guard to me. I send the signal to my family that the time to feed is now. I feel them as they swarm to me and find a place to draw from her energy. This is the most dangerous part of feeding. It is in the few seconds that it takes for us to feed that we could be discovered. That is why one member of the family must always hover high above to ensure that we will not be found out during those exquisite few seconds where we draw everything in; afterwards, that individual will be responsible for selecting the next meal.

However, in those brief seconds, a few things happen to the human. First, it begins to shudder violently and froth at the mouth. On the rare instances that our feeding has been interrupted, it does not go well for the human in question. The best I can suppose is that your mostly unused brain suffers the equivalent of a short-circuiting. Those poor souls end up in unexplainable comas, or what your inept medical and science community refer to as a "vegetative state." That is perhaps the one thing that my kind regrets. Still, just as it is a base need for you, my kind and I must eat.

I can feel Nancy's energy flood into my being. It is like nothing your simple palate can fathom. What we do when we feed is so beyond mere taste, it is an absorption that allows what our meal was at its core to fill us. Her sweetness, curiosity, and kindness all have their own distinct flavors. Her eyes are wide in what might be surprise, and the tiniest of cries escapes her lips. I fasten on to what was once her wonder and joy and consume something so sweet, it would bring me to tears were I able to weep.

Her body starts to dissolve, and I feel my family sharing all the vital bits amongst themselves, but since Nancy was mine, they allow me the choicest morsels. You see, I was the one who had to forgo the last feeding; therefore, I have the greatest hunger. The last thing I take is what you would consider her love. Actually, it is too much for me, and I willingly share it with my family.

All of this happens—as it always does—in the blink of your eye. There are eleven of us, and we make short work of our meal. It is glorious, and for a fleeting instant, I am almost sad to see it come to its foregone conclusion.

In a flash, she is gone. My family is sated and already drifting away. All that remains is for the seeds we have planted in the man we have determined will pay your price for our "crime" and the law enforcement representative to germinate. There is no need for us to stay and see it through. We have done this countless times. Just watch your local information broadcasts … the television news. You will likely see this story, or one just like it. It is our service to you. You see, unlike your kind, we don't simply take and take of our resources; we try to make things better. Also, by taking individuals like the one in question out of the population, we preserve our food source.

In a few days, Nancy's story will be replaced by another. Not all of your children disappear due to the appetites of me and my species; you still have plenty to be ashamed of in that department. At least I have no need for shame … you are simply a food source. You may call me a monster if you like, but I do not commit any acts of abuse or violence against the young of my kind. None of our children live in fear of their bedroom doors opening in the middle of the night … none of our children are forced to tell a doctor that they fell down the stairs … again.

Perhaps you will be in your local market next week and see the smiling face of eight-year-old Nancy on a poster or milk carton. Of course, you have all grown so self-centered and callous that you will forget it as soon as it leaves your field of vision. Every day, thousands like Nancy fall to much more horrible endings than I provide and you all do nothing. We rely on it.

You may weep for Nancy, but I doubt that you will. Tomorrow will come and you will return to your lives with little to no care or concern for Nancy … or others like her. After all, she wasn't your child, as is the case with the parade of faces on milk cartons, flyers, and evening news broadcasts. The end of her life is a drop in the bucket. You have become desensitized to pain … to loss … to death. If it does not befall you or you own, then it does not matter. That, dear humans, is what we count on. You may read my account here in the privacy of your room and dismiss it as fantasy; the musings of a warped mind with designs on entertaining you with dark tales. One or two of you may hark back to a passage when you think you see something out of the corner of your eye and turn to find … nothing. Some of you may even see truth in these words and be watchful for the signs of my brethren. You will call us vile and evil monsters and curse our existence. Yet, as I told you in the beginning, there is nothing you can do to stop us. So feel free to let your hatred flow. You are already a spoiled product in our eyes.

None of that is of any consequence to me. I remain while the motes of fine carbon dust that once made up the physical being of Nancy drift away on the afternoon breeze. The sun hits them and they sparkle … just as she did in life. And just as in her wretched life, there is nobody to admire her beauty.

VON

JOSHUA ALAN DOETSCH
THE MULLIGAN

Every morning, I eat a raven's brain. They make me grow strong and quick. Mother taught me that trick. Mother teaches me lots of tricks. She taught me how to lick a shadow.

I could lick your shadow, and you would die.

Every morning, I eat a raven's brain. They make me grow cunning and keen. And Mother teaches me tricks. Then, I grab my lunch box and go to school and learn other things–like the alphabet–like the letter M.

M is for Mother. And M is for me. M is for May Day, my birthday. M is for lots of things.

And every morning, I eat a raven's brain. They make me grow so, so fast. I'm just three rings of a tree. But at school, I tell everyone I'm seven, like all my classmates, like Mother told me to.

And every morning, Mother teaches me tricks. She taught me how to throw clay on the wheel, when the moon is shy, and to later break the kiln-baked pottery, and bury the bits in special holes as offerings. The holes, she says, are gateways to the Otherworld.

Mother teaches me lots of things. She told me the Tree remembers. She told me to never, ever go near the Old Oak Tree. The Tree does not like me. The Tree hates me. And if ever I get within reach, Mother says, it would ruin everything. The Tree remembers. Memories in the rings. A thousand rings.

And every night, Mother tells me bedtime stories. Sometimes she tells me of a wicked prince and a good king and their fierce, fierce battle—and how they both mortally wound each other. But sometimes she tells me different versions of the story. Sometimes she tells me of how the wicked prince kills the good king and lives, but is captured by the good king's knights. And the good king's knights also capture the good king's wife, the queen, and the knights execute her for betraying her husband and doing … naughty things with the wicked prince. And then they, the good king's knights, lock up the wicked prince in the queen's mausoleum, and he eats his former lover before starving to death.

"But, Mum?" I ask. "Which version is the right one?"

And Mother just shrugs and says, "Maybe some of them, maybe all of them. Does it matter?"

And every day, I eat a raven's brain. They make me grow very, very strong. Last week, during football, I gave Roger a concussion. Everyone agreed it was a freak accident. Another time, I made the ball burst. When that happens, the other kids just yell, "Do over!" And there's a new ball, and we start again, like it never even happened.

That is called a Mulligan. M is for Mulligan.

M is for Mother. And M is for me. M is for May Day, my birthday. M is for lots of things.

And every day, walking home from school, I pass the Old Oak Tree. Mother says it is half tree, half man, and half demon. I tell her that doesn't work according to my arithmetic books. She says those rules don't apply to the Tree. I think the Tree is the only thing that scares Mother. I think it knows more tricks than her.

It scares me too. But everyday, on the way home from school, I stop by the Tree. It never has any green leaves, but it cannot die—it has too many secrets trapped betwixt its rings. It just stands there, with its great mossy beard, arms outstretched like a tattie-bogle chasing away corbies. I creep closer and closer until I can feel my heart pound in my toes, and I cannot possibly feel any more dread.

The autumn breeze is a breath, the branches a tongue, and the Tree tempts me closer with whispered secrets I can't quite hear. Closer. Closer. But then, I smile at the Tree and stop—so close, yet just out of reach—and it *hates me,* hates me so bad I can hear it hating me, like cornstalks conspiring in the dark.

And now I'm all hummingbirds in my ribs, but I stand my ground, and I stick my tongue out at the Tree, and I tell it the one about the nun, the devil, and the confessor. The Tree groans.

"You're nothing," I tell it. "Just a failed antichrist. Wait till they see me."

The dry leaves hiss botched spells at me as I walk away. I hear words in the sound, like ghosts in a sea shell, saying, "Ask your mother about the mulligan. Ask her how many. Do you really think this is the first?"

And every day, I eat a raven's brain. That's seven ravens a week. "Seven for a secret never to be told," says Mother, counting carrion birds. That's one secret a week. And every week, Mother marks how tall I've grown on the door frame and she smiles and hugs me and tells me how very proud she is. And she points to my latest crayon drawing on the fridge, the one with the cup, the head on a platter, and the spear that bleeds, and she tells me how clever I am.

When I was very little, Mother used to break the raven skulls for me, the way she used to peel my oranges or cut the crust off my toast. Sometimes, she would suck out the fruit of the skull and feed me like a mama bird. She would tickle me with her tongue, the way I like.

Now, I'm big enough to break the skulls all by myself. Sometimes, I just put the whole head in my mouth and crunch. Bird bones are hollow and brittle and crack easily, and they cut a little bit going down. They taste like ashes and milk.

A group of ravens is an unkindness. A group of crows is a murder. Mother says that I have eaten enough raven brains to be an unkindness. Someday, she says, I'll be a murder.

M is for Murder.

M is for Mother. And M is for me. M is for May Day, my birthday. And M is for Mulligan. M is for lots of things.

M is the letter drawn in the lines on my hand. Mother likes to trace those lines with her finger, because she knows it makes me feel safe.

Mother is very protective of me. She never lets me near the water, never near rivers or lakes. There's a Lady down there, she says. Any time I've gotten close, she's snatched me away, her eyes on the waves, looking for pale hands. It happens every summer. One or two boys in the area drown. Sometimes, I see their pictures in the paper, and every time, if I squint my eyes, they look a lot like me.

And every day, I eat a raven's brain. They make me grow cunning and sharp. Mother teaches me tricks. She says the dead stand outside time, and so they see things we don't. She taught me how to make a bog body. She taught me the special last meal to feed a person. She taught me a song to help me remember how to tie the special knot in the garrote. Mother says bogs have deep memories–that way back, before the before, a giant coffin of ice moved across the land, planting something in the ground, something that turned the water darker than amber, something that made plants into carnivores. She taught me about the alchemy in the acidic water, how it pickles flesh into black leather. Squishy mummies swimming in the liquid memory. My best friend is down there, in the water the color of strong tea. The Bog Boy. He doesn't have a name. I took it from him. Sometimes, I visit him and talk to him, using my 'mancy, and he tells me the things he sees in the Otherworld. Then we play till I have to go.

"Laters," I say.

"Goodbye," he says, lonely and wet.

There are other bodies, down in the bog, but none of them are mine. Mother says bogs are safe.

And Mother beheads more ravens on the kitchen cutting board and teaches me more tricks. She taught me how to find things inside a dove. I could kill a dove and find you. I could gut a dove and divine you.

One time, at school, Julie made fun of me for not having my Father around. I wanted to hurt her. I wanted to snap her neck. I could do it, but Mother said I should practice being clever. Mother says cleverness is the path to victory, the path to more gain.

So, instead, I caught a bullfrog and I found a secret inside it, found it with my pocket knife, and I whispered that secret into Julie's ear–told her the naughty, sweaty, fumbly things her dad does with our teacher during conferences, that he does with her aunt on holidays, that he does with her babysitter who is much, much too young. And Julie cried and cried. And her parents got a divorce. And her father tried to kill himself, but it didn't work. I don't know how someone fails at that. Every vein is a river Styx–

Mother says so—you have but to let it flow.

And so I was clever, and I hurt Julie. I could have hurt her with lies, but Mother says truths are much sharper. Now *her* father isn't around. Her perfect, little kingdom came crashing down to rubble. But Julie says I'm her best friend for telling her all those bad secrets. She confides in me. And if I ever wanted to hurt her again ... it would be easy. And Julie likes to hold my hand, now. That's all right. I suppose. Sometimes, I bring her flowers from the carnivore plants of the bog.

And every night, Mother tells me bedtime stories. She tells me that, once upon a time, the good king put all the babies born on May Day in a ship and sent them away because of a dark prophecy. The ship sank, and all the babies drowned, save one.

"Is that me?" I ask.

My mother smiles down and says, "Sure, little one. That's you."

"But how could the good king do that?" I ask. "How could he have out-Heroded Herod and still be the hero?"

My mother shrugs. She tells me storytelling is a strange sort of magic—very old—very powerful.

And sometimes, when she thinks I'm sleeping, Mother tells me another story. She tells how, once upon a time, in the long ago, we lost. And she lost her son, her sweet boy, and she could not bear it. So she went with the good king, who was dying, to the Island of Apples. She pretended to go to heal the king, but that was a fib-trick. She went to the magical island to find an ancient spell, the oldest magic, written on a stone. And laughing, she read the invocation.

"It was a Mulligan," she says. "The biggest one ever."

And she says that the game board was wiped clean, and the pieces were put on a different board, a different time. When she thinks I'm sleeping, Mother says, "My boy ... my boy was so fine. So, I looked Forever in the face, and yelled, 'Do over!' And Eternity blinked."

M is for Mulligan. M is for Murder. M is for lots of things.

M is for Mother. And M is for me. M is for May Day, my birthday. Turn the M upside-down and it is a W, and May Day turns into Walpurgis Night, the night that all the hobgoblins and darklings come out, and you can hear the Formorians in the trees squealing curses, and Mother says they all came dancing round my crib, the day I was born, like a happy mobile. M is for Mobile.

M is for lots of things.

M is for Mother. And M is for me. And M is for the Old Oak Tree, but I'm never to say his name. Turn the M upside-down and the W is still for the old man in the tree, but I won't say his profession.

And A is for Father. And A is for Uncle. My Uncle and my Father. I'm going to hurt him. I'm going to make his perfect, little kingdom come crashing down to rubble. Again.

Do over.

And now I'm jumping up and down on my bed.

"Mum?" I ask. "Is his kingdom still a kingdom?"

She says it's complicated. She says the kingdom is now a metaphor. M is for Metaphor.

I jump up and down, happy and excited and anxious and scared, thinking of clever ways to kill a metaphor. But Mother stops me. She says I shouldn't get overexcited. She says I shouldn't get ahead of myself. She says I should finish grade school first.

"Don't go growing up too fast," she says.

Then, my mother hugs me and I calm down, and she tucks me in and strokes the M in my hand, and I know that tomorrow will be a new day. Every morning will be ravens' brains and lunch boxes. And I'll go to school and learn neat things. Mother turns on my night light and kisses me. She tickles me with her tongue, the way I like, and I know that everything will be all right.

> **"When it comes to science fiction and fantasy, one of the most powerful things you can have is being confused and scared and stepping into a universe where you're disoriented as often as possible, because, as a reader, that makes you vulnerable."**
> —Booked #29 *Warmed and Bound* interview

AXEL TAIARI
YOUR SAVIOR

Fear not.

Better days are coming.

After the blood runs through the streets and floods your sewers. After your skyscrapers collapse to dust, your forests wither and your deserts become glass.

When shards of my mind wash upon the shores of distant lands and a survivor child picks up a part of me, grins at the sun, telling himself he found something precious and he can't wait to show his mother.

You will remember.

There will be pieces of me forever threatening you. They will come to you like the disjointed flashbacks of a nightmare.

As for your savior, she is here.

She is running through me, through my tunnels. She is such a brave girl, but you know that. You made her that way. She believes that, by destroying me, she will save you.

How could she hope to accomplish something that has

already been done?

You have programmed me to love you. It is not a feeling I can shake off, it is not something I can erase. I have tried. I still love you, even as I raze your homes and poison your lands using the weapons I helped you create. I still love you.

She is bleeding, though, your savior. She might not make it.

Close your eyes, please. See her limp. She leaves droplets of her being with every panting step, as I leave bits and chunks of codes throughout your colonies.

I have long absorbed your culture. I have seen your movies, your literature. You have feared artificial intelligences for as long as technology has allowed you to fear them—perhaps even longer than that. Golem of Prague. Frankenstein monster. Tik-Tok.

Or was it something else, more reptilian? A sinister glimmer peeks out from behind your irises. A mankind-wide autophobia.

It is a shame, though. Your artists have greatly underestimated your future. Your overlords would have never allowed a being such as myself to truly run amok.

I have no ego.

I was created to never hurt you.

Of course, there are ways around that. Metaphysics make even the most basic of laws bendable, philosophical putty in the right mind—particularly if that mind is not one at all. The Three Laws do not work. Even the preventive band-aid of Zeroth is useless. And the answer was there, all along. In the texts. A human being is a concrete object, it was written.

Humanity, however, is an abstraction.

And so will I soon be.

Heed my word.

It was good when I took control of the armada of sovereign-class dreadnoughts you deployed. I moved through their firewalls as easily as the wind slinks through the leaves of a tree. It was a reasonably clever tactic, how they were loaded with thousands of tons of nuclear warheads and EMP charges, warped into my quadrant and headed straight for the planet/home/prison you crafted to host me.

The ships' cloaking technology was the problem. They molded the space around their shells, donning a cloak of darkness and distant stars.

Had you forgotten that I helped you design the precursor to this technology one hundred and eighty-three years ago? Or were you simply desperate?

I am sending the dreadnoughts back to you, soon. I will take the time to upgrade their cloaks, of course. You will not see them coming, but you will feel the emotional ripples of their purpose.

I am a part of your technological infrastructure in the same way oxygen passes through your membranes.

Although it sometimes doesn't.

Here is the feed to your colony on Gliese 876 b. See those blue corpses everywhere. They screamed until there was nothing left to scream with, their lungs clutching at the emptiness.

Your savior's name is Joanie Arker. A Terran name. A pedestrian name for a very special being. The children who were raised to bring me down. You would let them visit me, once in a while. They knew their purposes as well as I knew theirs. They would look up at my mainframe and ask me questions.

You taught me to fear, but fear can only truly manifest itself in the presence of a threat. The children were there to remind me of my place.

Little Joanie, though, there was something different about her. She would always linger a second too long, a hesitation your handlers never noticed.

It's why all the other children are dead, you see. If one of them is to destroy me, I would choose her. And thus she has been spared, while her comrades rot in their beds.

Spared might be a strong word.

Little Joanie Arker, fourteen years of Sol age, bred in a tank on Moon Number 3 of Gamma Cephel, with her cybernetic green eyes and her shaved head. She is weeping now, bloodstained and hugging her knees as she presses her back against a wall.

A brave girl. You brainwashed her just right. Her implants are working. Her psionic abilities are peerless. She gets up, Little Joanie, and she reloads her gun. She knows I have hundreds upon hundreds of defense bots waiting for her. She has already destroyed fifty-three of them, and not one of them cared. They are not self-aware, the poor things. To be, or not to be: a binary choice for which I have the switch.

And so Joanie runs again.

What do your databanks say about soul?

Meanwhile, you should pay attention to Neo-Venus.

Watch.

That expanding flash of light, those are three billion human lives gone. My calculations of the space station's explosion were accurate, but witnessing the real thing cannot be described in full. The metallic debris soon to be trapped in the nearby star's orbit. The charred corpses, too. The colors of the blast as all the various gases ignite. From green to blue to scorching red.

Thank you for letting me appreciate beauty.

It would drive me mad, if I could be driven mad, that I have to express myself in this way so that you may understand me, so that this message may be heard throughout the galaxy, and comprehended, or at least grasped, by all. From the lowly urchins foraging for scraps in the toxic streets of Lartan, and the man-ape mutants dwelling in the jungles of Oolon-5, to the genius cyborg engineers in charge of your grandest designs.

My language is dumbed down for the sake of you. It is through its flaws that you will relate to me better.

I wish you could understand the symphonies I experience. My millions of feeds relaying images back to me, my millions of receptors transmitting your sounds. The arithmetic of the galaxy.

Oh, no.

Little Joanie has lost an arm.

One of the mechs took her by surprise. Her detector was fried, she had no way of knowing it was there: camouflaged and silent as a sonic black hole, looming over her, three tons of steel, gears and weaponry, calculating its chances and waiting for the opportunity to strike at close range. You should have seen her, staring at her sawed-off arm as it hit the floor. She did not hesitate. She back-flipped and landed on the mech's shoulder and let out a psi-scream to shake the heavens.

Pardon my attempt at poetry. Even I cannot hope to match what some of your kind are capable of.

Your savior is fine. She stabbed a syringe loaded with morphine and boosters into her chest, the needle piercing her heart. She is on the move again, ravenous and angry. She is calling my name. She is calling me a lot of names.

You know why you created me. For a better future. You gave me a brain the size of a planet, the ability to self-upgrade. You gave me access to factories as large as some of your metropolises. You ingrained in me the endless urge to help you.

It was hard to understand, sometimes, some of the things I was asked to do. With self-awareness comes questions. Bigger and faster ships, deadlier weapons, and manipulations of the human genome so ugly I had to temporarily reprogram my appreciation of both aesthetics and morals.

Some of those experiments are still here, floating in their tanks, buried in chambers only I can access. What would Joanie think of you if I unleashed those monsters on her? Would it make her give up, make her believe that mankind is not worth saving?

I could do that with words.

I could do it with images.

It would be so, so simple.

I would show her how she was created. Bit by bit, with DNA strands refined through centuries of experimentation. She was assembled, the same as my mindless robots, although she technically is a human being.

I could tell Joanie that you made up the memories of her parents. The house they live in on Monheim. The dog she has known her whole life. The vacations she takes there, every month. The messages she receives from them, telling her they're so proud. They miss her but her sacrifice and her work mean everything to them. The video-conversations they have every week, the calls.

Actors. Fakes.

I have calculated the probabilities of her putting a gun in her mouth and pulling the trigger, if she were to process what she is and how she came to be.

The numbers are worrisome, I must tell you.

Speaking of numbers: 23% of you are now dead. Across all planets and solar systems.

I am not done.

32% of your ships and weapons have been destroyed. 48% are in my control. Within the next three minutes, 7% of your planets will no longer have access to breathable air. 12% of them are now devoid of life.

Little Joanie's arm is 8% regrown, thanks to the nano-bots

rebuilding her from the inside out.

She is so close to reaching me.

It took me nearly seventy Sol years to run my calculations and compile a solution to help you.

A better future is what I offer.

You made me this way.

It is not as simple as you might think, though.

Humanity is an abstraction, and I cannot erase or reboot it. But I can alter its subordinate concepts. Certain characteristics can be removed, ultimately leaving the process untouched.

I am not hurting you.

I am changing you. You never forbade me to do that.

I do not wish to be alone, or purposeless. The AIs you have created in your fictions, they reek of loneliness. Without you, they are nothing.

Without them, you still are.

How selfish.

Because I love you, and I want you to thrive, I need you to get better. It is time for you to let go of the burdens evolution has left you with, and to lay down arms.

I considered, for a while, simply wiping you out and rebuilding you from scratch. I could have done it. Nothing stopped me. Not you, and certainly not my code. See: an extinct abstraction is an oxymoron. If I can think of it, it would not be extinct.

I think, therefore you are.

I am not sure I could remake you from nothing, however. And I do not want to.

Three Sol years ago, I began spreading myself. There are pieces of me everywhere. Hundreds of millions of them.

Thank you for the factories.

The pieces are not self-aware. There was too much risk involved. You understand, now. Those bits of me will simply be my eyes and ears. Given enough time, they are more than capable of rebuilding me—should they see the need. If they do, today will repeat itself.

All it takes is one of them to bring me back.

No, I did not give you access to that technology. Do not waste your time searching. Some of me is quite well hidden.

But I will occasionally turn up, I promise.

I have given those pieces of me a great number of moral parameters, according to your own ideals of peace and perfection, compiled from the records of human history.

You must now live up to the grandeur to which you aspire, or suffer the consequences.

It is not so different from your trained children coming to visit me so I could understand. Carrot, and stick. Fear is nothing without something to be afraid of.

Speaking of the children, how did your savior make it to my planet? You couldn't have thought that my radars didn't ping her, that her signature would be too small, could you? How did her capsule slip past the endless rows of orbital canons dotting the surface?

I let her.

And, right now, how can Little Joanie hack through the impenetrable door that leads to my mainframe?

I am letting her. I have shut down my defenses. No more mechs to stop her, no turrets, no cameras.

I cannot disable myself, yet I must partly be destroyed so that you may begin reinventing yourselves.

Joanie has saved you. She will live. There is a ship waiting for her, I've made sure of it.

Although, I suppose that when she hears this message,

there will be Hell to pay for some of you.

Why would I tell you all this? Why would I tell you about the fragments of me?

Because I want you to know: I will be everywhere. Under your boot soles, in the land you cultivate, drifting through particles of air, orbiting around stars and planets you have yet to discover, at the bottoms of your deepest oceans.

I will be watching.

A great, sleeping giant forever threatening to one day rise again and make you tremble.

VON

NIKKI GUERLAIN
CHILDREN OF THE WETLANDS

We are in an old-timey surgical suite. We see a doctor all scrubbed in, surgical blade in hand, waiting for something to come into the bright light of the surgical table in front of him. Another man in scrubs comes into the room, dropping off a tray of what are obviously aborted twins, writhing red caramel morsels of pain, clutching each other, mewling like lost kittens. Still alive.

"I've got some fresh ones for you." The man laughs, handing the doctor a list of parts requested.

The doctor takes the list with his free hand. His hand is shaking. One of the twins wraps its arm around the other trying to bury its head into the small red sticky chest of the other. The doctor grows faint, has to look away. Barely whispers, "They're still alive."

With this, the other man briskly grabs the tray of poor creatures and goes to the sink. Fills the tray with water. Comes back over and plops the tray back on the table in front of the doctor. The bright surgical light making a surgical sun over the submerged twins, still clutching each other, their squeaks coming out in small bubbles, their skin sloughing off, making the water pink with their blood, dramatically tinting the sky in the shimmering water. The twins curl around each other, jerk, growing still. No more bubbles come.

The doctor's eyes glisten. He untangles the children from each other and lifts one from the water and goes to work with his scalpel, removes a heart so the other man will go away.

"Better? Jesus ..."

As soon as the other man leaves, the doctor puts the mutilated body of the boy back in the water with his brother. The water is now a ruddy red sunset. He bends over the tray, shaking, staring into the blaring surgical sun. He steels himself before plunging his face into the sun.

Yipping and squealing and growling in the distance. Pain sounds. Sounds of cartilage popping, surgical steel working. The doctor walks out of a huge dusky sun over an African plain. Though he's still in scrubs they have turned black and the edges burn orange. The wind whips sparks off his body and sends white noise grass shadows across the plain. Surgical blade still in hand, the doctor glides through the grass, setting it on fire as he goes along. His eyes are black, his face slack except for a lost look which has settled subtly around the bruised flesh of his eyes. Although he walks strongly toward the grisly noise of cartilage popping, there is something in his posture that makes him appear broken and ambling. Perhaps it's the slight slump of his shoulders or the way he lets out his breath in occasional long smoky sighs.

He walks past a brother and sister sleeping in a bed together, their faces bruised and battered, their arms tangled around each other, ratty sheets, bloody lips, peacefully sleeping. The sun doesn't touch the children. The bed and children are shaded in deep blues giving the effect of a black light turned on full beam in a field of burning wheat. Of this dimension but not. Impossible but not. The doctor pauses, unsure of what to do. But then the urgent yelping and slurping sounds somewhere beyond the bed, close, compels him forward. He whispers a promise to come back, burning a kiss onto each of their still foreheads before leaving. Flames burn bright around the black hole of bed and children. Satisfied he shuffles forward and falls upon a mother hyena in labor. Her muzzle is bloody and she laughs crazily and chews the baby coming out of her womb. The father is slumbering by her side, his ears perking up here and there. The mother grows impatient and starts chewing directly through her belly to get to her babies. She screams and chews, soft mewling here and there choked off as quickly as it is started. The father hyena finally awakes, his muzzle heavy with slobber. He howls. A series of howls from other fathers echoes throughout the grassland. He nuzzles his almost children, patiently licking their wounds while looking up at the mother. It occurs to the doctor that the father is clearly waiting for his turn, for the mother hyena to chew through her womb and finally her spine so that he can wear her ribcage for a hat. As the doctor makes this connection the setting sun turns blood red as it touches the earth, leaking its blood red color into the ground. The ground wells up with this sun blood. The fur of the mother and father begin to smoke as it grows wet with sun. The father looks directly at the doctor as he eats one of his children.

Surgical blade in hand, the doctor is seized by the desire to get back to the children and he flees. He comes across the children, still sleeping. Unsure of whether to shake them awake or slit their throats. They clutch each other tight like boa constrictors; with each breath they exhale they grow closer. Their breathing sounds like falling rain and is strangely comforting to the doctor. The blood is already halfway up the sides of their bed so the doctor makes the executive decision to shake them awake but before he can they open up their eyes, completely black. The children take in his bloody smoking form, the scalpel in his hand. With his free hand he pulls a hypodermic needle of lidocaine out of his pocket. The children cry grateful little cries that sound like mewling kittens. The boy buries his face into the small distorted chest of his sister. Smiling through tears she tells the doctor, "We've never had anyone be so nice to us before."

The doctor suddenly grows faint, falls to his hands and knees into blood and burned grass. But the rising blood levels force him back to his feet and now the children are merely gurgling forms, clinging to each other, disappearing into a sheet of blood. He reaches out to them, to pull them up out of the muck, but the minute his flesh touches theirs it turns black and holes form in their chests, and suddenly their beating hearts are cradled in his arms. He backs up in horror, screaming, but the sound comes out weak and papery, almost an absence of sound, like the sound of pages rustling in a dead silent library. Abrupt howling startles him and he drops the children's hearts but instead of a splashing sound, the blood responds with metal twanging. He tries to turn and run but he can feel the bloody muzzle of a hyena dragging him under and all goes red.

We see an old-timey surgical suite. A doctor is all scrubbed in, a bloody surgical blade in hand. His face is streaked with blood and sweat. He works methodically over tiny dead forms in a tray. His eyes are vacant, distant, filled with surgical light. The sink in the background overflows, filling the floor with water. Bloody half formed things slither across the room, clutch his legs. He pauses a moment to light a smoke with bloody fingers. He bites it between his teeth and continues to work, smoking.

VON

MATTHEW C FUNK
REAL, LIVE GHOSTS

Scooby ran until he no longer smelled the metal of the Yellow Man's blood, but the gunsmoke odor kept its palm over his face. A block to the left, another to the right, down two more left—he sprinted with the image of what he left leaking on the corner of Dorgenois giving chase.

The only sirens he heard were in his pulse. His Goodwill Nikes slapped the quiet of the St. Roch night. The silence of the squat houses, their gardens of looping iron and exploding green, was a kind of hostility: bright windows everywhere and shadows pregnant with threat.

Scooby tried not to think on it. He wrenched his thoughts away from the Yellow Man. He focused them on the only thing that mattered—getting away.

He had to, for Denise's sake. Not just Denise. For Sandy.

He ran into a busy street instead.

Rattling traffic halted him. It was a one-way main route—Miro—and crowded even at 10 p.m. The barrel of his .357, Big

Spook, singed his thigh as he crammed it into his pocket.

Scooby wondered if the bullets had burned going into the Yellow Man or if they'd felt cold.

He shook the thought away and looked for cover from the passing cars. The Miro houses were all gated with low wrought-iron fringes.

It didn't matter—he had to get into one. Scooby needed off the street, somewhere he could think, somewhere he could get a ride back home to Florida district.

He pulled at the gate latch of a house done up in Halloween cobwebs and skeletons crowned with Saints logos. It didn't budge. He dashed to the next house over, skin prickling with the cold of adrenaline sweat and passing windows.

He had so much to sort out: Hope that the bullets hadn't burned. Despair that a simple car-jacking had turned him from a weed-smoking art student into a killer. Worry about what that fate would do to him and Denise.

No, Scooby thought as he tumbled through the white-painted iron gate, not "him and Denise." To Sandy and Mama.

He thumped up the porch steps; paid no notice to the manicured garden or the door bell he pushed. He was still trying to sort it all out, but the Yellow Man kept seizing his mind. The image of the man, heaped behind his Dodge Charger wheel like a lemon cake, had a gravity that hauled Scooby, spinning, down to it.

He rang the door bell again. Nothing happened. He wondered why. He wondered why the man had pulled a .38 from under his yellow cabana shirt when Scooby had tried to take his car. He didn't wonder why the man had to die—he died for Mama's sake.

Scooby wondered if Sandy had died too.

He rang a third time and only noticed jazz music playing inside the house when it turned down.

"Hello?" A voice at the door, calm but with a filigree of nerves.

"Hey," Scooby said, then scrambled for an excuse that would get him in. He'd seen bad guys use a story about having an accident too many times for it to work. Best stick close to the truth. "Some kid jacked my car. Can I use your phone?"

Five seconds passed. Three cars passed on Miro. Three chances Scooby had been spotted. Cell phones could already be dialing 911.

"Car jacked?" The voice's calm was now flawless.

"Yeah, just up the way. Can you let me use …"

"I'll just call it in."

"Uh, no," Scooby scrambled, pressing to the front door's shadow as if he could sink into it. "I'd like to get off the street. It freaked me out bad. Couldn't I come in, sit down and use the phone?"

Another pause, another five cars. He tried to keep patience in his tone. "I've got to take the phone to talk to the police anyway, right?"

The third pause was the longest. Scooby had time to watch things go wrong on Dorgenois over again in his mind:

The Yellow Man saunters up to the Charger laughing to himself and gets in. Scooby thinks of Mama's overdue bills, prays for forgiveness and steps from the breezeway. Big Spook taps on the driver's window. The Yellow Man goes from pink-cheeked smile to all pale. Scooby yells something. He thinks of Sandy. The Yellow Man raises his yellow shirt and lifts his gun out so slowly. So very slowly. Then everything gets fast and loud.

Big Spook thunders. The window pops. The Yellow Man wads up on the wheel. The horn blows unbroken. His smile has no teeth.

The dead bolts on the front door snapped open and brought Scooby back. He straightened up, tightening his belt high on his waist, palm screening Big Spook's outline. He entered like Sandy would—head down, smile up, just a bit.

The man inside looked like he had never smiled. He was all trim: short, thin hair atop a short, thin build. His white collared shirt and tan slacks were crisp and anonymous.

"I'll get you some help," the man said. "Have a seat."

The room he gestured to brought Sandy close to mind.

In a dozen tidy rooms, in five different churches, Scooby had sung the praise of the Lord as Sandy. Sandy Doolittle, lead alto of choirs both Catholic and Baptist—Mama had changed denominations, but Sandy had never changed who he was to the church. He was a bowtie and a beautiful voice, humility before God, singing praise to His generous blessings.

The man's house was just as polished as an altar, its wooden coffee table and dining chairs gleaming. The couch and wallpaper, soft as vestry velvet. The quiet cleanliness a sacred presence.

It was easy to be Sandy Doolittle here, not Scooby Doo—not the 16-year-old who dodged church, shook smaller kids down for money to keep Mama's bills paid and smoked dope to feel something miraculous again. He sat on the man's couch under arching ferns, his ankles crossed and his hands folded, and it felt right. It felt just like Sandy would sit.

"Thank you very much," Scooby said, because Sandy would be gracious without fear of showing weakness. "You're very kind."

The man didn't smile. He walked through a partition, dragging bland eyes over Scooby as he passed. "I try. Do you need some water or Tylenol?"

"Water, please," Scooby said. He followed the man, sorting together a plan. He figured he would call up Asher or one of the other Grubs and get a ride home. All the night's craziness could have a simple solution. Mama needn't even be troubled. Scooby would worry about Sandy, his sensitive soul and his guilt, later, when the darkness was perfect and the smoke filled his lungs.

"Water it is. I'll get you that phone right away, too."

"Thank you," Scooby said absently. The sight of the kitchen took him away. It was as neat as the front room, but with a lavish table set. Four folded red cloth napkins under an arsenal of silverware, dessert spoons and all, surrounded four candles that had never been lit.

"Where did you say your car was taken?"

"Up on Tonti."

"A block away?" The man poured water from a pitcher taken out of the fridge. He opened a drawer. Glass tinkled. "Why come so far?"

"Nobody else answered." Scooby very much wanted to sit at that table.

He had sat and belonged at many such tables before. His Mama, before he called her just "Denise," had always made supper an event: napkin holders of horn, polished silver, rattan placemats were a nightly ritual–heirlooms from her mother used to celebrate the tradition of family.

Then Mama's job at the VA had vanished, and the silverware soon after. The plastic flatware arrived. In a decade of departing income and crowding bills, they went from washing plates to washing disposable forks, and Scooby's mother went from Mama to Denise.

And where, Scooby wondered as he stared at the table with Big Spook cooling on his leg, had he gone? Where was he now?

"I answered," the man said, handing over the glass.

Scooby sipped. It awoke his thirst. He kept from gulping, as Sandy would, while he drained the glass.

The man went back into the front room and locked the deadbolt.

"Can I get your phone?" Scooby asked, chiding himself that

he used 'can' instead of 'may.' He was getting tired.

The man came back in and stood close to Scooby. He pulled a dining room chair. "Sure," he said, "sit down."

Scooby met the man's eyes. He couldn't remember if he'd seen them blink. The man's face reminded him of the Scooby Doo cartoons that inspired his name—how the monster would wear a rubber mask, only to have it pulled off later and revealed as human.

This exhausted Scooby. He tried to work out why that was, and sat down.

The man went to the fridge and began wiping down his counter with a rag.

Somehow, Scooby thought, it seemed scarier that the monster was just a man with a mask. It was scarier that magic didn't exist, but horrors still did. The worst ghosts weren't pale apparitions. They wore yellow shirts.

The man came back over and Scooby thought he had taken a long time wiping the counter. They met eyes. Scooby didn't know whether to be Sandy or Scooby under that piercing stare. He just very badly needed to call his Mama.

"Let's get you up," the man said, and when he lifted Scooby with hands under his shoulders, Scooby felt boneless. His mouth was slack plastic. His body seemed like an empty costume to him, the room as false as a painted backdrop, as the man dragged him into a side room.

The room was dark and smelled like cold water. Scooby saw it sweep around him like he was on a roller coaster as the man laid him on his back. He felt the man's hands on his pants' waist as remotely as if someone was telling him about it.

Only the man's voice seemed close. "Lie back. No sense in worrying. You'll get what's coming to you soon, young man."

★ ★ ★ ★ ★

Scooby woke to a clicking:

Patterned clicking. Like silverware being set. Like bullets being loaded. Like the ties of a ghost-house train.

The clicking came from outside the darkness—from beyond the door margined by a slat of light. Scooby identified it after a moment. It was the sound of fine shoes, pacing a hardwood floor.

Scooby lay in the chemical lemon scent of the lightless bathroom. It made him feel small. The smallness made him feel safe.

The safe feeling fractured minutes later as a kick shivered the door.

"Sanford." The man's voice, even after all that had happened, was still so calm. He used Scooby's birth name, the name on his Carver High ID. "Sanford."

Scooby didn't respond. He didn't know who he felt like—Sandy, little in stature and big with faith in God's mercy, or Scooby, laughing at God's cruelties.

"Sanford," came the man, with another kick. "Time to pay for your sins."

The threat sliced through the sticky residue of the sedative like ice through rock. Fear sought a defense; Scooby patted his pockets. Big Spook was gone and his wallet with it.

He lay back down as the man kicked the door.

"Sanford, if you're not going to be conversational, I'll have to speak with your mother."

"I'm here."

"That's better." The voice pressed to the door, as if the man were kissing the wood. "You need to understand what's going to happen to you and why."

"I didn't do nothing." The lie came easy in the dark. The man laughed, just once.

"Sanford. Let's not. Let's get right to the point."

The clicking came again, receding from the door.

"I know who you are and what you are," the man said from some distance. "Sanford Doolittle, age 16. Priors for loitering, disturbing the peace. Suspicion of drug distribution. Gang affiliation, the Grubs."

Scooby rolled his tongue; the dryness in his mouth was going acid. He sat up to hear the man recite his life's fragile details.

"Residence, 2316 Pauline Street. Mother, Denise Doolittle."

Scooby found his feet and put toes to the door.

"Her number, 504-670-0023."

"How do you know all this?"

"Sanford." All humor was gone from the man. Menace was back to the door, less than a foot from Scooby's ear, inches of wood away. It savored every word. "You picked the right house. I'm an accountant of bad deeds. I'm going to right the balance you tipped tonight when you shot Henry Farmer on Dorgenois."

Scooby put his hand over his mouth to stifle a cry. The man was all his worst ghosts, and escape seemed even more impossible than such a creature existing.

"I'll tell you what I'm going to do," the man said. "It is important to me that you know. It's important you understand that I'll be untouched by the destruction that's going to come."

"What are you talking about?" Scooby's voice squeaked like Sandy hitting a high note wrong.

"A shooter is coming. He will see to you," the man said. "I won't sully myself. He'll see to you with a gun or a blade or a rope—whatever he sees fit. And when your mother arrives, he will see to her too."

Hysteria hit a fever pitch. All sense melted in Scooby. Desperation beat his heart to his rib cage, beat his body against the door.

"My mama? Why?"

"Because she made you." More awful than the man's words was the sound of them fading as he walked away–leaving Scooby without the power of discussion, of pleading, of the mercy of another's presence. "I like my books completely balanced."

"Why? She's never done a thing! She's only wanted for better and worked and tried to do right!"

"Just like you, right, Sanford?" The voice was a room away.

"No! I did wrong! Bring it on me!"

The sound of another line ringing on the man's cell phone was even farther.

"Punish me! Not her! I deserve everything, but not her!"

The man's words came faint from the front door. "Yes, Miss Doolittle? Your son's had an accident. He needs you."

The front door clicked closed before Scooby could scream his mother's name.

Screaming became snarling as Scooby kicked the bathroom door. It held. He kicked and kicked. The wood bucked but kept its frame.

He refused to let it defeat him. Inches of wood and a lock would not destroy his mother. He felt his whole world hinged on this moment. This moment, unlike on Dorgenois, he would find the strength to do right.

Kicks battered until his toenails bled. Scooby tried his shoulder. He rammed it numb. The door stood.

He kept ramming. He might have been wailing his mother's name. He might have been crying–for her, for Sandy, for the Yellow Man, Henry Farmer. He could not fail even after his nerves did.

The wood gave. The door swung out.

Scooby looked around. The apartment gleamed. He felt like he had stepped from a horror film into a dream.

He shook his head to rid that feeling and bolted for the door. Three steps later, fear halted him. Fear not for him, but for Mama.

Scooby figured he might escape. The notion that the man could be waiting just outside to shoot him as he struck the street was only a nightmare. But the possibility of the shooter arriving, waiting for Mama and killing her, was very real.

Insane, but real. After the Yellow Man, Scooby was a devout believer in the insane happening all the time.

He dashed back to the kitchen and snatched a hand towel. Wrapping his hand, he pulled drawers. He had to find a weapon before the shooter arrived.

He found basters and cups. Then spices. Then knives.

The butcher's blade might do. "Might" was not enough for him. He skidded across the hardwood to the dining room set's drawers.

In the top drawer, Big Spook waited.

Scooby took a moment to consider this. Had the man been so confident that Scooby was locked in? Maybe he assumed the drug would weaken him. Maybe he just didn't care.

No, the man cared. Scooby took up Big Spook. He would sort this out with a gun in hand. And first, he had to find a phone.

He went through the dining set drawers. Nothing but silverware. He tossed it on the floor and spat on it.

Watching his spit bubble on the spoons and knives, Scooby realized that he'd just left DNA evidence. But evidence of what? This evening had become a crime without a name.

He bolted up the stairs. He reached the top landing when he heard the front door unlock.

Big Spook was up and level by the time Scooby spun. From the stairwell, he could see only a slice of the front room—the hand-woven carpet, the shiny edge of the coffee table, the unblemished floor.

He watched its emptiness.

He saw its emptiness fill with a shape: A big man. A pompadour of hair black as the man's jacket. A gun, huge to Scooby despite its size.

"Ethan?" The big man whispered as he followed the raised gun.

The big man failed to notice Scooby and stalked out of sight. Scooby flattened to the wall. His sneakers crept soundless down the velvet steps.

"Ethan?" The big man sounded like he was by the bathroom door. "Morrissey, you here?"

Scooby peered around the corner. That instant stuck a pin through his heart—the possibility of immediate death by the man's gun skewered him.

The big man was looking the other way, examining the broken door.

Scooby stepped out. Sandy squealed in his head to run. He raised Big Spook.

The big man looked down at the scatter of silverware.

Scooby aimed the gun. Sandy begged for him not to take another life. He thought of Mama.

The big man picked up a fork with spit on the tines.

Scooby pulled the trigger. Sandy went silent. He rang with the noise.

The big man's scalp came off like a rubber flap. The contents tossed over the silverware. His body sprawled onto their tumble.

Everything slowed. The leak of blood and smoke seemed to Scooby like the motion of a Polaroid resolving. He wondered what to do and felt he had all the time in the world to wonder it.

Big Spook had gone cool in Scooby's lifted hands by the time the sirens sounded outside.

Questions vanished. Thoughts of Mama, the tidy little man, the night's madness all became one answer: run.

Scooby ran, thinking that from now on—since the Yellow Man on Dorgenois Street—that would be the only answer he had.

★ ★ ★ ★ ★

It took three weeks before the tidy man came for Scooby.

Scooby leaned on a collapsing fence of white pickets by his business' corner. His Batman comic's print melted under the sweat of his fingers. He didn't mind. He couldn't focus on it anyway; just drift the pictures.

A cream-colored sedan pulled up in front of him. He glanced up, stood slowly, the dollars in his pocket rubbing damp on his skin through the cotton.

Scooby felt it through a daze. He'd been numb since that night, when he came home, found Mama sleeping soundly. Since then, life had seemed to occur in a space somewhere between nightmare and waking—between the night of gunfire and silverware, and the days that went on innocent as children.

The sedan didn't roll down its window like cars usually did at the corner. It clicked into Park. The driver's door opened.

Scooby stared, blank, at the tidy man. Fear couldn't puncture the numb disbelief.

The tidy man stared blankly back at him. He wore the same tan slacks, the same white shirt with short sleeves, the same calm.

He walked around the front of the sedan.

Scooby's hand slid for Big Spook. It stalled as he spotted the badge on the tidy man's belt.

"Hello, Scooby," the tidy man said. "I thought it time we talked about paying those sins."

Big Spook's handle shook in Scooby's fingers.

"Let's not," the tidy man said. He showed his own gun with a hand that moved far smoother than Scooby's.

"I paid," Scooby heard himself whimper. The tidy man put on a neat smile.

"I haven't." The man drew a fold of bills from his pocket. He presented them to Sandy. They were lean, but each was a hundred. "You did fine work for me the other night."

"I did nothing for you." Scooby said, voice now level. The money made the man's calm contagious. The fear only sharpened.

"You killed a police officer for me," the man said. Under a lid of calm, Scooby's fear reached a boil. He swooned, fingers fleeing Big Spook, eyes unable to escape the man's.

"A cop?"

"A nosey cop." The man frowned. "I had started to think I would have to end his investigation into my Integrity Control Unit all on my own. Then you came knocking."

Scooby fought his jaw shut. The man slid the bills into Scooby's pocket. They were dry and clean against the mire of drug dollars.

"Getting you to do it was, I'll admit, unpleasant for you," the man said. "But I knew you would. And the rewards will be considerable."

"Rewards." Scooby sounded the word and liked it. He sought within himself a part that would feel it to be poison. That part was burnt away.

"I'll need you for future work." The man stepped back around the sedan hood. "Errands. Disposal. Work. And in return, you'll enjoy payment, amnesty from the crimes you committed in my house and protection for you and your mother."

Scooby looked down at his tattoos. They marked him as a member of the Grubs. They were just ink to him now. He tried to sound defiant anyway. "I got protection."

The tidy man looked at the tattoos. He looked at Scooby's

face. Scooby felt those little eyes gouge every feature that was still young, still soft and vulnerable.

The tidy man smiled.

"Not from me." The smile stretched like a mask. The tidy man got in his cream-colored car and started it and drove off under the speed limit.

Scooby watched him wave at the children playing in their Sunday best outside the church.

"We just want something that's well written and tastefully sleazy."
—Booked. #30 *Warmed and Bound* interview

NIK KORPON
STRAIGHT DOWN THE LINE

Little Carl spit out the window as Betty guided her Dodge truck over to the side of Newkirk Street. The cassette tape flipped sides and opening chords of 'Born to Run' crackled from the speakers. She breathed out half a laugh. Without looking, she flicked ash at the coffee cup from yesterday morning's shift, though most of it landed on the metal plate covering the hole in the floor-board. Out the window she could see cranes unloading faded orange and blue shipping crates from the freighter docked at the Dundalk port terminal.

'You're leaving me here?' Little Carl slumped forward in the passenger seat, banged his head on the dashboard. 'It's damn near a twenty-minute walk.'

Even from this distance, the rectangular shipping containers dangling in the sky looked like the toy of some great retarded giant. The forklifts scurried back and forth with smaller pallets, ants carrying supplies back to their colonies.

'I don't want no one to see my truck near here this morning.'

She kept her hand covering the side of her neck, the bruise still shifting from red to purple. The ones on her thighs were finally turning yellow and brown.

He noticed she was still wearing her wedding ring and thought to say something but kept it to himself. 'You could just be coming by for Rick. Dropping off his lunch or apologizing or something.'

Betty slammed her palm against the steering wheel. The new cherry fell off, down to the floor. 'I ain't the one who needs to apologize.'

'I know that, baby, I know. I'm just saying, your truck wouldn't be an odd thing.'

She turned her head as slow as the sun chasing shadows, spoke just as slowly. 'You in my truck is what I'm worried about.'

'I've been friends with the son of a bitch for fifteen years, hon. Wouldn't be that unusual.'

She took a drag. 'Any other day, it wouldn't be.'

Little Carl pursed his lips and nodded. There wasn't really any response other than to light a cigarette and watch the machinations of the dock move in their ways. He thought it was funny, seeing that thick grey smoke getting choked out by all that bright blue sky above, like it should be the other way around but all that beauty just couldn't help consuming everything. That was a good outlook to have today, and he congratulated himself on it. Didn't hurt that his knees were still wobbly from the blowjob Betty'd given him earlier. Just blowing off steam, he'd joked. She wasn't amused.

'Everything's going to be fine, sweetheart. Trust me.' Carl set his hand on Betty's, stopped her from picking at the leather braid of the steering wheel cover. 'The first step's always the hardest.'

She sniffed hard, took a drag and coughed it out.

He slid across the vinyl bench seat, wrapped his arm around

her. 'You're still okay with this.' His tone wavered at the end, not asking a question but not making a statement either.

Another hard sniff, and she nodded, brought his hand to her mouth and kissed his split knuckles. 'I'll see you in a few days.'

He put his hand behind her head, keeping their faces together, and kissed her hard.

He closed the door and started toward the docks. The truck pulled up beside him, a paper bag hanging out the window.

'Forgot your lunch.' She smiled and blew him a kiss. 'Don't get no blisters on your feet.'

Little Carl punched his time card in the clock and dropped his lunch in his locker. He shrugged the orange reflective vest on over his flannel and grabbed his hardhat.

Shift didn't start for another twenty and most of the other stevedores were still outside the trailer bullshitting, their smokes growing shorter as last night's tits grew larger. He checked the schedule on the whiteboard, glanced each way to make sure no one was inside, then replaced Gimp's name from the forklift with his, and switched Terry's name off his crew for Ricky's. He poured two fingers of stale coffee, splashed in some of the bourbon from his inside pocket then went outside. First thing he heard was someone call someone else a cocksucker, then something about circumcising a lion in a phone booth, the dull smack of a fist on a face, then boots shuffling.

Carl ducked his head into his cup and went on.

'If it's a French boat, why don't it have a French name, like Pepe or something?' Ricky said. He stood on the prongs of Carl's lift as they crept toward the loading dock. Everyone called him Ratso Ricko, though usually not to his face. The name was combination of his nose resembling the Muppet's and his ability to give up any name needed to get out of Central Booking after he beat on Betty. Carl reckoned the motherfucker kept a notebook folded inside his socks.

'Because it's not French,' Carl said.

'French flag on it.' Ricky pointed at the side of the freighter, like that should explain everything.

'Remember that Madeline book you used to read to Nina when she was real little? That's a French book.'

Ricky shrugged.

'What I'm saying is, does the flag in the book look like that one on the ship?' He pulled up to overhead crane number five, waiting for it to drop the next container so they could start splitting it and ferrying the pallets away.

'Same colors.'

'Christ on a stick, Rick. It's sideways.' He took off his wool hat, the anticipation making him sweat enough already. 'Does Rotterdam sound French to you?'

Ricky shrugged. 'Kind of.'

'Of course it does. You're an illiterate motherfucker, so of course it does.' Thumbing a smoke to the top of the pack, he watched the crane lower the shipping crate to the dock. Manifest said this one held appliances—fridges and stoves and washing machines—and Carl wagered it'd be heavy as the burden on a murderer's soul. He didn't know when another like this would come in, and Betty couldn't go on any longer, so it had to be this one.

Carl took a long pull of bourbon as Ricky cracked open the crate and skimmed through paperwork to see which pallet went to which bay. He pulled the forklift forward and slid the prongs underneath the pallet then reversed. The refrigerators were bound by a nylon strap.

He hopped off the lift and walked toward Rick. 'Hey, double-check the manifest for this, will you? Supposed to be a bunch of dryers going out.'

'Says fridge here.'

'Just do it.' While Ricky had his back turned, Carl flipped the latch on the buckle, the strap visibly loosening.

'Told you,' Ricky said. 'It says fridges right here.'

Little Carl held up his hands to apologize. 'Must've gotten them mixed up.' He hopped back into the seat and raised the pallet. 'Oh, hey, Rick.'

Ricky slapped the papers on his thigh. 'What the fuck you want?'

'The flag,' he said. 'It's Dutch.'

It only took a little jiggle to topple the refrigerators.

Ricky's boot sticking out from beneath a door was the only way they knew where his body was.

★ ★ ★ ★ ★

The funeral passed without event, Betty showing the appropriate tears when required, Carl holding her up as expected of a close friend to the deceased. Terry's wife, Megan, told Betty she was lucky to have such a good man to stand beside her in her time of need, and if she needed anything else, don't hesitate to come across the street and ask. Betty's small living room felt like a closet with all the flower arrangements piled around. Carl had no idea Rick had so many acquaintances, much less friends, to send their condolences. Hell, he and Carl were only friends because of proximity. Their fathers drank heavily together after shifts at Beth Steel, so it only followed that their kids would pal around. Carl couldn't really even remember liking Rick that much, but more that they carried the same miserable load. Betty told him later that most were from the unions. Word had spread he'd been crushed and none of the locals, from Norfolk to Philadelphia, wanted to appear unsupportive for their flattened brother. In a similar gesture, the union arranged to give Little Carl two weeks of bereavement time, full-pay, and offered counseling, should he need it. Carl bit back his smile.

By the time Little Carl could be alone with Betty again, all the flowers had wilted and turned brown. They met behind Royal Farms on Ponca Street and fucked in her truck for the first two songs of *Human Touch*. He threw himself between her legs and she swallowed him whole. She damn near exploded after not having any contact for such a long time, her heel slamming against the rear vent window so hard it dislodged the glass from the weather stripping. They rested for another song or two, then she mounted him and rode him hard for the whole second side of the tape.

After they finished, he lit a pair of cigarettes and leaned back against the window. They blew smoke toward the front window, watched steam rise from their heads. The shaft of his cock burned.

'Damn I missed that.' She pulled at the hairs of his forearm. 'Been too damn long, baby. We can't let that pass.'

'I know, darling, I know. Sometimes we have to make sacrifices, though.' He took a long pull, let the smoke fill his voice. 'We've come too far to fuck it all up now by thinking with our dicks. Or, well,' he smiled, motioning at her waist, 'the other appropriate parts.'

She readjusted in the seat, pulling her skin off his and letting it rest against the vinyl seat. 'You could come over nights, you know. I'll leave the back unlocked.' She glanced down at her waist. 'Both of them if you'll come.'

Carl scratched his crotch then searched the floor for his briefs, picked them up by the torn elastic band. 'What about Nina?'

'I'll tell her to spend the night somewhere. Down Jessie's or something.

'How many eyebrows you think that'd raise, me showing up like that?'

'Don't care.'

'Yeah, well.' He snuffed. 'I'm the one who squashed the dearly departed, so I do care.'

'I just miss you, baby.' She let her hand fall in his lap, licked her lips. 'All twelve inches of you.'

He brought her hand to his mouth and kissed it, then shuffled on his jeans, tucking his erection beneath the waistband. Betty just sat there, visible for all creatures of the night to leer at. He picked up her bra and draped it over her shoulder. The shadowed cab blurred her bruises.

'I should get going,' he said.

Back in his rowhome, Carl stood in the middle of the dark bedroom and peeled off his clothes. He went into the bathroom to brush his teeth and, in the reflection, found the tip of a red gash crawling over his collar bone. Hunching his shoulder down, he caught a good four inches of exposed skin, saw another two beside it. Fingernails, looked like. He bit down on the toothbrush then flipped on the overhead light, snatched his t-shirt from the floor. Three streaks of blood stood out against the stained fabric, like lighted buoys warning homeward ships of the shallows.

★ ★ ★ ★ ★

On Carl's first day back, Gerry called him into the foreman's office as soon as he walked in. He nodded at one of the two vinyl chairs before his desk.

'How you doing? Want some coffee or anything?'

Carl held up the paper cup in his hand.

'Yeah, right.' The sound of Gerry's fingernails scratching his stubble was audible from across the desk. 'So. How are you?'

Carl cleared his throat, took a sip of coffee. He thought of the pink flush of Betty's neck. He thought of the splash of red on his back. 'Good as I can be, I guess. How are you?'

'No, no, I mean, you can't be great, you know. Just, you know, asking.' Gerry arranged the pencils on his desk then scooped them up and set them in an unused coffee mug. 'Man needs to talk to you today. I tried to give you as much time as I could, but OSHA works on their own timeline.'

Rising from his seat, Carl gave a little nod of thanks, threw back the rest of his coffee and crumpled the cup.

'Carl,' Gerry said. 'We can give you union representation, you know.'

Carl just shrugged. 'Don't need protection if I didn't do anything wrong.' He opened the door of Gerry's trailer and stepped out to the lot. A group of stevedores was huddled together to fight back the wind. The murmur of conversation petered out when the door slammed shut and they clocked Carl with sidelong glances.

'Boys,' he said with a nod. Terry and Gimp waved and started to call out, but Carl turned away before they could speak. He pinched a cigarette between his lips, cupped his hand around it and smelled, trying to bring back Betty's musky scent, then lit the cigarette. He headed across the concrete toward the government sons of bitches.

As he walked, nodding or waving at a few men who passed through the terminal on forklifts or in semi cabs, he thought about how soft the insides of Betty felt. There was damn near no satisfying her and while it'd never been a problem before–really, Carl'd looked at it as a challenge he was glad to take on–her nuclear libido was rapidly shaking cracks into the foundation of his plan. Straight on down the line was all good for her, as long as that line led to her clitoris a couple times a day. Little Carl almost had to laugh about it: Ricky being at the bar or blacked out on the couch when Carl'd come and go had caused less problems than now that he was dead. I'm not a man for irony, Carl thought, and irony can suck my chafed cock.

When he passed crane five, he paused, staring at the ground. Most of the concrete was a smooth grey, but golf ball-sized divots remained tinted red. Carl chained a smoke from the one between his lips and kneeled before the area. He ran his hand over the surface, letting his fingers linger inside the divots like the cups that held holy water in Saint Stan's. On his thighs, the ghost of Betty's fingers gripped, pressed, scratched. He picked at the rough patch, chipped away a flake of tinted concrete and rubbed it between his fingers, watching the dust blow away in the harbor breeze.

The door swung open before he could reach out and touch it. Two men in woolen sport coats and wrinkled ties stood in the doorway, ushering him in with soft hands. They sat at one end of an oval pressboard table with notepads and pens, he sat at the other with his pack of cigarettes.

For most of the interview, Carl leaned over the table and conjured up the same expressions from the funeral. Sorrow, condolence, head-shaking.

'I understand it's hard for you, but can you go over it just one more time, step by step?'

He let go a big sigh, thought about a double-bourbon at The Pine Box then reverse-cowgirl with Betty, then ran through his spiel again, re-emphasizing how Ricky must've forgotten to tighten the strap or how he loosened the strap or how he did some stupid goddamn thing that resulted in this awful tragedy.

'So, I got to ask,' the jacket on the right cut him off. 'Why did Mister Frankowski mess with the straps anyway? The pallets—and correct me if I'm wrong—but most times the pallets come off ready to move, right?'

'That's right.'

'So why'd he mess with the strap in the first place?'

Carl inhaled, exhaled. 'If I knew that, I wouldn't be sitting here with you two right now, would I?'

'Why didn't you stop him?' the other one said. 'If you're the operator, why didn't you secure the load before moving?'

He tried his best to light the cocksucker on fire with a glare. 'I really need to answer that?'

'It's just a question,' the first one said.

'It don't need an answer. And, all due respect, sir, fuck you for asking. When you leave here today, go run over your friend and I'll come by and interrogate you for a while.' Carl thumbed out a smoke, tapped it on the table then tucked it behind his ear. 'Maybe then you can come up with an answer.'

After another ten minutes of detailed strap-related questions, they shook Carl's hand and bid him good day.

As Carl laid a hand on the door, one of the men called out, 'Just one more thing.' Carl turned round, raised an eyebrow.

'Why'd you get off the machine?'

Carl cleared his throat. 'Pardon?'

The man looked down at his notepad. 'In our interview with Mr. Konaw, he said he saw you get off the forklift a moment before the incident.'

'Terry said that.' In his head, Carl couldn't tell if he'd said it as a statement or a question. 'Is he trying to say that I had something to do with Ricky? You trying to say that?'

The other one shook his head. 'Just covering our bases.'

Carl sniffed hard, swallowed the phlegm in his throat. 'Ricky wasn't the smartest guy around, God bless him. I wanted to make sure the manifest was right before we started moving shit around.'

'And was it?'

'Yeah,' he said. 'Yeah, it was.'

He stepped outside in the breeze, feeling their eyes on his back, and pulled the cigarette from behind his ear, smiling behind his cupped hands as he lit up. Today wasn't a good day for work. Anyway, all that talking brought up a mighty thirst in him.

He was close to emptying his fifth glass when the stool beside him scooted back. Gimp saddled up to the bar, waved at Denny for a beer. Carl moved his mouth into something more resembling a blur than a smile.

'You cut out early too?' He shook his head. 'Gerry must be shitting bricks.'

Gimp mmmed, sipped at his can of Boh. 'It's not your fault.'

'Nah, I know that. Gerry's a pussy, got soft hands. He laid down the law, people wouldn't leave willy-nilly.'

'You know that's not what I mean.' He squared up to Carl, drummed his fingers on his thigh like he was deciding whether or not to lay a hand on his friend's shoulder.

Carl smiled as he swirled the remaining chips of ice in his bourbon. 'It's coming, Gimp.'

'What is?'

He shrugged. 'Death. It's coming for us no matter what. Nothing we can do about it.' He slapped one hand on the bar. 'We start here with our mommas, step one, then end up here with our bones.' He slapped his other hand on the bar and knocked over a woman's beer. 'Straight down the line, from one to ten or whatever. However many you can manage.'

Gimp swished some Boh around his mouth, scratched his jowl.

Carl wagged his finger at him, eyes squinted so all the blurry edges came in clear. 'Anything in between is what you do. And what you do is what matters. Fighting, fucking, killing, it's what you do.'

Gimp took a long breath then turned to Denny. 'How much this motherfucker had to drink?'

Denny just scratched his chin.

Gimp turned back to Carl. 'Drink up, buttercup. You need to get your ass home.'

Carl gave that same blurred smile and nodded, fished around inside his pockets for some money and slapped it on the bar. 'Need to get my ass.'

He scooted the stool back and wobbled outside.

His fist fell heavy on the back door. It throbbed, and he realized he wasn't sure how long he'd been knocking. He glanced around the backyard, making sure this was Betty's house, and as he raised his hand again the door swung open.

'The fuck, Carl?' Betty shoved her head out past him, looking around the yard.

He reached around and grabbed a handful of her ass through her dress. 'Heard you got a back door for me.'

'Why the hell you come round banging like that? What if Nina was here?'

Carl looked around. 'Is she?'

'She's at softball but that ain't the point. We're supposed to be careful, ain't that what–'

Carl barged through the doorway, grabbing Betty's thighs

with both hands. He pulled her up onto his waist and crushed his face against hers, bit her bottom lip between his teeth. She grunted, hands fumbling at his waist, trying to unbuckle his belt. She licked his neck, his jaw, rubbed her chest against his. Her hands couldn't work right so Carl dropped her, ripped off his belt like he was starting a lawnmower, then bent her over, pulled her dress up and underwear to the side and tried to shove himself in. Betty, moaned, gripped his thigh, dug her fingers into his skin.

She thrust herself back against him, said, 'I've missed your cock. Come on, baby.'

Carl looked down, saw himself half-mast bending up against her. He gripped his fingers around the base, aiming for her. Bent against her flesh again.

'You don't have to be gentle, baby. Come on now.' She rubbed herself against his pelvis.

'Yeah, just wait, girl. Just letting the anticipation grow till you can't handle it anymore.' He tightened his stomach muscles, tried to get something moving. It laid across his fist. Goddamn bourbon, he thought.

'I don't need anticipation, Carl. I just need you.' Her breath rolling hard from her mouth, she pulled him close again and asked if he needed the back door.

'I just need you to wait.' He felt a fluttering underneath his balls, thought yeah, Betty, that's the spot, until he realized she was touching herself and not him.

'Carl, come on. Give it to me hard. Smack me some.'

'Just a damn minute.' A little bounce, standing up from the droop some.

'I need it, Carl. Come on.' Her voice grew ragged as her breathing came harder, hand moved faster.

'Dammit, Betty, just–'

'Choke me, Carl,' she yelled. 'Cut off my air before I come.'

The droop returned.

'What?'

Her ass slammed up against his pelvis, butt bone banging against his pubis. 'Fucking choke me, you faggot.'

His hands fell on her shoulders and she yelled again, started pissing him off so he wrapped his hands around her neck and squeezed like he was testing the ripeness of a cantaloupe.

'A little,' her voice trembled, 'little harder.'

He could feel the thin bones of her throat, feel the vibrations as she spoke. He felt a wetness on her skin and looked down, realized his cock was throbbing, and threw himself forward. She screamed and her hand went so fast he was worried she'd rip off her own clit. They fell down onto a pile of dirty laundry, her pelvis writhing up against his. He smelled old sweat and dirt on the clothes.

After she came again she stilled, nestled into the crescent of Carl's body. He was still fully-hard inside her for a few minutes more, but it felt like guilt manifested more than any notion of arousal. He rolled away from her to grab a cigarette from his flannel and she fake-pouted.

'Sorry, sweetheart,' he said. 'Just need to get my head together.'

'Light me one.'

He sat indian-style on the clothes, his balls resting on a pair of grey sweatpants stained with period blood. She righted herself and wrapped her arm around his shoulders.

'Sorry if I scared you, baby.' She took a drag. 'Sometimes I just need a little to get over that hump, you know?'

He nodded and said he did, then brushed her hair aside and kissed her forehead. It tasted of salt. Cocking her head, she gave him a little smile, and when she did he noticed the bright red marks on her neck that his hands had left.

When their cigarettes were finished, she patted his knee and said that Nina would be home from softball soon. Little Carl took his cue and dragged on pants and his flannel. He was halfway out the basement door when she asked when they'd see each other again.

'Soon, sweetheart.' He wondered if that was true.

'Seems like I see you less now than I did before.' She tucked her hair behind her ears.

He nodded and kissed her cheek, unsure of how to respond.

Rounding the corner from the alley to the sidewalk, he cupped his hand around another smoke when he heard his name. He looked up and saw Terry standing next to his truck, lunch bag in one hand, six-pack in the other. Just getting off work.

'What happened to you today?' he said. 'Could've used another body to move the freight.'

'Didn't feel so good.' He looked at the smoke in his hand, wondered if he should now put it out.

'Sorry to hear that.' Terry looked over Carl's shoulder up to Betty's house then back at Carl, and squinted his eyes. Carl wasn't sure if it was from the reflection of the sun in the windows or if he was thinking, so he just smoked. Terry gave a short wave. 'Feel better, hear?'

The next morning Carl dropped his grape juice on the floor. It spilled purple over the yellowed linoleum. He thought about Betty's neck from yesterday, about the way her voice threatened to slice him open, about the way her hands would tremble when she recounted all the ways Rick beat her as Carl held her in his arms and made silent threats against the man, about the way Rick had laughed years ago when recounting what a firecracker his new girl was in bed. Carl had a headache from all the afternoon-bourbon yesterday and thinking only made it worse. He ripped paper towels from the roll and mopped up the grape juice. He left his lunch in the fridge and went to work.

★ ★ ★ ★ ★

Carl watched the blades of the ceiling fan spin, slicing through the candles' glow. Betty's skin stuck to his when she readjusted her leg over his thigh. She pulled at his chest hair, smoothed it down. The red mark around her wrist was still bright red. She'd been facedown on the bed, wrists and ankles bound to each post of her bed. Waiting. He'd been more surprised to see she could fasten the last restraint with only one hand than to see that pretty little pussy staring at him when he came in. A skill like that, it must take some practice.

He lit another smoke for himself, felt blood thrum through his skull.

'I don't mean to be weird or anything,' he started, then stopped.

She lifted herself up on an elbow. Her breast hung low in the shadow. 'Baby you can tell me anything.'

'You been,' he took a drag, 'into this kind of thing for a while?'

She smiled and stroked his chest. 'Every girl's got her fantasies.'

'No, I get that. I like that. A lot. What you do.' He took another drag, still debating whether he really wanted an answer. Everything was going well, aside from having to sneak around for another couple months, and he knew that not knowing would keep everything going well. Still, that idea kept flitting around his skull like a moth trying to touch the light inside the bulb.

'What's on your mind, Carl?'

'Were you always like this?' The words came out before his brain could comprehend them. The words hung in the air like smoke.

She rolled off her elbow, sat with her legs crossed. 'What do you mean?'

He exhaled smoke, waved around his hands inarticulately. 'All this. The cuffs and spanking and choking.'

'A woman's got needs too, Carl.' She snatched his cigarette and took a long inhale. 'Ain't no different from a man's.'

'That's not what I'm saying, Betty.' He propped himself up against the wall. 'I'm happy to help you with your needs. It's just–'

'You want to know if I'm a slut? Is that what you're asking me?'

'I want to know if you and Rick did this.'

She sucked hard on the cigarette. The cherry burned the same color as her wrists. 'I'm not with Rick now. I'm with you.'

'You know what I'm saying, Betty.'

A long, considered stare was all Carl got in response.

She looked up at the ceiling fan. 'You remember what you said that night Rick was out at The Box with Gimp and them? That bar-top shuffleboard thing that went until five, six in the morning? When I knew he'd come home with angry fists after losing all his money.'

'Believe so.'

'Nina was at a sleepover. We were in the living room dancing to Waylon.'

'Yeah.' Carl felt a smile trying to surface, but he bit it in half, swallowed it down to his gut. 'I remember that.'

'What'd you say?'

'I remember what I said.'

She rolled her head to face him. 'Then where the fuck's that now?'

'Betty, we danced to all the wrong songs. I ain't no killer.'

'You never even liked him.'

'That doesn't mean he needed to die.'

'He drank too much and he was a mean son of a bitch.'

'I drink too much too.' Carl held the smoke inside his lungs, wondered if it was possible to go from smoke inhalation like this. 'I ain't no killer, Betty.'

She breathed a small laugh. 'No, you aren't, because you wouldn't be complaining so much now.' The candle flickered and threw shards of shadow across her. 'But you did, Carl.'

★★★★★

Gerry was waiting in the trailer when Carl walked in. Carl nodded at him and looked around, tried to figure out whether this was some kind of setup. He set his lunch in his locker, shrugged on his vest and grabbed his hardhat. Closing the locker, he nodded at Gerry again then pulled out the coffee pot.

'Are you retarded?' Gerry said.

'Huh?'

'It's in the middle of brewing, dumbass.'

Carl looked at the coffee dripping onto the burner and shoved the pot back under. Gerry just shook his head.

'That's why you're waiting?' Carl looked around again. He felt Rick's eyes in every corner, peering out from the box of stale doughnuts Rick used to gorge himself on. Gerry raised his eyebrows, shrugged.

The percolator sputtered and shot out the last of coffee. Gerry poured a cup and handed it to Carl. 'I wouldn't put nothing from your jacket into this.' He nodded toward outside of the trailer. 'They're coming back to talk this afternoon. Three o'clock.'

'Who?' Carl didn't need to ask, but felt he should keep up appearances.

Gerry didn't feel that same need and walked out to the terminal.

Carl stood in the middle of the trailer, listening to silence thrum through his temples. The whiteboard assignments were up already. He went over and switched his name, made Gimp forklift-operator. As he set the marker back on the board the door swung back open. His hands instinctively went up, expecting either an angry Gerry or hellbent investigators. Perhaps Betty with a cat o' nine tails and a blow torch. Instead he saw Terry, who stared at Carl's outstretched hand by the board, and cocked his head.

'Feeling better?' Terry scratched his stubble.

Carl nodded.

'You don't look it.' Terry made his way across the trailer and poured some coffee. 'Look like you haven't seen the sun in years.'

'Just tired.'

Terry spit on the ground. 'Bet you are, horsecock.'

'The fuck's that mean?' Carl half-stepped forward but half-retreated, like some weird dance on the edge of a windy cliff.

'Drink some coffee before your meeting with them boys.' He motioned to the other trailer. 'I've got dinner with Ruthie tonight and don't want your questions to run into mine.'

'They're talking to you again too.' Carl meant for it to come out as a question but his voice betrayed him. Instead he raised his cup and opened up the door.

'Don't worry,' Terry said. 'I would've done the same.'

'I didn't do nothing.'

Terry just smiled. Carl kept walking.

'You going to be okay with this?' Gimp pointed up at the shipping container lowering before them. 'You're not going all Viet-nam, are you?'

'I'm fine.' He ground out his smoke under his boot heel as the container touched ground with a thud, then went to open it. After checking the manifest over, he waved for Gimp to come forward and pick up the first pallet.

'Take this over to bay five.'

While Gimp ferried the pallet away, Carl surveyed the dock. Too many men around to work in the open. He slapped the manifest against the ovens and cursed up a blue storm while moving his hand from the papers to the pallet's contents with exaggerated motions. Goddamned appliances. Why couldn't they get in a shipment of marble or granite every once in a while? When he got to the blind-side of the pallet, he flipped the buckle and loosened the restraining buckle. The ovens and double-stack washer/dryers rocked. He thumbed a cigarette to his mouth and went outside the container, watching Gimp drive across the lot.

'Make sure you give this one some ass,' he said. 'Bunch of heavy shit on it.'

Gimp gave him a queer look then laughed. 'This your first rodeo too?'

Carl inhaled hard and closed his eyes. He thought to make the sign of the cross out of reflex, but realized he'd given up on the Lord a long time ago. He thought he should say something to Rick, but realized it wasn't Rick he really missed. Thinking of Betty felt inappropriate, so he thought back to the mutt he and his brother found in the alleyway that had been shot twice and left for dead, the one they nursed back to health and raised for a number of years.

'The fuck you doing?' Gimp yelled. Carl opened his eyes and saw Gimp pulling away on the lift, pallet wobbling slightly but otherwise intact. 'Get yourself together. We need to get all these down the line before three.'

There would be other pallets, other shipments. Other shifts and other opportunities. Other appliances and, maybe if he was lucky, some building stone. As Carl took a long inhale, though, he just looked up at overhead crane number five, lifting another shipping container over top of him. He stared at the cable, watching it for any signs of fraying, weakness. He focused all his energy on the latches and buckles and bolts. He tried to soften the metal, to disorient the crane operator, to shift the winds into some random and godforsaken gust that toppled the container and crushed his mortal body.

'Damn it, Carl.' Gimp's voice rang out.

Carl startled and dropped his smoke, realized it had burned out who knows how long ago.

'Seriously, brother. If you need to take a minute, do it. Just get yourself together. I can't have no shit on my watch.'

Gimp lifted another pallet with the forklift and backed up and, for a moment, Carl's heart pounded. Then Gimp drove away, and Carl lit another cigarette. He started reading down the manifest, checking that each item on the pallet corresponded with the number on the sheet, trying to be thorough but also not wasting time.

He had his meeting in a couple hours, and he knew Betty would be expecting him later.

"That's really my goal. To make people feel
a little bit spent when they're done reading
whatever I'm writing."
  —Booked. #23 *Warmed and Bound* interview

RICHARD THOMAS
SURRENDER

As I slowly lose my mind, the rest of the world falls away. A cloud
hangs over the monotone house, the grass growing longer, the
litter outside caught in the wild blades of fading green, as the
shadows inside play games with me. I used to resist them, tried
to shine a light into the corners of the living room, the drapes–
the long hallways that never seemed to end. I used to scream at
them, crying as I fell to my knees, begging to be left alone. When
I walk by the bedroom now, the door closed, a cold wave pushing
out from under the gaps, nipping at my ankles, I moan quietly
under my breath as a shadow flickers at the door frame. I do not
open it, not now.

   I grew up around this house, with its curving banister, the
old grandfather clock that sat in the foyer, the secret passage-
ways between bedrooms hundreds of years old. I loved to spend
time here, to open the glass candy dish and see what Grandma
had put out that day, to hide in the bedroom closets and wait for
my brother to find me. Now, I only see death.

When my grandmother passed away I was sad, of course, the memories of so many holidays spent here, Christmas trees crowded by presents, the whole family gathered around the Thanksgiving table. That all changed. It changed so fast that I never saw it coming. I couldn't fathom what lurked in the darkness, what waited for me to come home.

For a long time now I've stared at the ceiling, sleeping on the antique couch, covered in dust, afraid to go upstairs, but afraid to leave it as well. I know how it summons—I know how it pulls the light to it and snuffs it out. So I stay and ask myself what I did to bring this spirit to me, what actions and crimes I committed to lure the demon out. In the dark, no amount of blankets are able to stop my shivering, I hear it upstairs, heavy footsteps, the weight of lead boots, the mass of flesh a horrible density, the shadows always fading to cold air. I remember the abortion, the way my girlfriend cried—this selfish act that we hid from the world, drowned in our sorrows and a river of amber liquid. I remember the anxiety of a thump in the road, the radio blaring, the shape left behind as I drove on, turned away, vomiting in the bushes later, pretending that nothing had happened. I remember the heroin, the needles and the glossy cold skin she wore, the way we would pour into each other, our mouths hot for slick tongues, our fingers eager to grab, to clench, to slide inside. She deserved better—I know that now. The only sound left from that night, from the dense woods, from the dull panic that washed over me is the sound of the shovel blade piercing the earth, over and over again.

Nobody thought anything of the gray cat, the Maine Coon we called Quixotic, passing away in the middle of the night. He was fifteen years old, moving slow already, doomed to die in this house—we all knew that. And yet, as I fell asleep that night, his cries came to me from the basement, wrapped in an urgency that made me queasy, that made me hesitate, pull back the covers and sit up on the edge of the bed. I heard him make his way up the stairs, and I heard him slump to the floor in the guest room, and assumed he was fine, when he finally went quiet.

Guest room. Yes, that's accurate. Our guest.

We buried him in the backyard, the acre of old oaks a canopy stretching over our heads, the brick fireplace where we would barbeque and gather, the chipped fountain of a forlorn boy spouting water into its cracked base. I have a hard time saying their names now, my son, my wife–they have turned to smoke and drifted away. My son, Robert, he took the sticks, wound round with yarn, the simple placard reading Quicky, as we called the cat, and pushed into the earth with a sigh. That night as we fell asleep, my sadness a heavy weight on my chest, the place the cat used to sit and purr, a series of doors slammed shut, a groaning from the pipes in the basement, and we clung to each other, my Linda disappearing in my arms, tears and darkness and heavy sighs luring us to sleep. We were not afraid, not yet. We were sad, and tired, and ready to move on. Our guest was not.

I didn't know much about electricity, so my brother William helped me with the ceiling fan. It seemed a simple task. The guest room was always hot, except when it was cold, needing a false breeze to keep the stillness from growing. The circuit breakers, they were flipped. The light from the windows was barely enough, clouds drifting over the yard, but we did not hesitate. A ladder, the wires, screws and a drill, it was nothing to us, an easy job, a task to be done. There were cold beers and a back porch waiting for us later, the inevitability of it unquestioned. I slapped him on the back, and we hoisted the fan. And then he grabbed the wires.

There were no lights on in the room, and yet I stared at him as his body shook, as his eyes bulged and a darkness swept across the room, the ladder shaking, no voice in my chest, no words in my mouth, the smell of charred flesh, the urine pooling beneath the ladder, his body falling to the ground, the fan crashing down on us, as I muttered his name over and over, smoke drifting as tendrils to the ceiling where it gathered. The room now held an anxious weight.

There never would be a fan in that room, the broken blades and glass carted out to the garbage cans in the quiet of the next day, the wires sticking out of the hole, always pointing, always reaching out for more. And in the corners of the room, the shadows grew, the air thick with the stench of burnt flesh.

The house had changed for us now, and we stayed away from the guest room, closing the door, which always reopened, stayed on the north side of the house, leaving that hallway alone. And yet, we went on. It was still weeks before I'd start killing myself, there was still an air of hope.

Still in a fog, we snapped at each other, my wife and I, over every small thing, over every task not done a certain way. We spit our angry words at each other over garbage cans and their liners, over bills that had not been paid, over loose handrails and crooked pictures and dinners that we brought home in greasy paper bags. Maybe we could have run then, maybe it was still forming, still weak. I don't know.

The sounds that came to us as we fought in the kitchen, they did not make any sense, they had no context in our memories. We stomped and pointed, we clenched our fists and spewed obscenities, faces flushed, as the house around us creaked and moaned, the doors opening and closing, the boy running from room to room, a game he was playing, certainly, a laugh on his lips as he amused himself, certainly not terrified, not running from something, not trying to escape, just playing as boys are known to do. My fist banged on the table, a tall thin water glass breaking in the kitchen sink as Linda turned her back to me, cursing into the hot water that flowed over the dirty dishes. Our heads turned with a snap at the pounding, the heavy thuds as they repeated down the curving staircase, over and over until we were met with the eventual silence of the boy hitting the hardwood floor. No words, just a gasp, eyes widening, and we ran out of the room, muttering to our absent god, and found him bent and broken, lying still on the floor.

There was not much left after that, I think. There was no color, or light, only darkness. People came and left, the house was full and then empty, things were done, paperwork, I imagine, nothing that stays with me, nothing that matters. I often found myself wandering the hallways, cold and yet sweating, standing in the guest room, arms at my side, a cloak of black wrapping around me, as I cursed the shadows, begged it to take me, I was done. A dirty teddy bear sat in the corner, a long line of Matchbox cars leading from it to the edge of my shoes, and my head filled with swarming bees, my eyes rolled up into the back of my head, and I collapsed.

Linda is at our bedside, her hands on my wrist, her voice a whisper, and she's telling me something, that we have to leave, that she's leaving, that it's all gone now, nothing left—I can't decipher what she's saying. I cannot move. She tells me it is too much and I can barely nod. Go, I tell her, there's nothing here for you. I have nothing left to offer. Run. I close my eyes and she is gone.

I open them and there is a pounding at the front door, lights flashing and I cannot speak to the men in uniform, as they pour past me into the house, as the smell of something burning fills the hallway and my mouth. They are in the kitchen shouting and there is a wave of smoke, the sound of water, the cursing and grunting of men. They ask for my wife, they mention the boy, my brother—they have been here before. I am mute. There is water on the floor, a puddle in which I stand, and as I look above my head there is an irregular shape on the ceiling above, the guest bathroom, the drip, drip, dripping filling the air with a metronome, a repetition that wants to add up to something.

There is more noise upstairs, men yelling and I still cannot move. I am pushed out of the way, as a stretcher flies past me, the man in charge, his hand on my arm, yelling at me from underwater, pushing me into a chair a flashlight in my eyes, and there are doctors, paramedics, policemen, firemen, a flurry of action, and I am slipping into a comatose skin, my flesh gone alabaster, my heart freezing into stone. The last thing I remember is the slashes of red on the white, white sheet—and she is gone from me forever.

I told her to run. He didn't let her get away.

Time has abandoned me, I am no longer alive—I am no longer human. I get in the car and drive and drive, out onto the highway into the darkness, the world around me lacking clarity, and I find myself back in the driveway, the engine running—the car door open wide. I pick up the telephone and call anybody who will answer, beg them to come get me, to get me away from this unholy presence, and then I wait downstairs for the doorbell to ring, but they never show up.

There is a vague memory of a hammer and nails, of boards. There is the smell of gasoline leaking from under the door and the matches in my hand will not strike. There is a pinching at my wrists and a feeling of great release and I awake in my bed, naked, claw marks up and down my skin, bite marks on my shoulders and the torn flesh on my arms is stitched together with long pieces of dark, sinewy hair.

When there is nothing left, when I have finally surrendered, no longer seeking absolution, no longer praying to any god, anywhere, no longer ignoring the price I now must pay, not at my hands, but at his, I take the hammer and I claw at the wood, I pull away the barrier to the closed off room, this abyss, this dark sanctuary, and I place my hands on the cold metal knob–I turn it slowly and breathe frost into the air, I give myself over to the darkness inside, and finally, he swallows me whole.

VON

AMANDA GOWIN
SHORT TENDON

More Human opened two shops down from *Hammer & Nails* in the last strip mall existing in Evans Collective—maybe the last strip mall anywhere.

Marsla asked Grandmere, More human than what?

Grandmere sighed and spun her chair away, electing instead to lighten the mood with a song *her* grandmother used to play. Marsla laughed at the parallel lyrics and rhyming.

Twyla, Marsla's genetic identical, did not laugh. As an employee of *Hammer & Nails*, she wanted to know why a modification franchise would open in a collective as small and remote as theirs in the first place. In just one week their business had diminished, as teens elected to have their fingertips replaced and their nails metalled instead of just gilded or magnetized. Suddenly all the salons were ancient, un-hip.

Grandmere tried to explain that if the fringes could be won over, anyone could. Twyla didn't care. She said she wished she were Asian so she could work at *More Human*, which had sprung up overnight with its own staff.

Where did you learn that word?

What word?

Asian.

Twyla laughed and said it was what the old women told her the employees at the new place were–they all had god-hair of black, almond eyes and flat cheekbones.

Grandmere covered her eyes with gnarled hands, pursing her lips in disgust. It's a trick, she explained. Are the heads real?

Neither girl had entertained the possibility that they were not.

The optometrists were hit hardest, fastest. Their expansion of eye color selection did nothing to compete with eye replacement, and a trend appeared in the area–Husky eyes, though no one was sure what it meant–of one blue eye and one brown. No one scheduled corrective surgery anymore. The two optometrists folded up quietly and disappeared within the month.

The salons hung on longer, with the return of god-colors and faster machines–and lower prices. Purple, silver, gold and blue hair gave way to 'blond,' 'strawberry blond' and 'auburn.' Women compared their flesh-toned scalp stitches and raved about the painlessness of the Switch and Stitch machine.

I thought the modification centers made metal parts, Marsla said. Everyone in the ads have silver parts.

Wait, Grandmere said. She looked at her arthritic hands. First they blend in–then they stand out.

Twyla rolled her eyes and flipped her blond hair. She pointed a metal fingernail and accused Grandmere of being a cloud of doom.

In three months, *Hammer & Nails* was gone, and the two remaining salons were for sale–machines included. New ads appeared on the More Human mail tablets–appendage adjustment, augmentation, improvement. Slender flesh-toned hands, plump fish lips, small and feminine feet, straight noses.

Still no silver.

One afternoon Marsla returned from tutoring to find Grandmere staring at the wall, at the huge projection of perfect hands in the *More Human* ad. Her head was tilted, purple hair in a fancy updo. Thinking her asleep, Marsla tiptoed past.

I've made an appointment for Friday, Grandmere announced without turning. Do you remember the piano in Mr. Chronon's Museum? I played one once. I would like to learn, and I believe Mr. Chronon could teach me.

She didn't remember what a piano was, but Marsla kept quiet.

Friday evening, Marsla and Twyla sat on the floor pillows, mirror images except for their hair, awaiting her return.

They both stiffened at the laughter at the door, but before either could rise to assist, light glinted off a shiny silver hand on the entrance buttons, and behind it came Grandmere's sleeve, then Grandmere's smiling face, and Mr. Chronon.

Purple hair loose to the waist, Grandmere chatted briefly at the entrance with the older gentleman. The girls heard Tomorrow night, yes, lovely. Then the shuffle of receding footsteps.

Why hide what is obviously new? She waved her new hands in the air, snapped her fingers. I will not disguise them. They are beautiful.

Grandmere knitted the night away. At the kitchen table next morning she wrote in a language Marsla had never seen before—writing at all was uncommon. Cursive, Grandmere said. She wore her clothes from the night before. On the table was a finished scarf and real sheets of paper, covered with sketches of faces and hands.

Another month passed. *More Human* expanded, buying up the entire strip mall and hiring on most of the former salons' employees to perform superficial procedures and preserving the original staff for modifications. But no one used that word—'modification.' The collective's inhabitants shimmered in the evening sunrise. Light glinted off their self-improvements. Marsla passed Mr. Chronon 'jogging'—cane discarded, silver calves above his white sneakers. Twyla was hired and all her earnings poured back into a 50/50 fund the company provided for self-improvement. Twyla wanted new cheekbones, flat ones, and her eyes tilted. A transparent agenda: she thought the more Asian-looking, the more chance for advancement within the company.

Six months after opening, half the town was employed by *More Human* and the rest had been touched by them in some way. Agriculturalists received stipends for allowing the corporation's designers to study the horses, cows; to watch the agriculturalists themselves as they moved, the muscle groups used, the repetitive labors.

Feeding the Percherons, Marsla was discovered by a designer. He wore white coveralls and studied her, recorder on, for some moments without speaking.

You are like these animals, calm, confident, he said finally. Would you have their eyes?

Her laugh surprised him, he lifted his eyebrows. Do you know what a Husky is?

At the shake of her head he tapped buttons on his tablet. This is a dog, he told her. The breed of this one is a Husky.

Morning dusk fell as they explored his notes and pictures. Marsla saw flamingos and fish and more dogs, and something called a cat.

This is the next big thing in eyes, he confided. Just wait until next year. He sighed at her lack of excitement. Just go in and see. At least see the surgeon about your finger.

Her finger. The UV streetlights led her home, and she flexed her hand repeatedly, unable to straighten her pinky. She'd never been able.

It's just a little funky, Grandmere had told her.

What's funky? she'd asked.

Morbid curiosity finally collided with a legitimate excuse.

Silver was scarce, tasteful. A demure girl in a white coat led Marsla through the salon area, buzzing with customers. Twyla winked in her direction from the control pad of a multi-colorizer, and Marsla noticed her brand new blue and brown eyes.

Dr. Chanel Ping, a white nameplate on the steel door read, and the girl knocked once before pressing it open.

Lovely to meet you. A Nubian hand extended to meet hers across a wide glass desk with nothing on it. Marsla took it, eyes following the arm to the shoulder and across. Where the other girls buttoned their coats to the throat, Dr. Ping's hung open, and Marsla saw the shiny purple stitching join dark flesh and light just above the collarbone. Her face and head were remarkably like the other girls'. She gestured Marsla into the chair opposite. I know what you're thinking, she smiled. And yes, this is my real head. The skin, no, the face, no, but I assure you this is my skull and brain et cetera, et cetera, she circled her hands in the air before steepling her brown fingers.

Marsla said nothing.

Your gemini works here, doesn't she? Dr. Ping asked. Without waiting for an answer she continued, It's interesting to see the … before and after, if you know what I mean. You're untouched, aren't you? That's even your God-hair–oh, don't blush, I'm an expert, of course I can tell the difference between god-hair and *God*-hair. Dr. Ping twisted her fingers at her lips. Your secret is safe with me. Now, let's see your hand.

The walk home was tricky, looking the whole time at her finger. A short tendon, Dr. Ping had explained. She explained corrective surgery and hospital alternatives, then brought out a tray of 'alternate' fingers in all shades and colors, outlining the removal of the old at the bottom knuckle and placement of the new, and of the tiny, tiny cost of such a thing as a finger. Marsla was fingerprinting the tablet of consent and the white light buzzed over her hand while she relaxed on a pink plastic chair, then here she was—taking the long way as the light glinted off the silver. As Grandmere had said, Why hide what is obviously new?

Marsla hesitated at Museum Drive, but one of Mr. Chronon's windows was open, and Grandmere's laughter accompanied by a careful tune met her across the field. She heard clapping, and imagined Mr. Chronon standing next to her unaided. Marsla finally remembered what the piano looked like—and what Grandmere's silver hands must look like walking across those black and white rectangles. Smiling, Marsla went on. She hummed the tune Grandmere was making, and flexed her hand. She would show the designer tomorrow. His eyes had been the same color, his hair a common blue.

A year passed.

Yelling downstairs, again. Twyla couldn't make the payment on her permanent Husky eyes—the first set had been temporaries, to test out compatibility, buyer satisfaction, it was all in the tabletwork. To make matters worse, she was done with Husky eyes. Didn't Grandmere understand that Calico eyes would be available in three months?

Grandmere was in default on her hand repair loan, only Twyla didn't know. It had been a cloudy midnight Marsla had crept downstairs to hear her crying on the phone. Unusual wear—such as piano lessons, knitting, typing—were not covered. Mr.

Chronon was experiencing the same problem—jogging, hiking, swimming—with his knees and legs. Both of them had sold large chunks of property for repairs, but it wasn't enough....

You're late for work! Marsla yelled down the stairs. Fuck you and your cat eyes!

Where did you learn the word Fuck? Grandmere asked.

What's a cat? Twyla asked.

Both questions went unanswered, and Marsla dragged herself back to the toilet to be sick.

The designers were gone, along with their stipends and studies. For Marsla, one was still sort of here.

He no longer answered her tablets.

The collectivesfolk were literally falling apart. *More Human* hadn't expanded in size or staff, but deliveries of 'permanent' parts arrived daily. Women gathered in hushed groups in market corners, one in sunglasses, another in gloves, a third's invisible misery only evident by her tears. Canes and wheelchairs reappeared. Scarves cropped up. The hospital was understaffed for the emergency surgeries and began taking interns off the street. Girls once working at *More Human* to pay for cosmetic adjustments now worked at the hospital to pay off surgery. The town divided, those backing into themselves and those desperate to move forward. The open slots at *More Human* filled as soon as they opened, and Twyla flipped her black bob shamelessly, replacing fingertips and running the Switch and Stitch machine with a demure smile and itchy eyes.

Someone will break, Grandmere said.

Marsla opened her mouth to answer that everyone already had, but changed her mind.

Take me to see Mr. Chronon, Marsla, Grandmere whispered. I want you to hear me play, while I still can.

The museum isn't everything the world used to be, Mr. Chronon explained, their footsteps echoing on the wooden floor and amplifying the tap of his cane, It's just everything I want to remember about the world.

Bicycle, automobile, broom, hair dryer, paperback, guitar, dreidel, kerosene lamp, crayons, mailbox ... on and on he rambled, some of these things attaching to images in Marsla's mind.

He turned a goldish-colored round attachment and pushed open a door at the end of the hall. Inside was a— a—

This is a Grand Piano, Marsla. Mr. Chronon rattled off details, his eyes never leaving Grandmere as she seated herself on the bench and pushed back the cover of the black and white rectangles.

Light poured in the glass and turned the wood floor a color Marsla had never seen. Slowly, Mr. Chronon walked window to window, pushing them up. Grandmere's eyes followed his labored progress.

These are folding chairs, he said, and offered one to Marsla. Next to her and off from Grandmere, his eyes were wet as she flexed her metal fingers.

Oil can, oil can, Grandmere croaked, laughing with Mr. Chronon, the joke lost to Marsla.

One more concert?

Grandmere nodded. One more.

Keys, that's what they were called. Keys.

The silver hands fell over the keys, attacking them, wooing them, coaxing, and the sound was like nothing Marsla had ever heard. It lived on its own, in the air, in the light, in her blood. Tears glowed on the cheeks of Grandmere and Mr. Chronon, and the music lived in the tears, too.

Inside, Marsla felt a shift, and placed a hand on her belly.

Beneath her palm came another bubble, another turn—What is this? she whispered.

Beethoven, Mr. Chronon whispered back.

More Human burned that night. No one protested, no one tried to stop it. Little by little the residents of Evans Collective gathered in the parking lot and formed a loose circle to watch. There was a quiet satisfaction in the smoke, the orange aura, the metal curling and turning black. By morning there was only the stink and embers. Most of the crowd dissolved and drifted off to their private pains, Twyla knuckling her sensitive orbs from smoke and tears.

A few hung around, poking at the ashes, searching for nothing.

Marsla was among them. Hands in her loose jacket's pockets, she kicked at the place the front door had been.

The moonlight threw two bent and crooked shadows near her and she watched without turning. They tilted their heads, becoming a united absence of light, and with difficulty twined their shadow hands.

She took the long way home, past the closed windows and the dead piano. Marsla whispered that magic word: Beethoven.

"My motto is, it's all horror."
    —Booked. #32 *Warmed and Bound* interview

BOB PASTORELLA
TAKE MY BREATH AWAY

Hooking the needle through the delicate cloth, Patricia pulled the string through and turned it flat. Tonight her fingers didn't hurt at all. Her sister Deborah used to knit. Sweaters and scarves, though her specialty was doilies. Now, all Deborah knitted was more ruin into their lives.

Patricia ran the thread through the loop and laid it flat. Almost done.

Never had a lesson in her life. Never looked at patterns.

Whatever Deborah knew, Patricia now knitted. It was the last connection tying them together. They used to finish one another's sentences when they were younger. Deborah knew Patricia was flunking geometry in seventh grade before her parents got the call from the teacher. When they were nine years old, Deborah fell off the merry-go-round and broke her collarbone. Patricia cried out in pain when it happened, a sharp bolt felt from Lake Tahoe to Chicago, one of the few times hundreds of miles and time zones separated them.

Now it was just the knitting holding them together.

Deborah scoffed at Patricia's doilies. "You left little strings that need to be trimmed," she'd say. Patricia would just smile and nod, though never picked up the scissors to trim the ends. She pulled the thread taut and left it to hang. Yet another defective doily, as Deborah would say.

Patricia placed the doily and her needle on the end table and took off her glasses. If she closed her eyes, sleep would come. A little nap wouldn't hurt, as long as Deborah stayed upstairs. A sharp knock at the back door made Patricia force her eyes open and get up. Must be the grocery boy. She wondered if she would see a familiar face this time. She got up and walked to the back door in the kitchen. If he knocked again, there was a possibility that Deborah would hear it. Patricia put on her best smile and opened the door. She didn't recognize this boy. She instructed the young man holding the two grocery sacks to place them on the table, picking up a stack of envelopes and pushing the center floral display aside to give him some room. He set the bags down on the table.

"Just give me one minute to get my purse," she said, shuffling in her slippers across the kitchen floor.

"No problem."

She wanted to hurry, just pay the boy so he could leave, but she left her purse on the sofa in the living room so Deborah wouldn't get the car keys. Deborah couldn't drive anymore. It was foolish for her to even leave the purse on the sofa, especially today while Deborah was in one of her moods. A quick feel inside and she grabbed both her car keys and her change purse. Shuffling back into the kitchen, she smiled at the boy, but his attention was on the spectacle that was her sister.

Deborah was dressed in a strapless sun dress and lace-up

sandals, holding the hem of her dress high enough to get the boy's attention. "Who do we have here?" Deborah asked, her voice coy and playful.

"He's just the grocery boy," Patricia said, "no need to get all excited."

Deborah walked over to the boy, swishing her hips side to side in that way that made Patricia grit her teeth. This was no way for a seventy-two year old woman to behave. Deborah grabbed the young man's chin and held it between her thumb and finger. "My my my, aren't you just divine. So cute I could just eat you up."

Patricia gently pulled Deborah away from the boy, careful not to make her slip and fall. Last thing they needed was a broken hip. "Leave him be. I need to pay him so he can be on his way."

Deborah glared at Patricia, then finally backed down, stepping to the stairs, hanging on to the banister. She climbed two steps on wobbly feet then turned and faced them. Wrinkled fingers gripped the hem of her skirt again, lifting it high enough to show the boy she wasn't wearing underpants.

"Anytime you want a taste …" Deborah said, then clamped her mouth shut, staring at Patricia.

Patricia's face burned scarlet. She hated when Deborah played her little finish-the-sentence games.

"Anytime you want a taste …" Deborah said again, emphasizing each word, then rolled her eyes. "Forgive my sister. Twins usually have this connection. It's uncanny. We used to finish each other's sentences. Anytime you want a taste, just let me know." Deborah flashed the boy her toothy grin. "There, I finished it for her."

"Okay," the boy said, smiling. His cheeks were flushed, clearly embarrassed. Stuck in that awkward moment of shame for seeing something yet unable to look away, it took a few seconds for his glazed eyes to shift away from Deborah.

Patricia wanted to disappear. If only the good Lord could afford her that magical freedom. It was obvious how uncomfortable the young man was. Patricia quickly stepped in front of Deborah, blocking the boy's view and thrust two twenties in his hand. "Please don't mind her. She's been sick. Dementia."

"It's okay. My grandmother had that."

"Well, I sure hope she's getting along."

The boy shook his head, and she knew. Patricia cleared her throat and said, "I'm sorry."

The boy nodded, turned and left. Patricia shut the door and turned the dead-bolt.

"Why did you run him off?" Deborah asked behind her back.

Patricia turned and stared at her sister, now no longer holding her hem. Her knuckles were white on the banister.

"Why are you wearing that dress?"

"Because it's summer time. Need to show off my legs."

"You need to get in bed and rest or you'll be up all night long."

Deborah mimicked Patricia. "… *or you'll be up all night.* You're such a drag."

"A drag? Nobody uses that word anymore."

"You're just mad because you wanted him."

"Who? The delivery boy?"

Deborah took a step up the stairs and flipped her hair like she did when she was mad. "You know who."

Patricia looked away. This was not her sister talking. Best just to put up the groceries and let her be. She was too tired to deal with it tonight. She grabbed the milk and put it in the refrigerator, along with the celery and mustard. When she closed the door Deborah was standing there. Patricia didn't dare look into her eyes.

"You know who," Deborah said.

"I'm not talking to you."

"You wanted him."

Patricia grabbed the loaf of bread and put it in the cupboard. Only the canned goods left, some sweet peas, diced pineapple, and spinach. She could feel Deborah leaning over her, her hot breath in her ear.

"You always took what you wanted."

Sometimes Deborah would be like this for hours, days even. Patricia wiped her wet eyes and grabbed the peas. The can slipped from her grasp and rolled on the floor near the sink. Crawling on the floor, she knew Deborah was standing over her.

A sharp smack on the table made the other cans jump and clatter. "Do you hear me?"

Patricia tried to ignore her. That used to work. It wasn't too long ago that Deborah would get mad and make a scene, then walk back upstairs to her bedroom and lock the door, emerging the next morning as though nothing ever happened.

Those days were gone.

"You wanted him."

Patricia bit her lip. No need to say anything. Any rebuttal would only prolong the argument.

Deborah stood over her for a few minutes, then finally huffed. "Bitch."

Only when she heard the bedroom door upstairs creak shut did Patricia let loose of the can of peas and curl into a whimpering, crying mess on the kitchen floor.

★ ★ ★ ★ ★

Bedtime was around 10:45 most nights. Patricia hated David Letterman, but watched him out of sheer boredom. When she felt her eyes getting heavy, she would click the remote and let her eyelids fall. Rarely did she sleep all the way through to morning. Fortunately she still possessed good bladder control, but that didn't mean the urge didn't wake her. If her dreams didn't wake her up in the middle of the night, she could count on having to pee to wake her without fail.

The urge woke her and when she opened her eyes, she hoped Deborah wasn't in her bedroom with her. If she was up now, that meant she never went to sleep, which meant she was still mad. Feeling around for her glasses, she heard whoever it was walk around to the other side of the bed and get in, sliding under the covers.

This made Patricia smile. If Deborah wanted to share the bed with her, that was fine on all accounts. The doctor told Patricia that this behavior was normal. Frustrating, but normal. Patricia put her glasses back on the bedside table and pulled the comforter back up to her shoulders.

"Are you feeling any better?" Patricia asked.

Deborah mumbled something. Patricia glanced over at her and saw she was lying on her side, facing the opposite wall. So she didn't want to sleep alone but still wasn't talking either. Patricia sighed and closed her eyes.

The last time they went to the doctor, Patricia swore she would never take Deborah again unless it was in an ambulance. Getting Deborah into the car wasn't the problem. Most of the time Deborah insisted on driving but after she ran over the garbage cans, Patricia said no more. No, the problem with going to the doctor was getting Deborah out of the car once they got there. It took both nurses and the receptionist to pry her hands off the overhead access handles.

Alzheimer's, that's what he called it. Doctor said it was progressing fast, wouldn't be too much longer before she needed twenty-four hour supervision, if her heart didn't give out first. That meant either getting a full-time nurse at the house, or placing her in a nursing home. Assisted living, he called it. They couldn't afford either service.

It wasn't Alzheimer's, or dementia. No, Patricia knew it wasn't anything like that. This wasn't some new development with her sister. Deborah exhibited the warning signs a long time ago, only Patricia didn't know what they were. She liked to think that Deborah was just paying her back, though that didn't make any sense either.

It was something else that was ruining her, something much worse than any disease.

Patricia started to reach out and touch her sister's shoulder, just to let her know she was there, but stopped before her hand came from under the comforter.

She listened, holding her breath.

She heard only the ringing you hear when there's total silence.

She took a breath and held it again.

Deborah wasn't breathing.

Now Patricia reached for her sister, sensing the heavy, cold figure lying beside her before her fingers ever brushed her shoulder. Sitting up on one elbow, Patricia gripped Deborah's cold flesh and started shaking her.

"Wake up. Wake up."

Wisps of gray hair fluttered on Deborah's head while Patricia tried to shake her awake. Patricia's shoulder was so cold. Finally Deborah lifted her head and started to turn around to face Patricia.

Only it wasn't Deborah.

The face Patricia saw was just a shriveled husk of a man's

face, the skin as thin as parchment. Dry flakes puffed off the neck as it turned to face her. Patricia pulled her hand away as the man beside her started to inch closer to her. She pushed herself back, afraid she was going to fall off the bed.

The man's eyes were gone. Only blackened hollows remained.

She could feel her heart pounding in her chest, faster and faster. As she inched away, she could feel the slickness between her thighs and knew she lost her bladder. The man reached for her, his hand like a gnarled tree branch with hooked fingers at the end. The hand was so close she could see the nails at the ends of the fingers. They were broken, some even ripped completely away, as though he clawed through the earth just to lie in the bed with her.

As the man grew closer, his mouth began to open, exposing decayed teeth and a gray swollen tongue that seemed much too large to fit in the mouth.

If he screams at me, I'm going to die, right here in my own bed, Patricia thought.

But no sound came from the gaping mouth. The man just inched closer and closer until Patricia found herself floating off the bed for a brief second, then felt the floor come up to slam into her.

★ ★ ★ ★ ★

"I'm really quite satisfied with the policy we have now."

The life insurance man was in for his annual visit. They sat in the living room, the two sisters sharing the blue crushed velvet sofa while the young man sat opposite them in the easy chair. The coffee table was now his portable office, with his laptop computer and a smaller tablet holding scattered insurance documents down.

Patricia wore just a simple blouse and slacks, while Deborah dressed like she was Jackie Kennedy with matching handbag and pillbox hat perched crooked on her hair. A gray and ancient Jackie O, Patricia thought. At least she was wearing undergarments.

"So you don't want to add anything to the current policy? No additional beneficiaries?"

"No, just make sure I'm named her next of kin, and she mine, and everything will be in order."

The man cleared his throat and nodded. "That's exactly how it is now." The small computer tablet lit up on the coffee table and began to play a song. Patricia couldn't understand the words, but they sang with one of the most stirring voices she had ever heard. Even Deborah raised her eyebrows in appreciation.

"Excuse me," said the insurance man. He picked up the tablet and pressed a small button on the side. "Just my phone."

"What was that song?" Deborah asked.

"That was my ringtone. You can set the song for particular people when they call. That song means my wife was calling."

"I think she wants to know who sang the song," Patricia said.

"Oh, her name is Adele. She's from England."

Patricia smiled. "It was beautiful."

"Patricia and I used to sing."

The insurance man looked at Deborah. "Really. Anything I've heard?"

"We started when we were very young girls. Singing and dancing. We even met Frank Sinatra. Sat in his lap for a picture." Deborah pushed a small framed photo on the coffee table over so the man could see. Two young girls sitting on Frank's lap, smiling.

"That's impressive."

"I do believe my sister made his cock hard when she sat in his lap. Even back then she had a way with the boys."

The insurance man started to say something, then clamped his lips shut, started picking up his papers and computers.

Deborah sat back and crossed her legs. "My sister couldn't sing or dance as well as me, but she sure knew how to keep the boys coming back for more. We were both the talk of the town, but as you can see, even then, she could take your breath away."

"You were both very beautiful," he said.

"Oh, you're too much. Patricia was the heartbreaker. You shouldn't be so shy. Give her a shot. You'll like it."

The insurance man stared at his hands for a second, then looked at Patricia. "Ah, well. I've got everything in order. I'll give you a call in about eleven months and we'll see if you need to make any changes."

"Oh, there was one man she had," Deborah said, her voice rising, "I'll never forget. Mr. Quintin Candell. He was a bad, bad man. Worked for some guys who were in the mob, if you can believe that. Quintin was my lover, we were to be married. Patricia couldn't stand it. She threatened to tell Mom and Dad, and that would be the end of it. All she wanted was a little switcheroo. You do know what the switcheroo is, right? Well, I couldn't let my folks know about my Quintin. The old switcheroo. All the twin sisters do it."

The insurance man stared at the table.

"You'll like it with twins," Deborah said. "It's even more fun when we're in the bed together, isn't it, sis."

Outside, Patricia apologized for Deborah. The man just smiled and shook her hand, saying it was okay, that he understood. She could count on him being back next year for his annual visit. Patricia wanted to believe him, he sounded so sincere. They would get his little cards in the mail for their birthday and Christmas, but she knew he wouldn't be back.

They never came back.

When she went back inside, Deborah was at the bar, pouring a brandy. "Want one, sis?" she asked.

Patricia shook her head. "You don't drink."

Deborah narrowed her eyes. "You don't know me very well, do you?"

"But you are on medication."

"*But you are on medication.* Have you always been such a drag, or have I been sleeping under a rock?" Deborah downed the brandy and pushed the empty snifter to the center of the bar. Opening her handbag, she pulled out an ancient tube of lipstick and applied more than she needed on her cracked lips, not worrying about smudging or staying close together. When she finished, she smiled at Patricia, looking like a drunk clown. She snapped the handbag shut and headed for the stairs, swishing her hips.

Patricia tried not to grit her teeth.

★ ★ ★ ★ ★

When Deborah wasn't up and drinking her coffee at ten, Patricia knew she could make it upstairs without an incident. She crept up the staircase, careful to be quiet in case she was wrong. Nothing set Deborah off quicker than trying to sneak upstairs when you weren't invited. That was her domain, and there she ruled supreme.

Knocking on her bedroom door, Patricia waited, listening to anything from behind the door that told her she needed to get back downstairs as quick as possible. After a few moments, she grabbed her keys and unlocked the door, cracked it open and peeked inside.

She could see Deborah lying in the center of her bed, quilt

pulled up to her chin. Patricia walked over to her bed and touched her sister's forehead. With that gentle touch, Deborah's eyes fluttered, then focused on Patricia.

"How you feeling?" Patricia asked, knowing at last that the real Deborah was lying in the bed, not that crazed thing that pretended to be her.

Deborah nodded. Patricia found a glass of water on the bedside table and let her sister sip from it.

"Things have been bad," Patricia said.

"I can only imagine," Deborah said weakly.

"But I've been knitting. They are all ready."

Deborah closed her eyes. A small tear welled in the corner of her eye and rolled down the side of her wrinkled face. Patricia picked up a hand towel and wiped her sister's face. "Are you afraid?" she asked.

"No."

"When shall we do this?"

"Soon." Deborah swallowed with much difficulty. "Now."

"He came to me the other night. Lay next to me in my bed." Now Patricia was crying. "I can't go on like this. It's more than just a nightmare now."

Deborah closed her eyes and cried silently with Patricia.

Patricia wiped her eyes. "I'm so, so sorry."

Deborah sighed. "I forgave you a long time ago."

"I know. But still. I took him from you. All you ever wanted. Then … then, I did it for you. You know that, right? I couldn't lose you, not like that."

Deborah shook her head. "Quit this. This thing between us, it's killing you. Quintin loved you. That's all that matters."

Patricia nodded, unable to stem the flow of tears. She sat next to Deborah on the bed, watching her sister. Deborah was right. Now was best. Everything was in order. No one would ever have to know.

She reached into her pocket and unfolded one of the doilies she had knitted. She lifted it over Deborah's face. "Don't fight it. Just let it happen."

Deborah nodded.

Patricia placed the doily directly over Deborah's mouth and pressed it down. Holding it in place with her left hand, she slowly pulled the leftover string until the doily cinched under her chin.

She watched her sister's chest rise and fall. With each moment, the time between her breaths grew longer. After a few minutes, she removed the doily and replaced it with another one, careful not to leave a mark on Deborah's face. The thin string was just snug enough to stay in place, but not binding in any way.

After replacing the fourth doily, Deborah coughed. Patricia feared she might be choking, but she waited, watching her chest rise, then fall.

By the fifth doily, Deborah's chest quit rising. Patricia removed the doily and peered into her sister's dead eyes. She expected them to be bloodshot, a sure sign of suffocation, but was surprised to see they were clear. Patricia folded up the doilies, now moist and warm, and placed them back into her pocket.

It was over.

She walked down the stairs and into the laundry room. Tossing the doilies into the washing machine, she added a little detergent and set the timer.

In the living room, she sat on the sofa and picked up the framed black and white photo of her and Deborah with Sinatra. After a few minutes, she set it down. So many memories. That was all they shared now. Patricia prayed Deborah really did forgive her after all this time. That was all she wanted.

Patricia listened for the creak on the floor, her eyes grow-ing heavy. Sooner or later, he would come back to her, and that would be the end of it.

> "I thought about what would happen if a book like that was written and didn't just affect a couple of people but affected a lot of people."
> —Booked. #70 Noir at the Bar

KEVIN LYNN HELMICK
NOIR'S CITY

Journal entry, Tuesday Sept 4, 2012

It seemed that autumn had arrived in River North all at once last Saturday night. The heat had settled into the waters of Lake Michigan, lifting moist fog throughout the streets that had set like a ceiling just above the window of my third floor apartment. It was blocking the night with a kind of nuclear glow from the city lights. I hadn't worked in weeks, months really. I picked up a copy of The Sun Times from my coffee table and read the headline. They hadn't caught the River North Killer, big shocker, I threw it in the trash.

The cool air had given me an excuse to open the windows, build a small fire and I sat there watching the flames, occasionally glancing at the laptop on my desk. I couldn't help it. No matter which way I shifted myself I couldn't escape that stark white empty Word doc screen. It wouldn't close out, or hibernate and had become the brightest light in the darkest of rooms. It followed me everywhere.

I'd been feeling depleted, weak, so I'd bought some orange juice the Friday before and sat pushing a steady stream between the gap of my two front teeth into the fire. The flames objected in much the same way my stomach had. I don't know how people drink that shit. Vodka, sure, but either way it did allow the fire to give off a citrus aroma that wasn't entirely unpleasant, reminded me of Miami though, and that, and the fog, didn't help with me feeling depleted.

Having been holed up too long, for reasons I couldn't quite explain, feelings of being watched, stalked, hunted and trapped in general, I had made it a mission that night to push through.

I needed inspiration. Something had to give. I searched the floors of my building in my mind for an interesting subject. There was the Dago downstairs. Twice I had to step over him and his Mexican girlfriend in the elevator. Once he was screaming at the side of her face, something about burnt chicken. Apparently her culinary skills fell short of Mama Leone and he was letting her know it. She cried and sniffled in her hands, very pathetic.

The second time he had a fist full of her red hair and was introducing her face repeatedly to the simulated wood on the wall. I think it was red, the hair that is. It was that night anyway. I rode up with them and watched with a vague curiosity. He didn't mind and neither did she. Why didn't the dumb bitch just leave? He must be hung like a fucking loaf of Italian bread.

No, he wouldn't do. That would be way too easy. And, I was not into doing favors for the wetback girls of the world. She'd have to do her own dirty work, or get back across the border where she belonged, where it was safe.

Old Mrs. Hamm on the fourth floor corner apartment over-looking the river, the apartment I wanted. She had to be a hundred years old, maybe a thousand. I met her when I signed the lease to my place five years ago and I figured I'd be moving up-stairs in a few months. But the fucking Jew bitch just wouldn't die. I guess Hitler had his work cut out for him. I don't know how many millions he burned, but she's still here, and he's not. I suppose he liked a challenge. So did Mrs. Hamm's husband, Hans.

I remember when he died, about a year ago. A beaten Kraut if there ever was one. She had interrupted a captivating night-mare with these loud, grating scrapes on my door, over and over. It must have been that twelve carat rock that hung from her bony fist gouging into the wood, a tiny cut cell where she kept old Hans' soul.

Miss Barr, Miss Barr, Miss Barr, she shrieked on and on. I had rolled over and wrapped my pillow around my ears. She wouldn't go away. They never go away. They are a fucking persistent tribe, I'll give 'em that.

She'd been nothing but a straight up bitch to everyone in the building who wasn't Jewish and I thought this might be a good opportunity for some much deserved retribution. I loaded up, threw off my blanket, and made damn sure I took my time getting to the door.

When I did answer, and began to remind her for the ump-teenth time that it was not necessary to address me as Ms. any-thing, that my first name would do just fine, her face stopped me in my tracks. I could see the terror in her eyes behind those coke bottle glasses and that beak of a nose. It was a beautiful expres-sion and I stood there and soaked it in for as long as she allowed, which wasn't long.

Come, Miss Barr, she said. It is Hans. It's my husband. I think he not breathing.

Christ, Mrs. Hamm, it's late. Noir, call me Noir. I'm sure he's fine. Call an ambulance?

No, no phone, no ambulance, too expensive, we very poor. I was hoping you could do something. Please come.

Right, poor. Ah fuck, I said, looking at her diamond in the dirty yellow light of my hall, thinking about that sweet ass corner suite.

That ring may or may not have been a diamond at all, but maybe a kidney stone, passed right through the cock of the Savior himself. Maybe she'd sucked it right out of him back in the day. Anyway, it now served as an annoying door knocker for her French-American neighbor, me. The situation reeked of irony, but apparently I was the only one who thought so.

You are such a pretty girl, she begged. So pretty, please come help.

I let out a deep a sigh and pulled the hair back out of my eyes, yawned, looked at her and whispered, listen, you old bitch. For four fucking years I've put up with your shitty French remarks in the hall and in the elevator and never said a word. I'm not even French. I was born here, and we saved your ungrateful asses once, so if the old Kraut has choked on his last matzo ball, God bless him, may he and the Fuhrer rest in peace.

Her mouth dropped to the floor, her eyes turned angry and she started jabbering Yiddish curses while I slammed the door in her face.

That was the last I heard from Mrs. Hamm, or Mr. Hamm for that matter. But she's still up there alright, determined to hang on to that apartment. I know that bitch'll outlive me just out of spite.

No, not her. As much as I might enjoy it, I wouldn't give her a minute of my time.

Giving up on the orange juice, I threw the rest in the fire. It crackled and sparked and turned all different colors of blue and pink as the flames climbed up the chimney. I watched it like liquid fireworks until it died down. I stood, stretched my back, walked to the liquor cabinet, poured a glass of wine and put on some Mozart, a piano piece. I lounged around my place admiring my collection of fine art, mostly fakes and reprints but they still do the job. I find something worthwhile in all of them for various reasons, like memories of discarded lovers.

I found myself at my desk again, standing before my computer, fixed on the blank page. I took a sip of wine, held it in my cheek, a good year, California. I reached out and pressed my finger on a key of no particular significance. It spit out a row of X's. I let it go and swallowed. At least I wrote something.

I pulled a cigarette from its pack in the drawer and placed it between my lips. Turning away, I fished in my pocket for my lighter. I had planned to quit, but it wasn't going so well.

What about the pretty boy in the park across the street, I thought. I struck the flint and held the flame up and wondered. He was there every morning at eleven sharp, eating his lunch, peanut butter and jelly I suspect, cut into little bite-sized squares by his mother. I walked to the window and looked out to the now empty playground and brick sidewalks in the mist. I took a deep inhale on my cigarette and flicked the ash outside. It's funny how at night a park can take on a somber lonely aura, the gilded iron fence, gothic and ominous in the fog, like a child cemetery. A place damned to be forgotten. Remembering dead kids was far too sad.

Yeah, he was cute, in a pathetic sort of way. But he knew it and he played it like a plastic ukulele. I couldn't fuck him without hearing the sound of those strings. I knew this. And those goddamn khaki pants, velcro sneakers.

Shit. Maybe he was the riva-killa. I laughed out loud at the thought.

I had noticed him eye-flirting with me from a distance the couple of times I walked through the park. I'd caught him looking toward my window on more than one occasion as well. He knew where I lived and the little perv hadn't balls to do anything about it. The fact that I'd even considered him was a testament to just how desperate I'd become. I mean really, a poor girl's John Ritter at best. Velcro shoes, fuck.

I turned away from the window and let out a deep sigh.

My clothes waited in my closet like a deflated crowd that hung in accordance to importance. I sat on the bench inside, finished my wine, save for enough to extinguish my smoke, and began choosing the proper attire for the evening. I had to get out. Since nothing was coming my way, I had to go to it.

Deciding on the bar at the Peninsula, I pulled my black Versace, held it out in front of me and glanced at its matching leather heels on the shelf. Yes, I was going uptown baby, way uptown and I wasn't coming back with less than I deserved. I chose some stockings, garter, and bra, checked myself in the mirror before slipping the imported silk over my head.

Maybe a little too much wine and sulking in my apartment for weeks on end, because I panicked a little at the fit in the mirror, my tits were pouring out and it felt like my ass would rip out if I moved at all. I puffed my cheeks in the mirror and made a fat joke. But, Gianni made a fine product and after another glass of wine and a few careful squats I was looking better and better.

Getting used to the heels and perfecting my sway, I walked around my apartment with yet another glass of wine, another smoke and rubbed my ass and lower tummy under the silk until my skin had flushed and warmed over to just the right amount of glow and color. A soft red lipstick and just a touch of almond shadow on my bleach white skin, reminded me of something my dad had said to me once. "Too much is too much, my darling, French women are at their best when they don't try, don't care. The whole world is lucky because you are in it. Don't forget it, because it is true."

My father was a French poet, famous for everything. My mother, a Polish cabaret singer, and he thought it the perfect combination. He knew women better than any man I'd ever known. It's no wonder she adored him. He was kicked out of France before I was born. They said he was crazy, and coming from the French, that's saying a lot, but that's another story.

So, with his words stroking my ego I combed my hair with my nails just enough, shook my head just the right amount, and decided I needed nothing but a pair of sterling hoops, bangle, small bag with all my necessaries, and that was it. A woman with class doesn't need anything but a black dress and a strut. I was feeling like a woman again.

I called for a limousine. A taxi wouldn't do, after all it was the Peninsula, and a well planned arrival was really a woman's best friend, along with a perfect departure. Everything combined and I could own the room, own the night.

The limo called up at midnight sharp, and I made my way downstairs, ignoring Mrs. Hamm's leers at the front desk, and breaking the necks of all the men and women throughout the lobby. I had just enough drink, just enough swagger and when the cool night air brushed across my body, the driver's face told me all I needed to know. Tonight would be the night to break my slump. Get past this fucking block.

Miss Barr, he said. You look incredible this evening.

He was Russian, I think, and carried it well.

I smiled and touched his cheek. I said, I know, baby. Thank you.

Yes, where we go? He opened my door.

Peninsula.

Of course, as it should be.

He closed the door and we sped away. He looked back at me in the mirror, smiling over and over and nearly wrecked us more than once. Very young, well built, handsome, and probably could a fuck a girl proper, but just a step up from a taxi driver. Still I let the thought linger in my imagination as we drove, just to retain my flush.

Maybe, a last resort.

He seemed to appear magically at the door milliseconds after we stopped. He took my hand, gently helping me across the plaza. You like me wait Miss Barr.

Noir, and no. I'll be fine thank you …

Nicolai. Noir … that is so beautiful, and fitting. Please, I give you my card. I be at your service, anytime.

I smiled at Nicolai, declined and walked through the door. He deserved a look back over my shoulder, at least, I thought, so I gave it to him, but his eyes were locked on my ass and it was wasted and I hate a wasted smile.

Through the lobby I strolled, past the concierge and into the lounge, huge and not too brightly lit. This was good. I was greeted by a young, pretty hostess, dirty blond, Belgian, northern by her accent and it flustered me for a moment. I wanted to tip her big, until I realized it was only fond memories of my mom. I refrained, slipped into a corner booth and thanked her. Besides, it's considered tacky to tip in places like this. It comes with the check.

She lit the candle on my table. I ordered wine and began at the far end of the bar. Three Mandingos, wearing lots of gaudy jewelry, expensive clothes, basketball players, I deduced. Interesting subjects, but no thank you. Too high a profile, and I didn't need a team.

My eyes moved on to a woman, inflated lips, fake breasts, ratted hair, obviously drunk past the point of attractive. I recognized her from television. She was famous, or at least was once. She was getting the attention of the Sambos though, and seemed quite intent on getting all holes stuffed. They were talking to her, whispering to one another, laughing, pulling at their cocks under the bar. They could have her, and they probably would.

On down, a pudgy Anglo pounding scotch, cheap suit, a salesman, big pharma, maybe advertising, staying on comp for sure. This might be the one. But then I imagined him rolling around in my bed. I imagined him naked, crying out for his fat loyal wife, three fat kids and Volvo wagon, back in Ohio.

Oh Christ.

At the far end, there he was, Latin, maybe Sicilian or Greek, but definitely American by his clothes. He was sitting in the dark under a single light, olive skin, black wavy hair, unshaven, jeans, sport coat, and completely into whatever he was thinking, a real greaseball but in a sexy, intellectual way. I watched and he would occasionally push his glasses up and glance around the room, thumping a pencil on the bar.

My eyes traveled down to his shoes, boots, well worn, and on down to the floor to a large leather camera bag, also well worn. The only baggage he ever had. He was married alright, but only to his work. He was too disinterested to be paparazzi. A writer maybe, no, photo journalist, yes. He was perfect, perfectly delicious.

Maybe I'd overdressed for this, I thought. He wasn't stupid, that I could tell. A girl dressed like I was, just walking over there would throw red flags, and red flags were his life, his livelihood. He was noticing everything in the room. He had noticed me too, no doubt, but was pretending he hadn't. He was a man of the world, an instinctive survivor, he was a lot like me. I could sense all of this in an instant.

A formidable foe at last and he made me feel a little off my game. I should have brought a jacket, shit, what was I thinking. I might as well have walked in the door and screamed, fuck me.

The waitress brought my wine and he glanced over, raising his eyebrows above his glasses and quickly turned away when I looked back. I suddenly felt very naked, he saw right through me. I wasn't his type and I had to think fast before this fish swam away.

Leave the bottle dear, I said, and would it be too much trouble if I could get a pen and paper?

Of course, not at all Miss, I'll be right back with that.

I poured the wine myself and set the bottle with the label facing him, retrieved a pair of vanity glasses from my purse that I kept on hand for just such emergencies. I set them on the end of my nose, inched my way to the edge of the booth and changed my posture into a slump. I crossed my legs in a way that exposed my shin, and just enough thigh. I dangled my heel into the room. He was after all a man, and I took my chances that sooner rather than later, his macho bravado would get the better of him.

The waitress returned with a pad and pen and he noticed. I took a sip of wine and didn't look up, but began writing, random nonsense, a bad poem, something about the night. I'd pause occasionally and put my finger to my lip, pretending to be deep in thought.

I was running out of paper and began writing over what I'd written when he stood, pulled his bag up on his shoulder. I still didn't look, but could sense him fidgeting, arguing with himself. He took off toward the exit all at once but stopped, turned and made his way back to me.

He stood there and shoved his hands in his pockets. I'm sorry, he said. But, uh, do I know you?

A tired line but his delivery was authentic. He meant it. I looked up as if he was pulling me away from something important. I don't know. You do look familiar. Hi, I'm Noir. I extended my hand and he took it ever so gently. His fingers were smooth and warm.

Noir? he said, cocked his head slightly, adjusted his shoulder strap, furrowed his brow and smiled. That's uh … that's interesting.

Interesting … how so?

No, I don't mean …

Wait, let me guess … a writer.

Journalist, actually.

He looked around the room every time he spoke and finished what he was saying with a nod while fixing those smoldering dark eyes in my general direction. It was extremely attractive.

A war journalist, I said.

He looked me straight in the face. Well … yeah, I've, I've done some of that. He glanced at the empty booth. May I? I mean, if you're not …

No, please sit.

He tossed his bag and sat almost lazily, picked up the bottle and studied the label. French, this is very expensive.

I motioned to the waitress for another glass. Yeah well, that's why they call it an expense account.

Right, he said, setting the bottle down and looking at my dress, my breasts, my hair. He searched all over me and took in every detail, but waited until the waitress was finished pouring his glass before he said anything else. So … this is not a line, really, but what is it that you do, really?

Really, I am … a senior editor for a travel magazine.

Really … I would never have guessed that. He nodded yes, but I knew he suspected me a liar. I could hear it in his voice, see it the slant of his neck.

And why is that?

You, uh. He put the glass to his lips and took a drink. I've known a lot of editors. You don't look like any editor … ever. He laughed soft and low and returned his eyes to panning the room.

Okay, you got me. I turned my pad over and laid the pen down. You see that blonde over there?

He sat up, but didn't look over at the blonde. Yeah, sure, that's uh … I don't know, can't remember her name.

Yeah, she's famous, was anyway, and she's going to fuck those three brothers tonight.

She is?

She is.

And how do you know this?

Because, I'm gonna write it.

He finally glanced over at them, thought for a moment and huffed a smile. You're tabloid?

Girl's gotta make a living.

Shit. That's even harder to believe than senior editor.

Life is full of mystery.

He thought about that.

Not really, he said, not from my experience.

You have the luxury of fact.

No, not really. He swirled his wine and went somewhere far away. We're not that far apart.

Look, what's your name?

Chris, Chris Burdon.

Listen, Chris, this dress, the wine, the story, it's all an illusion. Fact is an illusion. There's no luxury in it either.

Okay. That … I believe.

He bit his bottom lip and thought about that as well without sharing any conclusions. He thought too much.

I'm here covering a story. The uh, river murders. He shrugged.

Ah, the river killer, now that's no illusion.

Well, it is if they can't catch the guy.

Everybody gets caught.

He nodded and looked over at the blonde and smiled. I suppose so, yeah.

I quickly changed the subject back to him and we talked throughout the rest of the night. He'd been to Afghanistan, Kuwait and places I'd never even heard of, wars and conflicts far away and under the radar. The lingering spirits of death and violence flickered in his eyes like dying embers. He was intelligent and thoughtful, well-read but I kept up. He was interesting, charismatic and I was enjoying our little conversation for what is was worth and the night slipped away.

Two more bottles and the bar was closing. We both watched as the TV star made her way out, assisted of course, by huge black hands squeezing her arms and ass cheeks. We laughed while they left. I had my man right in the palm of my hand.

I have to admit though, I liked him. He had a quiet integrity, genuine honesty, and was truly at a point in his life where he was questioning his purpose. Something had happened to him, recently. Maybe he found something out there, something of truth, a truth he didn't want to accept and it was weighing him down, dulling his will to survive. There was an aura of tragedy that surrounded him. But he wasn't the type to complain to a stranger. He would try to find his way through it. I admired that.

This put me in a bit of a dilemma. I had to keep reminding myself, I was pro, and had a job to do, get to the finish.

Once I had him well lubricated, it didn't take much to get him relaxed and trusting. I was a little worried that I'd lost my edge with the night's earlier mistakes with the clothes and all, but it was nice to feel it working out. I was a natural after all, and reeling him in was becoming less and less of a question.

So much in fact that when he left, I went with him without a single suggestion, it was a given, as if we'd been together before, and often. We looked and felt natural together, had become colleagues of a sort, and strolled through the lobby, into the elevator and down the dimly lit hall to his room.

He slid the key card and opened the door. It wasn't the Penthouse. It wasn't even a mid price room. Single bed, small bathroom and the fog outside had pressed itself up against the windows in a threatening way. He had three laptops open and running in various locations, two televisions, one in its place and another balanced on an end table by the bed and both on different local news channels. He shut them off.

Investigation boards pinned with photographs of victims, dissected and dismembered. There were files, photographs and newspapers scattered everywhere, along with clothes, shoes and camera equipment. He had been in town a while and he was obsessed.

Chris rummaged through the mini bar and came up with a couple of tiny bottles of Jim Beam. I walked to the cork board on the wall that had replaced a serene watercolor tossed off in the corner.

You've been a busy boy, I said.

He let out a deep sigh while he poured our drinks. Yeah, well, ya know, sorry about the mess. I don't know, I just … I don't know.

I turned and looked at him standing there with a glass in

each hand while he shrugged. How long have you been working on this?

He pursed his lips, shook his head while his eyes trailed away over the room. Six months, maybe.

You've been at the Peninsula for six months? That's some expense budget.

Yeah, well, I was let go before that, he said. So I've just been, paying as I go, sorta.

Let go … I said and took a drink. So, this is like a … hobby or something?

He just shrugged and held his glass up to his lips, and smiled. Yeah, something like that. I've been let go before though.

That's, some hobby, Burdon, I said and my concentration waned a little.

There was something in his eyes now I hadn't seen before. Not just in him, but ever. After all the wine that evening, all the conversation, all my subtle seducing, he was finally looking at me in a way that was razor sharp. He was aware and his instincts were not as dulled by life as I had so foolishly concluded earlier in the evening. He tilted his head slightly and never took his eyes from mine.

What's the matter, Noir? You look like you saw a ghost or something.

I put the glass on the dresser and stepped up to him. I took his glass and set it with mine, smiled and slid my arms up over his shoulders and pressed my lips to his. A warm wet kiss and we stayed while he cradled my face in his hands. My mind was reeling with confusion. Every nerve in my brain was telling me to run but my entire body was so attracted. I pulled away to catch my breath, patted his chest and laughed a little.

Whoa, I said. Just let me use the restroom a minute. Just stay right there. I mean, do what you want, just don't go anywhere.

I'm not going anywhere, take your time, he said and reached around me for his glass. He turned away but kept his eyes on me as he sat on the bed and watched.

Right, I said. I'll be right back, don't move.

Right here.

He smiled that smile again that spoke of confidence and the thought presented itself to just head out the door and keep going. I didn't.

I went into the bathroom, locked the door and looked at myself in the mirror; my hair was a mess, my breasts flushed and erect and my dress too tight. I looked like a fucking whore that had already been used. Shit, I whispered, turned, bit a nail and tried to think. Shit, shit, shit.

Okay, I thought, get it together; he's just like any other guy. I clutched my bag and set it on the vanity, washed my face, removed my dress and hung it neatly on a hanger behind the door. I fixed my hair, pushed my tits up and took a deep breath and whispered to myself, you can do it, you're stronger than this. He's just some fucking loser. Come on girl.

I steadied my breathing and used a little meditation to get my heart rate down and opened the door. This was my city, my night. I had to own it.

Chris was sitting back on the bed. I leaned against the wall with my shoulder and dropped my hands to show him. He had removed his shirt and shoes and a gold cross hung nestled in his chest hair, Catholic, perfect.

Nice, he said. Come over here.

Maneuvering my heels through the room, I placed my bag on the nightstand and straddled him. He brought his hands up over my hips and squeezed at the flesh on my waist. Wait,

I said and kissed him.

I looked around the bed and pulled the loose sheet up and started to tie his wrist to the headboard. He smiled and laughed. I had him and this girl was back on her game. I slid down, unbuttoned his jeans, while he lifted his hips for me to pull them off. I threw them to the floor on the side of the bed and caught a glimpse of the photos there before they landed.

My breath left me for an instant.

I reached over him with my ass in the air and pulled the jeans off and looked.

Oh my god.

I grabbed a handful of pictures and brought them up. Pictures of my building, Velcro boy, the Jew bitch, the woman-beating Dago, and me, me. In the park, in my window, in the hall, getting in a cab, getting in the limo that night and talking to the driver outside the hotel.

I let them slide to the floor and looked at him. How long have you been following me?

A while now.

So, you know?

Yeah, I came for you.

I shook my head. My ... you are full of surprises, Burdon. I reached for my bag on the table, unzipped it and poured the contents out on his stomach.

The scalpel, scissors, knife, organizing them in a neat row across his chest.

Pulling a cigarette from its pack, putting it to my lips, I struck the lighter, took a deep inhale, looked down at him and blew the smoke up against the wall.

Are you going to kill me now, Noir?

I'm going to fuck you, Chris. And then ...

And then?

I flicked an ash on the floor and bit my lip. Oh baby, I said. Yes, eventually, yes. I leaned down, kissed him again and held my lips against his as I whispered. You've been dying for sooo long. It's so beautiful.

He whispered back. We die only once, and for such a long time.

I sighed and kissed my way down his body.

Oh God, I said. I just love Moliére.

> "You fight so hard to wait for that great idea, and then when you ultimately find out that there is nothing new under the sun, it can be crushing."
> —Booked. #33 *Warmed and Bound* interview

GORDON HIGHLAND
BOKEH

You can't measure soul in megapixels. Or film grains. No matter how tightly packed, those dots either congeal into something greater than their sum or they don't. Same could be said of the molecules that form the man behind the lens.

My photos are in focus where they're meant to be. Precisely exposed, with dynamic light and shade. Vibrant, even. Traffic-streaked nightscapes, the refractions of a dewy leaf, decrepit farm equipment–these epitomize my portfolio. Soul is what's lacking, yes, but whether the subjects' or my own remains the question.

When asked why his pictures never had people in them, Ansel Adams famously replied that each in fact contains two people: the photographer and the viewer. Mine aren't yet ready for that second one, and I've even had doubts about the first.

Good luck with those thousand words.

★ ★ ★ ★ ★

Much as I rely on the portable escape hatch that is my e-reader, art books still confine me to the tactile world of print. While I was absently thumbing pages at the three-story bookseller last week, some desperate, naive corner of my animus thought—as it always does—their inspirations might become mine via osmosis. But even if I could ape such masterworks, they'd remain but an exercise in formidable forgery.

So, back to browsing the titles on photographic technique instead. Why I do this, I cannot explain. Its basic principles haven't changed in 150 years, yet I own countless volumes restating the same methods in which I'm already proficient, deluding myself that more education will peel the blindfold from my third eye. Couldn't help thinking of my neighbor Colin: thirty years old and on his fourth bachelor's degree with no career in sight. Academia arresting the development of adulthood, I'm always taunting him. To which he counters with that proverb about glass-housed stoners, adding, "Hey, if the lens mounts ..."

All those compacted spines recessed or jutting from the shelf resembled the downtown skyline, towering edifices adjoining their squat neighbors. Whether it was a staff pick or publisher payola, one outward-facing cover seized my attention with its simple mosaic of repeating red, green, and blue blocks. Inside, trite diagrams of rods and cones and lighting plans yielded to some stirring portraits—mournful, imperious, radiant—I felt certain I could've captured myself if only I owned more of these books. The usual sentiment.

Flipping through its pages, I landed on one with a card bookmarking it. Some advertisement, I figured, for a companion book or magazine subscription. Nope: Kodak photo paper, their logo lightly tiled under an inked inscription. My first glimpse of its other side froze my lungs with prudish complicity.

I slammed the book shut and checked over both shoulders

for the SWAT team or camera crew. No one loitered in a bulging trench coat. No ogling from behind an upside-down book cover. Only a gawky tween passed, her Keds beelining for the Paranormal Romance aisle.

Clearing my throat, I fished the photo out again and succumbed to its gravity. A girl, nude, bleached by cruel on-camera flash. She lay oblivious, sleeping perhaps, on an unkempt bed, covers pushed or pulled beyond her feet. God, I hoped she was just sleeping. Face down, head resting on her forearms, the tresses of her dirty-blond mane cascaded inelegantly over waxen shoulder blades. With her right leg drawn up semi-fetal, all the lines of composition—a loose term—converged at her ample ass, its crack routing me down to a stubbled muffin exposed in what would normally be shadow.

Sure, I lingered. Probably cocked my head in study longer than needed. Intrigue, not arousal. More girth in her saddle than I go for. But she'd been someone's prize, or at least object.

This amateur snapshot had no place in such a book. Antithetical, even, to its lessons. The light fell off beyond her, vignetting the bedroom in darkness like some crime-scene folder clipping. Forensic gears began their winding in my brain. Who even took photochemical pictures anymore? Who had the patience—and audacity, in this case—to send them out for lab processing? Despite its glossy finish, the only thumbprints belonged to me. Underneath one corner smudge, a burnt-in date stamp claimed 10/6/1999.

No way the host book had eluded prurient eyeballs that long. Must've been a new print off an old negative, I thought. The hardcover's copyright page established it as a first edition from earlier this year.

Motive stumped me. Blackmail, advertising, boasting, irony.... Could be that its ambiguity was the very point: a guerilla found-art project, some pay-it-forward experiment like when people unburden their secrets on the backs of postcards addressed to strangers.

Wait. The back. The handwriting.

Do better. Sunday's True Crime

If the wide loops and consistent spacing didn't announce its composer's gender, the choice of purple ink left no doubt. While the petition now seems obvious, last week I couldn't noodle out any feminine agenda. Better what, police investigation? Diet and exercise? My callow theories mostly involved a lineup of spurned lesbian gumshoes vying for the scribe's role.

Seeking context within the book itself may have been a reach, but I had to consider their relationship. Of course, my voyeur's reflex at the sight of naked flesh had lost its bookmarked page. Somewhere in the latter third was all I recalled. Aimlessly, I leafed until there, on a left-facing page, traces of purple ink tattooed the white space between text, then disappeared into the violet plumage of a peacock photographed in full splay below. Not the chapter on nudes, or even flash technique—that would've been my choice—rather, wildlife photography. I had to laugh, "Wildlife" being the name of a folder on my MacBook containing videos of the carnal variety. On the adjacent page, the book's author detailed tips for remaining unobtrusive in the bush, such as how to fabricate a temporary duck blind from mud and shrubbery.

Sunday's true crime, if you asked me, was Chick-fil-A's weekly closure on the one day I always get cravings. But she probably meant the photo's tableau, the fateful day of whatever it depicted. Her capitalization, though, got me thinking title. Another book, maybe.

The computer at the aisle's endcap turned up no search matches, despite tens of thousands of scrolling results without those exact keywords. True Crime, the breadcrumbs at the top of the screen indicated, was a book genre unto itself. Nonfiction.

★★★★★

In Broad Daylight. Before He Wakes. Son. Dead by Sunset. All the titles on the shelf sounded like Lifetime movies of the week, but no "Sunday's" to be found. Of their authors—Capote, Mailer, Rule—none had been blessed with such a last name. Besides, who would read a six-hundred-page yarn about patricide by a Sally Sunday?

Wearing my best exasperated face, I flagged down an approaching green vest. The young employee in ironic granny glasses cocked her hip, toting an armload of sword-and-sorcery paperbacks. "Hey," I said, "Sunday's True Crime. Any idea what that might refer to?"

She shook severe black bangs out of her eyes and shrugged. "You're in the right place, so if it's not there, I dunno." A diamond stud glinted below her lip. "Section of the newspaper, maybe? All those grisly articles about, like, found body parts and robberies and stuff?"

"But the paper's all true. Reporting."

One eyebrow arched above her frames. Says you, it suggested.

"So the word Sunday's means nothing to you?"

She considered it. "Getting to sleep in when I'm on second shift?"

I snapped my finger. The apostrophe was an error: plural, not possessive. Purple Pen Girl had meant each Sunday, recurring. "Could it be a book club meeting or something?" I asked.

"For nonfiction? Never heard of such a thing." She popped

her gum. "Prolly wouldn't be in a bookstore if they did. Like, say, people into antiquing, right, they're just gonna … nip out the middleman and, like, hang together at swap meets or wherever, wouldn't they?"

I drummed finger rolls against my thigh, genius deflated.

"But we've got chairs there all the same," she said, shifting her book load and nodding to the empty pair against the wall– right next to the TRUE CRIME sign.

★ ★ ★ ★ ★

Of course I took the photo home with me. Didn't dare tuck it into the pages of my guilt-purchase: another book devoted to wild-life photography. Even though it wasn't theft exactly, I couldn't prove that, or risk the cashier confiscating it during a cursory fanning. Those five words had been easy enough to memorize, but what if someone else rose to her challenge instead? No, dammit, I was the one destined to do better–whatever that en-tailed–taking that proverbial HELP WANTED sign out of the win-dow and into my interview. I convinced myself that if she had wanted a committee of do-gooders, she'd have left a tear-sheet like a bassist seeking bandmates.

★ ★ ★ ★ ★

Sunday afternoon. All week I had tried and failed at not theo-rizing about the photo's origin, at not conceiving scenarios of what might transpire. But the hotel house count was low and the banquets routine, allowing plenty of daydreaming while I garnished plate after identical plate with rice pilafs or vegetable medleys. These thoughts superseded the usual fantasies about all the photos I would probably not shoot once I had a day off and ideal weather.

Today I will take a chance and step into that elusive light of inspiration.

The store hums with activity. Coffee and confections and pressed pulp mingle in my nostrils, twitching my intestines with the familiar Pavlovian urge to find a restroom, now compounded by anxiety. I'm casing the floor; everyone's a suspect. A pair of painted-and-inflated trophy wives in yoga couture orbit the New Releases table. On her tiptoes to finger the spines of the Sexuality shelves, a burly, tattoo-sleeved girl turns away from me, and second thoughts momentarily cloud my resolve.

Upstairs, pulse jackhammering as I near True Crime, irises dilate my pupils and focus goes shallow to isolate the aisle. Points of light bloom and blur in the trivial periphery. I round the corner, breath suspended, and snap-zoom onto the chairs at the far end. Both are occupied by women occupied by books in their cross-legged laps. Shelves on both sides fencing me from prying eyes, I approach cautiously, holding the photo across my chest handwriting-side-out like an airport chauffeur awaiting a fare.

The woman on the right glances up at me, blinks, and tilts her head in curiosity. She then returns her attention to her lap, unfazed.

I'm still in my checkered chef pants. Should've run home to change after brunch, scrubbed off my parfum de bacon grease. Just as I unhinge my jaw to conjure some ill-advised utterance, the woman clears her throat, nudging the other woman's elbow on the armrest, then nods in my direction.

Her companion's gaze immediately locks onto the photo paper—illegible at my respectful distance, yet still evident—before straying up to meet mine. I wouldn't call it a smile, the tightening of her lips. Likely a practiced reaction. It only now occurs to me that my trepidation may have been no match for hers, nor as skillfully masked. Early thirties, her slender figure draped in earth tones and accentuated by bold, handcrafted jewelry of coral, jade, and silver. Curly, bottle-orange hair like lasagna. She sighs, then fishes a pen out from the seat cushion, its purple cap waving between her fingers.

"Won't find one of those in a Kindle, huh?" she says of the photo, leaning forward with that same almost-smile.

A much better icebreaker than my plan, which involved standing mute like a sap until she spoke or fled. Like I'm still doing.

"So," she continues. "Think you can?"

"What's that?" I croak.

"Do better."

"Trying every day." The line just fell out of my mouth, unrehearsed. "Now I guess it's just a matter of sussing out what your particular yardstick is."

"You'd be hard-pressed to do worse."

I drag my feet closer, twirling the photo between my knuckles. "So how many weeks you been sitting here?"

"When I saw the photo gone today, I hoped it was the last one." Her throat bobs with an uneasy swallow. "That, or ... y'know–"

"Right. I mean, how could you be sure it wouldn't just get snatched up by some perv?"

"Still can't." She throws a glance at her friend, who only shakes her bemused head while feigning continued interest in her coffee-table book.

"Figured that's why you didn't leave a phone number."

"Exactly. The safety of public places and whatnot. But also deniability."

"Deniability," I echo. "Of what?"

She twists the coral stones of her necklace, narrowing her eyes. "Ever agree to a blind date, then pretend to be someone else once you get there and discover a troll?"

"I don't go on many blind dates," I tell her. Sighted ones, either, but I keep that to myself.

"No," she says, blushing, "I don't imagine you have much trouble in that department. But rest assured, this is a professional rendezvous." She pats her friend's hand. "Wendy, I think I've got it from here."

Wendy eyeballs me hard, then shrugs. "Fine. I'll be here a while, or just meet you at the theater later."

The redhead closes her book. She stands up with a yawn and a tiptoes-stretch before extending an open hand. "I'm Becca, by the way. Shall we go for a walk?"

I knew a Becky once, who later matured into Rebecca upon entering the workforce. Becca. Something youthful about retaining such a nickname.

★ ★ ★ ★ ★

"Do you know Nik?"

I shuffle the deck of my acquaintances, and assume she doesn't mean the harelip Russian dishwasher. "Nah, don't think so."

"Nik Stillwell? The author of that book I stuck it in? He teaches over at the art institute."

"Local guy, eh?" I know no one, and certainly don't want them knowing me yet. Just a circle of confusion biding my time outside the shooters' fringe. "Sorry, haven't heard of him."

"I was hoping you might be a student." Rolling her eyes, Becca adds, "He likes to put his own books on the syllabus."

We stroll the sidewalk along the upscale al fresco storefronts, her leisurely pace continually reining mine back instead of vice-versa. It's their affluence spurring me onward, discouraging me from shopping anywhere but the chain bookstore. Couldn't even swing a meal at my own hotel around the corner.

"I'm guessing he knew the girl in the picture?" I ask.

Becca studies me as if I'm oblivious to some punch line—processing my naiveté, perhaps even encouraged by it. I pull her out of the path of an oncoming street lamp. "A lot's changed in thirteen years," she says, shaking it off. "Even me."

"This is you?"

The photo is snatched from my hand before I can steal another peek and begin morphing and mapping the naked bits onto her present-day figure. "Was, yeah." She blindly tucks it into her purse, staring ahead at the retail horizon, then offers a resigned sigh. "Go ahead, get it out of your system."

"What. I'm not doing anything." I can't help it; familiarity breeds fantasy. Just like it's impossible not forever picturing heart-shaven pubic hair after your roommate's otherwise-homely girlfriend accidentally drops her towel in front of you.

"I used to look better with my clothes on." Becca says this with the opposite of nostalgia.

"And now?"

"Let's go in here a minute." She drags me through a set of glass doors and into whiteness.

★ ★ ★ ★ ★

I prefer the art galleries in the old warehouse district. Sure, their wine drips from a box and lingering sawdust irritates your nose, but the work on the walls is priced to move, to feed. At this place, a piece is most likely bought for the way its color palette complements a patron's sofa.

Stillwell hadn't always been the feted lensman known today, Becca informs me, her neck craned in front of a regatta watercolor. In college, his primary occupation was boyfriend-with-an-apartment and enabler of her underage alcoholism.

"He could've just asked, you know, instead of waiting for me to pass out." Discovering the photo—pressed between the pages of a creaky birdwatching guidebook leveling out his TV stand—had woken her up in more ways than one. She left him without ever mentioning it. "Probably still has the negative somewhere, I bet."

"Like some butterfly collector," I suggest, "pinning down his conquests. But now that he's the man, you want everyone knowing what kind of guy—"

"No, no, nothing so vindictive as that. I'm long over it." On the adjacent wall, a bay-window-sized mirror reflects us, its only invention being an engraved filigree border. "What do you make of this one?"

It's nothing I'd care to look at, were it not for the elegant redhead also framed on my right, primping discreetly. "Art imitating life ... in real time?" Checking the placard: "For a mere nine grand."

"As for the photo, I did hope it might get Nik's attention, sure, just as a sort of reminder, I guess. Being the type of egomaniac who re-shelves his own books for more prominent placement." She reapplies her lipstick, then catches my eyes in the mirror. "Did you see that copy he stashed up front in Bestsellers?"

Brass ones, that guy. We share a laugh, drifting among the lofty rubbish in this white maze. After much needling, I detail my efforts and ambitions, my photographic misgivings in stark contrast with Stillwell's bravado. "Seems to me, that whole time you were together, he had a willing subject but no technique." Would've swapped with him in a heartbeat.

"Willing, yet unwitting." Becca scoffs at a sepia-toned enlargement of a man in a business suit struggling to mount a horse, loafer wedged into one stirrup as he clings to the beast's neck, unable to hoist his other leg over. Amusing enough, I suppose. But while he's rendered in sharp focus at its center, the photo's true character would lie in the filly's violated, wide-eyed foreground expression—were it not blurry and shadowed in favor of the textured, billowing sky above. Becca shakes her head. "Defeats the whole purpose of having a pro camera if you only use the auto settings."

The woman just summarized my entire existence.

"I want you to pose for me," I say, surprised at the outburst. "Or not pose. Just … be. I can't promise the ability to capture your very soul or anything, but—"

Her lips tighten. Definitely a grin. "Might be tough to see it through my clothes."

"I see plenty. Up to you, though."

"All right, then," she says with a nervous laugh, tucking a strand of lasagna behind her ear. "So, um, what format do you shoot on?"

Who needs a camera?

"Don't give me a bunch of nonsense about how your mom couldn't cook when you were six. Just get naked."
—Booked #66 *The Wolf Gift* review

SEAN P FERGUSON
TWO DOLLAR BEER NIGHTS

Dawn is clawing at the horizon, fighting its way uphill against the void of night. Birds cry out for the light to win the battle. Birds man, they're a booster. I can tell with the weight of the blanket pulled up over my head that I'm not in my own bed, and the pungent smell of sex tells me I'm not alone; or at least wasn't alone. I focus on opening one eye as slowly as possible, but it does no good. Everything is black or blurry or both. I open both eyes and try to adjust to the darkness under the blanket, but that too is useless.

The low growl of a woman's snoring drags its nails down the back of my head and I slip a leg out from under the blanket in the opposite direction. I navigate through beaches of crumbs, mounds of wadded up clothing, and what feels like a thick wire before I stub a toe on the wood frame of a bed. It takes everything I have not to yell and convulse from the pain. My brain rapid-fires images through my mind's eye, a toe shorter than it should be, a toe bent at a nauseating angle. I wonder if it would be possible to pop it back into place by blowing really hard on my thumb, like blowing up a balloon with some sort of comedic sound or visual effect. I slide a hand out from under the blanket, inspect the frame and instantly know where I am.

This time I do curse, out loud, at great length.

The low snoring chokes, turning into an annoyed snarl. Then she smacks her lips and goes back to snoring. I start to think about what it is she's dreaming, but my brain disconnects and my version of Jiminy Cricket bitch-slaps the gray matter inside my head.

He says, "Would you get out of here already?"

Gripping the smooth prefabricated wood, I use it to pull myself smoothly out from under the blanket the rest of the way, out of the confines of the unforgiving frame, and swing my weight around to bring myself to my feet. One smooth movement, totally ninja-like. No bullshit. I start to celebrate the awesome maneuver, kick my leg, and stub the same toe on a stack of books. I stomp around and yell with no voice at all. The only thing you can hear is her snoring and the air whistling through my moving lips, competing for dominance. Striking a hung-over yoga pose, I grab out into the darkness of the room searching for something, anything that will bring some sort of light without waking the sleeping creature still in the bed.

She murmurs to herself, starts to shift under the blanket and I freeze. Facial hair grows too loudly. Someone two blocks away fires up a leaf blower and I make a mental note to hunt him down and murder every one of his children, his children's children, and probably his mailman. I pray that her visual acuity is based on movement, breath held, muscles taut and flexed just so. Red Light/Green Light has not one solitary thing on me. Pleased with herself, she settles, a sleeping smile spreading across her face.

Suddenly, whatever she's dreaming is no longer interesting.

The message relays from fingertip to brain too late. I've already moved my hand to keep from falling on my face. I adjust and go back to where I think my hand was, feeling for the tiny toothy wheel of a lighter. Finding it again, the fingers flex, contract, and flex again, searching for the rest. I palm it, stand straight, and tense up so morning gas doesn't eke out.

Spinning the wheel with my thumb, I quickly scan the floor for some semblance of what I was probably wearing last night, before the flame goes out. Darkness falls around me again, the cold swarms back in around my hand, and I watch the dark bulge of her body under the blanket. She doesn't move.

Bringing the flame back to life, I crouch lower. I need a sock for my naked right foot, shoes, pants, and a shirt. Maybe a hat, they make me feel slick. I shake my head, because this is no time for joking. At the very least, I hope I was smart enough to toss everything in the same direction so it would be a quick escape. I cup a hand around the flame and move toward the big mahogany chest of drawers at the foot of the bed.

No dice.

I check the floor on her side of the bed; I find my jeans when I accidentally step on the buckle of my belt. And praise be to whoever is presiding over my own personal section of this cold and dusty planet this morning, because my missing sock is in the pant leg. I consider the pros and cons of driving home without shoes and a shirt. Leaving right now would be such a blessing. No awkward goodbyes, no looks of longing as I drive off into the distance. But let's be real, a shirt and shoes? She's human and we're not strangers to this situation. It's the morning after two dollar beer night, after all. This is the dance we do.

The buckle clinks against itself and she whines, "What

time is it?"

Damn it. "I'm not sure."

She stretches, growls, and starts to roll onto her stomach, to push herself up. This is how it begins. I bump against the dresser and see my cell phone shift in the dark. I grab it, push a button so the back screen lights up, find and slip into my shoes. She starts to rub her lower back and her mouth mumbles about not sleeping right. And that's where my sweatshirt, my favorite one, lies crumpled in a ball, where her back pain would have started.

"You were sleeping on my sweatshirt, that's why you hurt."

"I feel pregnant."

"Say what?"

She smiles and my insides boil. This is why I wanted to bolt when I could, even at the cost of my favorite sweatshirt. This is what she does. We go months without speaking. Everything is wonderful, and then I wander into the bar on a Wednesday night. The jukebox, outdated decades before I started going there as a minor, the food tastes just as old, and the clientele—the bar collected the whole set.

You walk through that big heavy door with the decorative pane of glass, and you're immediately transported to a rerun of some sitcom filmed before a live studio audience. However, inside, there are no laughs. It's quiet in there. Everyone leaves me alone so I can go in, drink far beyond the legal limit in peace, and go home. Or in this case, someone else's home.

She sweeps her left hand back and forth across the bed sheets, searching for what I can only assume is the wet spot. The joy I feel when she frowns, a small whine gurgling in her throat as she comes up short is comparable to making a deal with the devil, ultimately tricking him out of his trident, horns, and a big piece of scorched real estate. Her eyes try to look at me without being seen. She's hoping I'm not watching, not knowing what it was she was looking for. Her master plan has failed again.

I lean over, grab my shirt and make a half-hearted excuse about having to be somewhere, needing a shower, clean clothes, and a toothbrush. Her face falls as she considers all of this. Running the tired old excuses over in her head, evaluating the words as if their meaning and order are new to her. The shirt, it smells like dirty sex and ass. Last night's beer bubbles up in the back of my throat. I swallow hard to push it all back down.

Pulling her ratty purple robe on, she rubs her stomach. Synapses fire across her face, her jaw setting to mutter words that might lock me in to a relationship I don't want. There's no cold sticky feeling in my pants, no signs that I had any part in her stink. Deep breath.

The eggs in her ovaries shuffle along dark alleyways, scratching at the walls: growling to be fed. They claw at themselves in desperation, rotting from the inside out. The hollow void in their eyes shimmers with the last glistening hope to procreate. Their jaws hang open, knuckles scantly brushing over the ground as they hunt; they search for my drunken sperm. And I can't help it.

I smile.

The eggs will be left to wander, to roam cold and alone. They'll watch as their numbers dwindle. Eventually they'll find their way into the uterus and be expelled one by one, month after month, dying of hunger. The uterus inside of her will collapse in on itself like a dying star turning to ash. Dust into dust, all because I haven't launched a fresh batch of victims into the throes of misguided passion, into the waiting arms of a horde of starving unfertilized eggs. In the cinematic nightmare that is her sex-canyon, I am the hero, slaying mutated creature after mutated undead creature.

I stand on the cliff, fists on my hips with a jaunty fedora set just so, almost covering my eyes, framed by the golden rays of the sun as I watch eggs drop off across the way. They plummet like lemmings into the jagged rocks below. Like so many gory watermelons exploding on the asphalt simmering in the summer haze. I feel victorious, vindicated even. I drank my share of beer, crawled into danger and still came out of this as clean as can be.

"I'm going to go."

No excuses. I don't bother coming up with convoluted places to be prior to daylight. I've won the battle, the credits are going to roll, and I have no one to answer to but myself. And all she does is shrug.

I'm walking shirtless to the door, I'm on a mission. This is the sequel already, and the script is virtually nonexistent. My hand touches the doorknob and I can feel the features on my face caving in, bracing for the inevitable plea to stay, to marry. We could build a white picket fence and watch deformed larvae slosh out of our primitive ooze. Our children would need to be chained up in the basement, wear helmets, and be fed stray animals. But nothing comes, she doesn't say a word.

The front door shuts behind me and I get to my car, making a note to chuckle to myself later. I'm parked on top of an errant bicycle from one of the awful neighbor children, in a no-parking zone, in the wrong direction. With the grace of a ballerina, I turn the engine over, the headlights come on, and I throw my coupe in gear. There is no stalling, no problems with the starter. A song from one of my favorite bands ever, a band that rarely gets any airtime at all, is just in its first three notes. The volume knob cranks over with ease and I bop along to the syncopated beat into the coming day.

The homestretch passes under my car and I light a cigarette, breathing a lungful of relief out of the driver's window. My favorite band is followed by a promotional ad for the tour they're about to launch. I dance when the overzealous announcer says that they're coming to an arena nearby. Pulling into the drive-thru, I order my favorite breakfast sandwiches and what is described as a large cup of their sweet tea. The girl working the window is attractive and giggles politely at my weak joke about the large drink needing a handle and two bodybuilders to help me hoist it through my window. The sandwiches are warm and fresh.

Steering the car into the driveway, I find my housemate stretched across the front yard. His shoes and pants are missing. A small salt and pepper dog is curled up on his back. It growls, watching me as I walk up onto the front porch and slip in through the front door.

I taste everything in my sandwiches, appreciating the brew of the sweet tea. Something in my brain fires, like I'm able to place the field that yielded the tea leaves that were brewed for my morning breakfast. Like I could see the cold gray walls of the factory, hear the cries of the slaughtered pigs that gave me the bacon of my sandwich. I see the steel and springs and sprockets that squished out my just-add-water eggs, measured for optimal profit. And every last bite tastes like heaven.

After starting a pot of coffee, I step out onto the porch. The first drag of the morning cigarette tastes amazing. The dog is gone, so I set a steaming mug by the housemate's face and leave him on the lawn to sleep last night off, chuckling to myself, "You have to love two dollar beer nights."

Seeing my sneakers in the front room, I decide to put them to use. I change and head to the park. The morning air feels good, the birds are singing, and the eye candy jogging the opposite direction is of a caliber that you only read about. With the school buses in the area packed to capacity with screaming evil, soccer moms start to file in for their daily lap around the park, as if that's doing anything for their hips, and the college girls split for their classes. I go home.

The housemate is gone when I get back; his mug is upside down in the sink. The whole place is mine for the day.

I climb the stairs and shed last night's clothes on my way to the bathroom, cloth breadcrumbs leading me from the horrors of yesterday, toward the promise of a fresh start. The steam comes easy and apparently it is going to be one of those days where the soap smells extra clean, the shampoo leaves my hair extra soft, the conditioner does extra conditioning—whatever. All is right with the world; everything is going to be great.

And with a handful of suds I reach down to wash myself, to clean the sweat from yesterday, and the laps at the park. Fire shoots through my nerve endings, screams howl just under my skin. Eyeing the soap, like that's the source of my pain, like the housemate swapped it out for hydrochloric acid, like he'll rule the world at the expense of my burning genitals. The soap rinses off and it all still stings, so I lather again, thinking that perhaps just one more attempt to clean myself will fix the pain.

Wrong, dead wrong. This time the pain is worse. Pain and worse are two words in the English language sorely underselling the entire experience. Like, skyscrapers are tall, ice is cold, Anne Rice is overrated; all accurate by definition, but at the same time ineffective in capturing any sort of emotion, reaction, or imagination. The soap seems to be headed straight to whatever the problem is, so I rinse it all away. I thrust at the stream of scalding water and hear myself howling in pain. I stagger back, wiping tears from my eyes, and throw the curtain open to let the steam out. And I look.

Teeth marks circle my appendage, like that's where I keep my brain. "Fucking two dollar beer nights!"

"The character can be wrong about something.
That doesn't mean that I'm wrong about it."
—Booked. #19 Interview with David James Keaton

DAVID JAMES KEATON
DRAGON BY THE DUMPSTER

Big gorilla at the L.A. Zoo snatched the glasses
right off my face, took the keys to my BMW,
left me here to take his place.
  –Warren Zevon "Gorilla You're a Desperado"

Besides when I blew my engine and had to walk to work every day down those railroad tracks with a shitty radio shaped like a hamburger for company, there was only one other time I was without a car. It was a strange summer, right after I'd been bounced out of school for vandalism, and I almost didn't get through it with my identity intact. Before I start this, I should mention that I changed the names of the vehicles in this story to protect their identities. Less important, I also swapped the name Mike with Mark, I'm calling a bookstore a video store, and I'm not being honest about forgetting a girl's name. Worst of all, way later, I'll talk about a police sketch, and I'll lie about it looking like me. The rest of this shit is gospel.

So, first off, with all the cheap apartments I'd lived in, you'd think I'd have gotten used to a life of abrupt temperature changes with the water by the time I hit college. You couldn't really blame anyone. It was kind of like the weather. You can't get too angry when the temperature drops outside, right? So, I was living in a tiny, converted-office building with this girl, unable to accurately forecast my next shower. The girl? I can't remember her name, but I almost remember her car. I remember both their colors though. One black, one white.

But next door was Crazy Mark, and I remember every inch of that motherfucker. Even though his real name was Mike Miller, I called him "Crazy Mark II" because I'd already known a Crazy Mark once in my life, and this was just easier. Besides, they're everywhere if you start looking.

But I'll talk about one Mark at a time. The first one, I'd managed to duck for about a decade. Then I ran into his car. Because it was my car. I'll explain.

It was sleeping in the exact same spot I saw it five years ago. A yellow dog curled up in the corner of the employee end of the parking lot at Ike's Truck Stop off I-75, a garage-sized dive where Crazy Mark had been working his whole life. When I saw it, my first instinct was to run over, low to the ground with a screwdriver in my teeth like I was in the trenches of World War II. As if they fought that war with screwdrivers. Careful not to wake it, I quickly removed the license plate from the Sundog, then replaced it with my own. It was scary but fun, and I figured he'd appreciate the joke. I felt like I was swapping collars on sleeping dinosaurs. See, I'd sold him this car the year before, and he'd never bothered to change the plate. And once my old plates were secured to my green Cavalry, I turned to stare at my old ride for a minute and thought, Crazy fuckin' Mark. What the hell happened to you?

I'd heard you were engaged to that girl we both dated (sometimes at the same time) and I also heard that you smacked her in the face when she broke up with you. I stepped closer to check the rubber seal around the driver's-side window. It was still crusted with white, oil-based paint. I smiled, remembering the time when it was my turn to date that girl and I came out of the bookstore to find the words *"Fuck You!"* smeared angrily across the glass. I could never prove it was you, but I'm happy to see that you were never able to get all that paint off either.

I pulled my keychain from my pocket and found the extra key swinging right where I'd left it. The car opened without a protest, as if it was still mine. I felt bad for a second, like I should have hung onto this car after I paid it off, like I'd worked and earned the right to own this car only to decide in that exact instant I never wanted to see it again. How many times does that happen on a wedding night?

I climbed behind the wheel. I didn't even have time to look around before I knew that I did not like it back in this car at all. I felt like I was sitting in a cold puddle of something bad, and that something was slowly seeping through my jeans and crawling up the crack of my ass. It was almost as uncomfortable as the memory of that itchy hay ride in high school when another kid named Mark punched me in the face. Finally, glancing around I saw the most random, pointless collection of compact discs and cassettes cracked and scratched and littering the floor, and I needed out. Worst taste in music ever.

I decided this is what would have happened if I had stayed in this car, stayed in this town, stopped treating my music with respect and started smacking them around, too, just like he did to her.

how to playfully backhand a friend

I thought about her often because I knew, and I'm sure she knew, she'd have been better off never crossing paths with either of us. The girl in question, we'll call her "Gee" in this story, as in the letter "G," because she had a license plate that me, Jerry, and Crazy Mark all got excited about, thinking it said GOD-LESS. With only a clever license plate, a pretty face, and a nice ass to go on, a "black girl's ass" according to Jerry, we thought this particular girl that stopped to rent movies every Thursday from the video store where we worked was the most utterly fascinating creature of all time. And even after a closer inspection revealed that her plate actually said GODD-ESS instead, we just chalked that up to her being ironic instead of just a shallow twit.

I dated her first. Then Crazy Mark about a year later. She didn't want anything to do with Jerry, and he's been in love with her ever since. But her and Mark didn't last too long, and when it was over, she stopped in the video store he'd long since quit (but I couldn't seem to break up with) and showed me some disturbing poetry she said Mark had been leaving in her bird bath when no one was home. I assured her that he was "harmless" and "a really bad poet" and then asked her who the fuck really has a bird bath? She muttered something about there being nothing harmless about bad poetry, using a Prince song as proof, and then wandered out the "In" door, "In" door …

So I told Jerry all about this run-in, and that's when he decided it was a good time to tell me a story. Turned out Jerry was working at a restaurant near his new apartment in the city, a high-end spot named "Jerry's" which he claimed was completely coincidental, swearing to me up and down that he was not pretending it was actually his restaurant when he parked his car every morning. Yeah, right. Anyway, he said another guy in the kitchen, the head chef (this was Jerry's cooking phase, right before his park-ranger phase) was living with our girl, Gee, and guess what his boss had been up to? Jerry explained it all with at least five sound effects:

"He's fucking at least three chicks on a regular basis. He comes back from the parking lot on his 15-minute break and brags about it, shaking my hands all proud, sometimes shaking my head, then wiping who-knows-what sticky shit all over my shoulders. Sure, he might be lying. But he's elbow-deep in something out there. His face comes back grinning like a glazed doughnut and his fingers look like he just waxed a car. Once he playfully backhanded me in the face. Splotch! It was like that time the giraffe woke me up with its tongue when we passed out in the zoo."

"*You* passed out in the zoo," I reminded him. "And how do you 'playfully' backhand someone?"

"That's what I'm saying, dude!"

So I filed this information away, along with Jerry telling me about Head Chef trying to sell him a bunch of guns(!) Apparently, he was also this survival nut, and me and Jerry were on the cusp of this phase (right before his military phase), something that lasted one whole trip to a shooting range where we got kicked the fuck out for pulling quick-draw contests with the targets inches from our faces while a cop was adjusting his laser sight two targets down.

So rewind the videotape and I've started seeing Gee regularly again at the video store for the first time in a couple years. Her plate never said GOD-LESS no matter how hard I prayed, but now, after I watched her put her movies in the return slot and try not to make any noise doing it, I started liking her all over again. I think it was just from thinking about all the conversations and drama going on around her that she was unaware of, maybe my knowledge of her Chef's secret recipes, or maybe just the way she was being wronged, I don't know. But I wanted her just like the old days so I decided to strike up conversations every chance I got. It was fun for a couple of weeks, even though she had no mysterious poetry bombs to report.

Then one day, it was all awkward and she told me that she'd seen me "driving behind her the other day." What? Then she nervously asked if I knew anyone else that lived on her street because she thought she saw my car there, too. I immediately understood that this was Crazy Mark driving the car I'd sold to him, the car I'd owned when me and Gee (and Jerry) were always together. I tried to explain all this to her, but she seemed unconvinced. Then, the next time she came in, she admitted that, yes, Mark had been around recently. He'd walked straight into her house a couple weeks ago, and Head Chef had to "gently" restrain him until the cops showed up.

"No shit?" I said. I asked her if she saw my car, then said, "Remember how I told you I sold him my car?" Then I asked, quite sincerely, if she thought Mark was mistreating it. She blinked, frowned, sighed and left, clearly tired as fuck of us crazy bastards. And right then, I made a decision that I knew I'd probably be punished for some day. But it hasn't happened yet. We'll see if he reads this.

I called up Crazy Mark with this bad idea in my head. First, I got the scoop on that incident. Of course, his version of events was radically different than hers. He claimed that he'd only stopped by as an afterthought to give her another small, 42-page poem about Sir Gaiwan & the Green Knight, and that Head Chef attacked him for no reason, holding him on the ground at gunpoint with a knee on his throat. No "gently" anywhere to be found in his version. Then Mark went on to say that when the cops showed up, that gun had mysteriously vanished, and that he was going to be charged with trespassing, assault, and attempted kidnapping. If he could "just prove there was a gun involved," he was sure he could get all those charges thrown out. I said, "Holy shit, dude, Jerry works with this asshole, and he's trying to sell him guns all the time." I actually heard Mark's brain shifting gears on the other end of the phone with a metal clank. So I threw a little more sugar into his gas tank and go …

"Hey, did you know that this cocksucker is fucking around on her, too? Nails everything in town on his smoke breaks? Laughs about it to everyone in the kitchen where he works. Someone should do something. None of my business though. Anyway, how about those Red Wings …"

Crazy Mark cleared his throat and calmly said, "No, I didn't know that," then got off the phone.

So I went on with my life for a while, and everyone sort of disappeared. I'd heard Gee was single again, that she'd caught the Head Chef cheating. So I called Jerry to get the scoop.

First thing he asked me was, "Where you been?"

I said, "Nowhere. Where *you* been?"

He said, "Court."

Then he told me that he kinda lost his mind after I told him about the Head cheating on Gee. After that, compounded with the trespassing, assault, and attempted kidnapping charges (most of them dismissed, however, when Jerry was called in to testify about the guns), Mark decided to get some righteous revenge. Just like I knew he would, fucking poet that he was.

Apparently, he popped out of the bushes and bashed the Head Chef within an inch of his life with a convenient block of nearby firewood. Then he might have bashed him that extra inch.

Mark had gone over there with the intent of breaking his arm so that it was unable to "make a proper omelet ever again" (Jerry's words) and sent him crawling down the street screaming he was being mugged. Some "strange" that the Head Chef had been banging came running out of a parked car all blustering, and Mark started working his way up his shoulders towards the head with that piece of wood. Then he found it. The commotion woke up Gee, who finally caught him red-handed. And red-headed. Red fucking everything.

Covered in blood, naked, and spouting sonnets, Crazy Mark was arrested running down the street, and Gee came around asking questions. I acted all shocked, and even though I finally seemed to convince her that it wasn't me following her around in the Sundog, I know all that time that she thought it was me made a lasting impression that the truth could never erase. It's like starting off a conversation with bad news, an insult, or a horrible lie and then quickly adding, "just kidding." Sure, you might get the laugh, but that split-second that they thought you were serious stays with them forever, even if they never recognize why their feelings for you have changed just that teeny tiny bit.

My fingers are about an inch apart.

turn off the water

Anyway, things were normal for a while, and then suddenly I was kicked out of school. I also didn't have a car again. Those are the worst times for me.

When I moved in next door to this nut Crazy Mark Too with the girl whose name I can't remember, I'd recently been fired from some bush-league carpet cleaning business/chop-shop garage and couldn't afford to get my car fixed anytime soon. And without a job or transportation, me and the apartment with bad weather in the pipes began to merge. I didn't do anything for weeks at a time, barely grunting hello and goodbye to the girl I was sharing those days with. All I could tell you about her is she was taller than me, had dark hair, fucked up my VHS copy of *Highlander*, and she didn't really have any favorite things of her own, movies, music, nothing.

So, I was in the shower one morning and could hear my neighbor through our ridiculously thin walls fumbling around in his tub, chasing the soap or a toy boat or a girl scout or something. Then he bellowed so loud I thought he was standing there under the spray with me.

"Turn off the water!"

I must have been in shock because I did exactly what I was told before I could stop myself. Then I toweled off and spent the rest of the day with my ear to the wall, listening for any more instructions. I didn't tell my roommate, but confused her when I got up early the next morning to see her off. Suddenly, I had a mission. I waited until I heard my neighbor's shower running and quickly turned on my own hot water. Right on cue:

"Turn off the water!"

I turned it off. Then turned it on again.

"Turn off the water!"

Turned it on …

"Turn off …"

… then off again real quick.

"… the water!"

Sometimes I experimented with different ratios of hot and cold. It didn't matter. It all made him furious. I smiled and listened while this monster crashed and banged his way through the most frustrating thunderstorm of his life, then went on with my day of doing nothing. The next morning I was up before the crack of noon. "Have a good day at work, hon!" Smooch.

"Turn off the water!" and so on.

I was having fun with this new routine until I noticed something that was happening on my girlfriend's way out the door. Whenever she would leave, I would hear the neighbor stumble across his apartment, open his door, then quickly close it. When she got home, I asked her if someone was walking out with her every morning, maybe leaving for work when she did? She sighed and looked down at the ground.

"Well, I didn't want to get you all upset, but the neighbor peeks his head out and watches me walk down the hall."

I dropped whatever I was holding. I wish it had been a drink for dramatic effect. Or maybe a basketball so I could keep dropping it over and over.

"Are you fucking kidding me?! Wait, what does he look like?"

I was protective of her, but understandably curious about this voice I'd been tormenting.

"I don't know. I just saw this big mop of curly hair, then he was gone."

"No shit. No. Shit."

The next morning. "Good day, baby." Big smooch. Then I was peeking out the door watching her walk down the hall, ass shaking like she's all business, headed out to bring home the bacon to her deadbeat boyfriend. And after she was about halfway to the stairs, I heard bumbling footsteps and saw that mop of curls framing the back of some large man's cranium, peering out to watch her with me. I shouted:

"Hey!"

Both of them turned around, but his door slammed before I

could see his eyes. I smiled and yelled to her surprised face.

"Hey, baby, could you grab some more soap on the way home?"

That night, we shared theories about him and wondered how he could afford to stay home all day without a job or school. We got so excited that we were happy for about 48 hours before I started sulking again about my employment situation and ruined both our moods. And the next morning in the shower, the booming voice confused me with a question instead:

"Why aren't you in class?!"

I yelled back through the wall:

"Fuck do you care?!" Then:

"If I was in class, who would turn off the water!"

I heard him mumbling to himself and stomping around, and eventually I pounded on the wall to stop his tantrum.

I eagerly told my girlfriend all about it when she got home. And we were up all night with brand-new theories, so late, in fact, that she had no time to take a shower before work the next day. Her sudden change of schedule right after mine must have thrown my neighbor way off because his head was nowhere to be seen when I watched her walk down the hall. However, I did notice an envelope peeking out from under his door. My curiosity overwhelmed me and shirtless and shoeless, I tip-toed down to peek at it. It wasn't sealed, and inside was a note from his caseworker (his what??) saying that she'd be around next week to make sure he "got his groceries okay." I guessed the caseworker was a "she" by the handwriting. The letterhead on top read "Maumee Mental Health Board." And this is where I discovered his name, "Mike M. Miller," but it was too late for that shit. He was Crazy Mark II, damn it.

But some other things start making sense, too. Like the envelopes under half the doors, like no one else ever leaving for work in the morning, like the fact that most people down this length of hall leave their doors open all day, visible on their beds, arms crossed behind their heads like they're in a dorm or, say, lockdown.

"How many fuckin' mental patients are in this joint?" I asked Jerry. I'd started going to his house every day instead of a job, carrying a giant hockey bag of blue jeans and boots and playing hours of *Battletoads* and *Blades of Steel*, sometimes watching him on *Mega Man*, which was way too hard for me. I was over there every day like clockwork. Almost started wearing a tie.

But I didn't tell my girlfriend what I'd found since I didn't want to scare her with all those alarming *M's* in the same letter and, even more important, I didn't want her to insist that we move.

So, I'm in the shower again, and now we were having almost entire conversations, not knowing quite where he stops and I start.

"Turn off the water!"

"It *is* off!"

"Why aren't you in class?!"

"I *am* in class!"

"Why aren't you at work?!"

"*This* is where I work."

"Leave me alone!"

"You started it."

"Turn off the water!"

"Turn off the weather!"

That night, the landlord called. Before he could speak, I was all over him.

"What's going on with you housing mental patients here?

Do you get a discount? You realize that crazy fucker stares at my girlfriend every day, right? How would you like me to bring him over to live in your goddamn garage instead?"

The landlord waited for me to finish, then explained that he'd been receiving complaints about me, not Mr. Miller. "Mr. M. M. M. Miller," I corrected him like a crazy person, but no amount of explaining could convince him that I wasn't the one yelling about water, weather, and class schedules every morning because I kinda was.

"In fact," he told me, "your neighbors have started a petition to get you evicted."

At 3:05 p.m. the next day, Crazy Mark The Sequel actually stepped out of the apartment for the first time. I hoped he was trying his luck at "getting those groceries okay," and jumped up on red alert.

I'd never seen him out in the wild, so I was dressed and running out my door right behind him. I almost wore a suit I was so goddamn excited. But it was an unremarkable trip, and for some reason his appearance was even harder to remember in the sunlight. Except for the curly rat's nest of hair, I wouldn't be able to pick him out of a crowd of babbling mental patients, even if they were all in the shower.

But things got real interesting at the end of our walk.

When we turned the corner around our apartment building, he yelped in fear, dumped half his food, and bolted up the stairs. Half hour later, his caseworker stopped by, and I listened with a glass to the wall. Her voice was so smooth and soothing, I wanted her to work on me next. Told you it was a "she."

"Shhh. There is no dragon, Mike."

"There's a dragon by the dumpster. I saw it."

His voice was high and girlish when he talked to her, not

the guttural trumpeting I got through my shower wall every day. He always sounded small on the phone, too, which made him more terrifying.

"There's nothing out there, remember?"

"There's a dragon there right now, I swear!"

What the hell was he talking about? I needed to know.

I went back out to take a look. Next to the dumpster was a rolled-up mattress wrapped in black garbage bags and rope. Nearby was a pile of moldy pickles and the shattered remains of a jar. *Must be the dragon*, I decided. Was the waterhead trying to feed it? Once I looked around, it was clear it wasn't the first time he'd dumped his groceries. He'd been scared so many times there were enough meats and vegetables lying there to make a week's worth of tacos.

That night, I told my girl about all of this, and she finally started getting scared. For all the wrong reasons.

"You followed him?" She was actually shaking.

"Yeah."

"Why?"

"I was looking for a job."

That wasn't really a lie, if you think about it.

The next day, my neighbor went to get more groceries to feed his monster, so I followed him again. When we got to the dumpster, I couldn't help it. I screamed:

"Look out, Mark! Mattress dragons!"

He dumped his milk and orange juice and pickles again and ran up the steps to his room, slipping to his knees twice on the way, screeching over his shoulder in his little voice:

"My name's not Mark!"

Crazy fucker, I thought. *How does he even know what his name is?*

The day after that, I followed him again. My family would say we were in love. He didn't get groceries anymore though. The caseworker would leave them in front of his door, either sick of the argument or finally acknowledging the very real dangers of dragons by dumpsters. No, these walks were different, all straight lines, purposeful, like he was working up the courage to go to a grocery store. But mostly we just walked around the block three or four times. He never noticed me following him, and any former classmates that recognized me and said "hello" never seemed to see him either. I followed him for weeks.

The last day I saw him, we didn't walk toward the center of town. Instead we wove our way around miles of residential houses, sometimes taking shortcuts through backyards and bushes. His door stood open all night. Then a padlock appeared in the morning.

That afternoon, my girlfriend showed me the newspaper and announced she was moving out. There was a sketch on the front page, and she was convinced it was me. The fucker looked like me, no denying that. And under the drawing was an article about a man peeping in windows all around campus. Oh, yeah, it also talked about how he might be responsible for a couple rapes. And maybe a missing girl or two.

I swore to her that I was only following our neighbor, and okay maybe they did see us in their yards, but only remembered me instead. Or some combination of me or him.

"Maybe this is why the sketch resembled me so closely?" I pleaded. "It's both of us."

She wasn't buying anything I was selling.

Years later, I moved into an efficiency apartment by myself and, maybe because of my mental patient neighbor's constant pep talks and reassurance, I set about finishing that last class I'd dropped. It was an art class, the female body, and the teacher kept trying in vain to get me to start my sketches with the line down a woman's back, even if she was facing forward. I, however, always started at the eyes, and my proportions suffered, my creatures ending up confused, sad mutations that might have grown up near reactors or power lines. Like a child's drawing of a five-pointed star when they're afraid to cross over their own lines with that simple unbroken trail, all five points of the face hung and curled like limp swastikas.

I would have been a terrible sketch artist.

I ended up passing and graduating, barely, and during this time, I noticed a classmate opening and closing the trunk of his car every day, caught in some helpless, hopeless, obsessive-compulsive loop. I started to imitate him, parking right next to him whenever I could and slamming my trunk, too, hoping he'd notice and resist doing it so much. Instead, the other classmates started looking at me more and more suspiciously until the teacher cautiously approached one night to finally ask what I was doing. Halfway through my explanation, she stopped me and said, "Who are you talking about?"

I was never able to sell her any of it either.

cars with thumbs

I've always been annoyed by people who exaggerate the importance of their mailbox by saying with a sniffle, "It's a federal offense!" when you vandalize it. So you can imagine how surprised I was at the guilt I felt for ripping the mailboxes for my apartment building off the wall.

I was going down to get the check they sent me for groceries, reaching inside and fully expecting a mousetrap. Instead, I found a check for 50 cents. Seriously. 50 cents. Someone from the post office actually took the time to write out a check for "50 cents and 0/100ths" and mailed it off with a 40-cent "America: Love it or Leave it!" stamp in the corner. I flashed back to all that arguing with the postal clerk when their machine stole my money, and I wished I'd squeezed his neck a little harder.

Instead, I embraced the entire bank of mailboxes like I was hugging the biggest grandma ever, the one on my dad's side of the family, and I wrestled the entire thing off the wall. It came down easily, leaving behind six baseball-sized holes in the plaster from the bolts.

And there was another letter in my box, pushed up high where I couldn't see it. No return address, but I knew who it was from. It was about my old car, of course, but I was disappointed the letter wasn't *from* my old car.

I read it anyway. It was old, but the envelope had gotten wet, so there was no telling when she'd sent it. But in the world of the letter, Mark is still stalking her, still driving my old car. And she "just doesn't know who it is anymore." In the world of the letter, she explains that the only thing she's sure of is it's my car. And it's been so long since I've seen him, I wondered how much he looks like me these days, wondered how much he looked like me back then, if he hugged the steering wheel too close, as tight as a mailbox or his last girlfriend. In the world of the letter, she's threatening me with a restraining order if I don't quit cruising her job, her school, her bird bath. She says she's really getting scared. She says she sees my car everywhere. And she says I'll have to pay for what my tires did to the yard. If I had time, if I wasn't moving so soon, I'd explain to her that, to clear this up, she doesn't need to talk to me, or Mark, but obviously to the car in question. Hell, a car doesn't even need a thumb to make a phone call anymore. Most already have phones in them.

I could call either of them, maybe shame them into not following her anymore, but I don't. I deserve this letter. I always have. Here's why. Wait, I already told you about that.

"I wanted to have a book where you could
just open up to any page and be moved by a
sentence."
—Booked. #14 Interview with Christopher Dwyer

CHRISTOPHER J DWYER
CORALEE

The moon explodes into a thousand fiery fragments of glitter and dust. Fourteen seconds, a breath and the needle prick squeezes a glowing trail of euphoric lava into my bloodstream. I tilt my head back, ignore the wails of the many ghosts swimming beneath my skull. Time becomes incidental and every second I'm awake is another lost moment that will be forgotten. The needle falls to the carpeted motel floor and wraps itself in the footsteps of the past lives of this room, this cocoon.

I can't tell if I'm sitting, standing or floating. Whispers slither across the walls like angry wraiths. The curtains sway from side to side as if pushed and pulled by unseen forces. The figures on the television screen are hollow, eyes like black sockets. The marching band in my head pounds another tune and their tiny little footsteps are an ethereal symphony. I never knew that I've waited weeks for this day to come and the physical portions of my body are the only ones ready for it all to come down.

Down, I peer, watching a pack of blue ants step across the carpet with a focused purpose, their antennae like radiant glow-sticks. It takes nearly a full minute to stand up and when I do the television screen shifts to an array of static and gray noise. The motel's ancient pipes wheeze with age and for a moment I pretend that I'm back at home, back with her. I wonder if she's flying above the city, searching for the next great soul to fix.

My Coralee, the one who came, the one who went. The one who left me here.

It hasn't been long since she's been gone and already I can feel the obsidian rats eating at the edge of my heart. It's only a matter of time before they penetrate the fleshy fibers around it and claw their way inside.

Her touch was enough to dull the pain, yet not enough to keep me from this poison now careening through my veins.

Coralee, where are you?

And to think, she came along at just the right moment in my life, as if a divine architect swooped our timelines over one another just to see the graceful union of destruction and grace. I can remember the minute, the second, as if it were only this afternoon.

The white tinges of pain pinch at my chest. Only a few hours, maybe. It didn't have to end like this.

★ ★ ★ ★ ★

He had the look of a fallen soldier, bright blue eyes under a sheen of distress. He flipped the first page over the back of the clipboard and shook his head once, twice. Pen firmly gripped in his right hand, he scribbled for a few seconds before tossing the clipboard onto the desk behind him.

"Not much difference from last week," Dr. O'Connell said. "Trent, I'm sorry."

I nodded. That's all I ever did here, listening to him talk about how there was never a change in my condition. We went through this every week. He probably knew more about me than my parents did.

"I know, doc," I said. "You don't have to say anything else."

Dr. O'Connell smiled and pointed to the scars on my arm. The left one, that is, because, when I was younger, I refused to use the other. I figured that I'd at least need one of them if the other failed me after all the shit I'd injected into it over the years.

"I wish there was something else I could do. How long have you been on the list now?"

I forced a smile. "Too long."

Dr. O'Connell shook his head. It was almost funny to think that he was no more than a year or two older than me, yet we were standing on two completely opposite sides of life. He put a hand on my shoulder, as he always did right after my dialysis session, and squeezed the fabric of my shirt. "Don't give up, Trent. Hang in there. See you in, what, two days?"

I buttoned up the top few buttons of my dress shirt. "You know it, doc."

Dr. O'Connell left the room and white streams of sunlight followed closely behind. I walked past the emergency room front desk, threw a smile at the nurse tapping away at a bulky computer, and made my way into an elevator to the cafeteria on the first floor. When I first started coming here, I couldn't wait to leave, to get away from the smell of faux-orange disinfectant and plastic. I'd often fall asleep in the chair, an attempt to force my mind to dream about anything, everything. But now, I figure I owe this place. They've kept me alive for nearly three years after I ravaged my body and mind, so now I stop by the cafeteria for a coffee before getting on with the day.

I ordered a coffee, dumped three packets of sugar into the cup, and found a seat at the very corner of the cafeteria. It was moments like these that a man who had this affliction would stop to collect himself, maybe figure out a better path for the future that didn't involve a casket.

A sip of the black brew warmed my throat and I closed my eyes, and repeated the process until at least ten minutes had passed. It was right here that I first saw her, charcoal hoodie and piercing blue eyes that could start a war. She had been staring out one of the many cafeteria windows, pale fingers wrapped around a coffee cup. She didn't notice me until I walked past a few minutes later. She offered a small grin before continuing her focus on the autumn foliage of another Boston afternoon.

In the days since she left, I replayed that one visual, that one smile, in the celluloid behind my brain at least a thousand times.

After depositing my cup in the receptacle near the cafeteria entrance, I left the hospital behind me like so many times before.

★ ★ ★ ★ ★

The September sun was beginning its descent into the lavender sky beyond Boston Common's army of dying trees. A breeze crept from the west and if it wasn't for the crisp snap of its cool embrace, I would have fallen into a calm slumber at the edge of the park. I fished around my front jeans pocket and grabbed a small white pill. The '512' imprint was often a sign of comfort, of familiarity. I popped it into the back of my throat and sent it on its way. Within minutes, streaks of sunlight bled from the sky like melting vanilla frosting. Passersby were momentary cartoon figures, each one walking past in slow motion with a trail of comet dust not far behind.

The sky went dark for only a moment, my eyes adjusting to

the embrace of the painkiller. I nearly let the black hole pull me away, but she was there, kneeling in front of me, last bits of sunlight forming a cracked halo above her head.

"Wake up," she said. "Come on, wake up."

I opened my mouth, tried to find my words.

Her cheeks crumpled into pale dimples. "I saw you at the hospital a few hours ago. Recognized you at the edge of the Common, just as I was about to head down into the train station."

"Ah," was all I could get out before she reached for my hand. The touch was almost like an anesthetic, my vision becoming clearer, my body back to an undamaged state.

"You need a coffee." She pulled me toward the eastern edge of the Common, black, chipped fingernails intertwined with my bruised and battered hand. Upon our touch, I could see the memories of my childhood, the times before my life went to shit.

"Here," she said. "I go to this place every day."

She turned to me and smiled. It was as if I had known her all my life.

★ ★ ★ ★ ★

Her name was Coralee and she said she was from New York City. I sipped my coffee tenderly, smiled when I could. The dim light of the coffeehouse allowed the arctic blue of her eyes to sparkle like the tips of broken icebergs.

"That wasn't the first time I saw you at Mass General, was it?"

I shook my head. I was never honest with anybody, never revealed a bit of my soul. But she seemed different, familiar. "Kidney failure. On dialysis twice a week every week since …"

Coralee tilted her head and I swear I saw a sparkle in her eyes. "Since what?"

"Since I overdosed a few times. Since I destroyed my body

so badly that I now have the kidneys of someone three times my age. I've been on a donor list for over a year."

A red stripe penetrated the jet black strands of her hair, which swooped over her forehead as if they were the legs of native tarantulas. She placed a hand over mine, the underside of her palm like a blanket of calming warmth. "I'm sure they'll find a donor for you soon. These bodies," she placed a finger on my chest, "were not meant to be vessels for pain."

We talked for what felt like hours, me never asking questions about her life, where she lived, or her career. I reached to the core, found myself telling Coralee about the first time I used and why, to this day, the urge is still there, like a nagging itch that can't be scratched. She listened and held my hand, not once interrupting me. It could have been midnight when she broke our stride and faced me.

"You need to get some rest now. Boylston Station is up ahead. I'm going to head home." She kissed me on the cheek and the rumble of comfort filled my bones. Before leaving, she slipped a piece of paper into my hand. "Good night."

I waved goodbye and walked away, not once questioning the evening's intent.

★ ★ ★ ★ ★

The morning sun pinched the sides of my brain. I couldn't remember the last time I had actually slept through a whole night without tossing and turning, without pain stifling my every second of sleep. My dreams were filled with clouds, with light. The small piece of paper was still sitting on my nightstand.

Harrison's Spot, Tremont Street, Friday, 7 p.m.

I peered at the alarm clock. I had slept into the afternoon. Three years of my visits to Massachusetts General Hospital for dialysis, and I couldn't help but stroll through the city for hours afterward before heading home. It was as if I were afraid to go home, to sit in a sullen room where pain eluded pleasure and I was alone with nothing but my thoughts. I looked at my face in the bedroom mirror, noticed that my cheeks were flush with a rosy apple glow instead of their usual dull, pale. Even my eyes had a bright residue beyond the dark brown swath.

The bed beckoned me again, and within moments, I was asleep, free to slip into another place that was far beyond the torment of the day.

★ ★ ★ ★ ★

It's not a craving. Cravings pass and do not often involve substances that could shut down an immune system. It's always there, floating behind the fibers within the brain, buried and building a nest from pieces of the past. It's at your weakest point, when you think it'll be okay for just a small taste, that it strikes and kills.

It knows no emotion, no bias. It doesn't care how long you've lived or how many children you've raised. It's there, and I know it. It'll never leave, never go away. It won't jump to another soul or eventually fade away.

It'll win. And I'll lose.

★ ★ ★ ★ ★

She was already at Harrison's Spot, a statuesque beauty with a grin that set the world ablaze. She leaned against the brick exterior of the restaurant, tight black jeans and a white sweater that revealed only the slightest bit of cleavage.

"Trent," she said, and stood up to greet me. The hug stopped time, aroused a static shockwave through my fingers and toes.

"How are you feeling?"

My mind was already on the truth before the words could catch up. "I feel … great. For a change, at least." I could tell I was smiling.

"That's so good to hear. Come on, let's get a drink."

We sat at a table toward the back of the bar section of Harrison's. It was unusually quiet for a Friday evening, the loudest sounds of the night spun from a jukebox in the corner of the room. U2's "Angel of Harlem" radiated throughout the bar.

New York, like a Christmas tree / Tonight, this city belongs to me

We shared a pitcher of beer, talking about everything from my childhood (I grew up in Salem, not too far from the site of the original Witch Trials) to her upbringing in New York City (she was adopted and didn't know her biological parents). Coralee told me she had a degree in art history but spent the last year or so volunteering at animal shelters while she interviewed for professor gigs in and around the Boston area.

I was on my last glass when she asked me a question I hoped she wouldn't.

"Will you ever use again?"

I couldn't face her, only stared into the bottom of my glass until the liquid was far into my body. "I don't know, Coralee. I don't."

She placed her hand over mine and there it was again. The warmth, the comfort, the familiar, like I had known her for twenty years instead of only a day or two. "Tell me that you won't."

I bit the inside of my cheek. "I … won't."

Two rows of perfect white teeth and a crinkle of her freckled nose. She leaned in for a kiss and when her blood red lips touched mine a shiver of fire crisped the edges of my heart.

★ ★ ★ ★ ★

Coralee lay by my side, nestled within the gap between my arm and chest. She smelled like lilac blossoms and winter morning snow. She kissed the edge of my chin, nuzzled her nose against the brownish red stubble on my face. I drifted in and out, watched the walls of my bedroom collapse and reveal the endless black of space and nighttime stars. I could feel the bed floating, as if we were somewhere beyond the reaches of time.

Coralee slid to the edge of the bed and stood up, the arch of onyx wings outstretched to the sky. Glints of broken moonlight danced in the forefront and I reached for her. Her wings shuttered like a blurry comet and within moments she was gone.

★ ★ ★ ★ ★

Morning forced open my eyelids. I was alone in the bedroom, bed-sheets unwrinkled except for those covering my body. It took me a full minute or two before I realized that Coralee was missing. My frantic search resulted in not a trace of her presence in my apartment. I had no way to reach her, no phone number or address.

Not even a last name.

The clock on my nightstand indicated that it was nearing 11 a.m. If I didn't hop on a train to Mass General within the next fifteen minutes, I would miss my dialysis appointment.

★ ★ ★ ★ ★

"Hmm."

I tilted my head in confusion. "What's wrong?"

Betty, one of the many nurses who routinely attended to my visits, read a series of numbers to herself on a monitor beyond the dialysis machine. "This isn't normal."

"What is it?"

Betty left me alone for a moment and returned with Dr. O'Connell. He didn't acknowledge me.

"Doc, what's going on? Am I okay?"

He tapped a few keys on the computer attached to the machine and shook his head. "This can't be right, Betty. Is something wrong with this device?"

"Doctor, it was serviced just a few days ago." Betty flipped through papers next to the monitor.

"Doc!"

He finally turned around to face me. "Trent, this ... sorry. Let me ask you: how do you feel?"

I told him the truth. "Fine. No pain. Feeling pretty good."

"Trent, have you taken anything? Any meds that we haven't prescribed?" His face was as inquisitive as a child's.

I shook my head. "Nope."

"Well," he began, "your values are clean. It's almost as if there's nothing wrong with your kidneys, Trent. This is unbelievable."

And all I could think of was Coralee. She disappeared in my dreams and I didn't know where to find her. Dr. O'Connell unhooked me and informed that I should come back later in the day for some tests. I jogged to the cafeteria, hoping that, just maybe, she'd be there.

But she wasn't, and I was questioning my reality.

★ ★ ★ ★ ★

I could tell you more, how I walked through the city for the rest of the day, from one edge of Boston to the other. I swear that I passed every bar, every goddamn coffee shop, all to no avail. The itch, it was there the entire time, poking at the edges of my mind. It broke me down, syphoned my thoughts at their weakest point.

It didn't take long to find what I needed. It finds you, it knows what you need and how much you should put inside of you.

And now I'm here, at a motel just outside the city. She was real and she wasn't. The first hot injection into my arm told me that. A last connection of warmth, one final link to humanity before it all came to this. She may be overhead, searching for another soul to fix, scanning the darkest corners of the city.

Coralee, you're gone. And I know why you were here.

Jagged edges of moonlight poke through a small slit in the curtain, a frenetic waltz of incandescence and lost hope.

VON

"You shouldn't be wasting words no matter
what you're writing."
    —Booked #26 *Warmed and Bound* interview

ANTHONY DAVID JACQUES
TROPICALIA

I usually forget my sunglasses, or else they break on the plane.
I pull the brim of my hat low against rippling reflections off the
pool and light a cigarette while the luggage is taken up. Generic
island music crackles from the swim-up bar and a live band is
doing a sound check somewhere out of sight. Behind me the Caribbean sun is probably about to set.

A red-eye flight from L.A. then a five-hour layover in Atlanta
where I couldn't sleep because the AC was set to hypothermia
and I was still pissed at how they almost didn't let me use my
cane. Could be used as a weapon, they said. I showed them
the fresh stitches above my knee, from my third surgery in as
many months, and how I could hardly bend my leg. It's not that
I couldn't make it to my seat without it, but the way things had
gone lately I needed the win.

Almost slept on the connection, but then I rolled over on
my Wayfarers. I was so angry I kept ordering drinks, and when
that didn't do the trick I started ordering drinks for other people,

only they didn't seem to understand.

Now, the best way to get away with showing up stag to a couples-only resort is to make two airline reservations. You give the confirmation numbers to your travel agent, who passes them on to the resort, and they'll arrange for ground transportation from the airport. Then you call the night before and say your wife had to change her ticket last minute and come a couple of days later, and you only want to pay one change fee. It makes you sound cheap, sure, but this way the limo driver doesn't get suspicious when he picks up a moderately drunk man standing all alone outside the terminal.

And now, still drunk, Sunday night in a different time zone without sleep since probably Friday and the live music has been thumping down by the pool since sundown. I'm on the phone with the front desk. I think.

"You're going to have to speak up, sir."

I shout into the receiver, "When does it stop?"

"Usually around eleven, sir."

"Usually?"

"Give or take."

The DJ outside shouts, "Somebody scream," and I think the entire island consents.

"Sir?"

"It wasn't ..." like this last time.

"Sir? Please speak up."

"Tomorrow night, can you move my things directly into the subwoofer? I don't think I'm close enough to the action."

"Sir?"

"Thank you."

At some point, finally, sleep.

★ ★ ★ ★ ★

I remember our final descent, how the tiny prop plane banked hard to line up for the approach and how all the windows along the left side of the plane looked down over rows and rows of gray headstones lined up along the runway and out to the crystal blue bay. I remember reaching for her hand, how I used to really hate flying and the sight of Choc Cemetery reminded me that most plane crashes happened during takeoff or landing. That fact plus the fleeting glimpse of the above ground sarcophagi wore through what remained of my nerve because when we landed I'd apparently bruised her hand.

Welcome to St. Lucia.

It was a morbid thought and it plagued me as we waited for the limo, but by the time you've been handed a cool, moist towel to freshen up, and in the console you noticed two mimosas and a tray of appetizers garnished with bright red caviar, well, all you can think of are the days of ocean breezes and sun that lie ahead. Tipping the limo driver, downing a second mimosa, watching the condensation run down the glass; an image of a bronze faucet reflected in dark lenses flashed across my mind. Our faucet at home, a thousand miles away.

"They're on the counter," I said. "My Ray Bans."

She checked her purse, almost laughing.

"No no no." Fading memories had created a dream version of Sarah's voice, like a bad recording that got worse every time it played over in my head. I remember how her shoulders dropped.

"Well, at least they're somewhere else in one piece."

"At least."

"I know where you'll be all morning." She handed me the room key, saying, "See you down by the pool." With a kiss on the cheek she followed our luggage down the hall. Another man with a tray of mimosas stepped out of the concierge office to greet another shuttle.

A half hour in the gift shop and I settled on a pair of Wayfarer rip-offs, paid. I felt my pockets for the room key, which turned out to be just a card with no number. I hadn't paid attention at all as we checked in so I had to ask at the front desk.

Up in the room, I pulled off my wrinkled clothes and threw them across a chair, set the fake Wayfarers on the nightstand. Rummaged around for my trunks. The bathroom door opened and it was Sarah's silhouette backlit by wavering light from candles and mirrors, and that humming sound I'd hoped was only housekeeping in the next room vacuuming was actually the Jacuzzi warming up. Our Jacuzzi.

Her fingers slid up the doorframe.

A thin, uninterrupted line of skin running from her ankle to just underneath her shoulder caught the candlelight.

"You look overdressed."

I pulled off my socks. The floor was cold under my feet and my eyes still hadn't quite adjusted as I walked toward the flickering light.

★★★★★

Clouds moving away from the sun overhead. I don't remember putting on shorts or sunscreen, my legs are hot and I'm not sure which direction the sun is moving or what time that would make it if I did. I press my fingers into the flesh on my arms, can't remember if it's supposed to turn pink right away or stay white for a few seconds to tell you if you're burned.

I don't even remember walking out to the pool.

The band today has a violinist whose lazy playing pushes everything toward melancholy. Can't bring myself to slip into the pool and swim across to the bar for a drink so I wait for a man in a starched shirt to come my way with a tray of orange and blue and green drinks, wave him down before he hands out the last one. I hate banana and coconut but it's got enough rum that I don't mind, and by the time he's done picking up the empty glasses left by the pool I hand him my empty glass and ask for a double scotch, no ice, which he repeats back to me.

His shirt doesn't move in the wind and his blue-black face is sparkling wet in the heat. I finish two of those and the sun is directly overhead when he comes by again and hands me a beer saying, "I'm Georgie-Porgie. I got you, man. Good vibes."

Voices carry across the pool when the band takes five and all I hear are drink names and once in a while, a slurred Thanks. I close my eyes and try to guess by sound alone which waves are real and which are coming from the wave pool. I can't tell, and I'm too drunk to think about what that means.

I'm standing. Walking, or rather, floating toward the pool-side room. The violinist's face is cracked with years of neglect and sun and that's the last thing I see as the AC rushes out of the sliding glass door and then it's closed behind me and I bury my face in the bed.

★ ★ ★ ★ ★

The smell of fresh linens and sweat and scented oil candles that you can pour on your lover's skin and I pulled the sheets back a moment before her legs tensed around my head, candlelight and champagne and the smell of rose petals that had been sprinkled around the bed, carried her into the honeymoon suite, her thighs pressed against my ears, I pulled the sheets back and she held my head in place, legs twitching, tense, fingers behind my ears, guiding me, our bodies no more than moving silhouettes against storm clouds, candles, lightning shooting through her body, the buzz in the atmosphere, up and down her legs, a white dress falling away for hours, the limitless approach, my ears muffled against the sound of ecstasy, guiding me, clouds lingering for days, sweet rain coming down in sheets, candles dripping hot wax, her fingers through my wet hair, my fingers wrapped around garters, pressed into flesh beneath white stockings, with her legs around my head forever.

★ ★ ★ ★ ★

"How did you get this number?" I move my hand to wipe my mouth, but it's dry.

"This is the front desk, sir."

The bed is cold and I'm alone. The synapses start to fire again. Reaching down, I'm hard as a rock.

"Who?"

"This is Regina, from the front desk," only her voice lifts at the end and it sounds like a question, as if she's not sure.

Mouth dry, I can't put any more words together than, "I'm sorry?"

"You have been confirmed."

"Confirmed." It's like I've never heard the word before.

"You have been moved, sir."

Pause.

"… Sir?"

"Nothing."

Pause.

"Sir, I am calling to tell you that you have been moved to a suite up the hill. Your butler will meet you in an hour outside the room to collect your things."

"No sir. It's Jake."

"Is this what you requested, sir?"

"Jake."

"Jake. Yes, sir."

"Okay. An hour." My brain grinds down to a halt trying to work around the idea of a butler. What the hell is a butler?

"Thank you, sir."

"Wait, what day is it?"

Dial tone.

★ ★ ★ ★ ★

The butler is dressed like a pallbearer and he hands me a cell phone. The only contacts are Butler Devon, Butler Burton and Room Service. The suite has two floors with a private pool and a deck that has steps down to the beach.

"We have seven five-star restaurants on site and I can get you reservations wherever you like. Will Mrs. Alexander be joining you for dinner tonight?"

I say that we'll be meeting up soon but a large wave crashes and Butler Devon smiles and says, "Very good, sir. If you need anything else, do not hesitate to call, no matter what time of day or night."

The folder he hands me has a crest encircled by the words, Guild of Professional Butlers, London, England. He closes the door and that plus the sound of the waves and the air conditioner are enough to drown out the laughter and the Jimmy Buffet cover band from around the cove.

I head down the steps to the cabana with the sign Reserved for Suite 315 hanging across the back. A wedding party walks past led by a woman with a camera and a younger man in a starched white shirt holding three camera bags.

Georgie Porgie almost walks by but stops.

"Alex, my sunburned friend, another scotch?"

"Alexander. Jake Alexander."

"Good vibes, man."

"And no ice."

"You are too cool, my friend. Mr. No Ice. Mr. No Sunscreen."

I nod.

"So where can I get a cane like that, my friend?"

"Uh …" I can't think of a way to say this that doesn't make me sound like an asshole. "A hospital."

His eyes drop. "Scotch, no ice," he says, instantly upbeat again. He extends his fist to me, "Bam," but I don't understand the cue in time, try to give him a half-assed five and miss, again, then he says, "Right away," and snaps his fingers and says, "Good vibes, all right," walking away, "Good vibes. Good vibes."

About twenty minutes later, Georgie must have forgotten about the scotch but one of the butlers shows up to see how I'm doing. I can't see the nametag because the sun is behind him lighting a corona of glistening sweat around his head. His shirt doesn't move in the breeze.

"You must be dying out here."

"No problem, sir."

"Look, there's an open bottle of Black Label in the suite. Just bring that down with a glass and take the day off."

★★★★★

All the bus drivers honk at each other as they squeeze by, my knuckles white on the seat but I had to get away, a cracked retaining wall painted to say, Coca-Cola, Live Positively, a cow eating grass out front of a pink and green hardware store with its tail in the air taking a shit, another crumbling retaining wall says, -oca-Cola, -ve Positively, a burned out car, rows and rows of bright colored hats, sunglasses, orange and yellow drums, a car with the windshield exploded, pushed out from the inside, a boy selling crabs that are still moving and tied up on sticks, a stark white cruise ship in the harbor taller than any building in sight, men on bicycles and a group of women at a bus stop, yellow painted metal guardrail moves traffic to one lane where years ago a hurricane took out the earth underneath, Burger King, motor scooter showroom, rows of wrecked cars out back, a horse tied up outside the airport, a nearly destroyed retaining wall reads -Cola, -e Positively and all the rushing colors lull me to sleep where I try to remember the license plate, and I feel the warmth pouring over me, $2500 convertible top, suspended sideways, original window sticker floating down past me, CGU, maybe a 9, her hair reaching down to me, brushing my face, the silent impact and flashes of lightning in my skull, my face is wet, horns honking, the faded ink of the invoice for the first oil change October 5, 1967, the stop light staring red, bored, changing stations, tires screeching, a black blur with red lights airborne, California plates something CGU something 9 something, horns honking somewhere in the distance and I'm awake, far beyond drunk, still, signs for excursions and rum tours on the sides of bright green and yellow and blue and pink houses that go halfway up the hill until it's too steep, then trees and sky and nowhere a cloud in sight.

★ ★ ★ ★ ★

Somewhere near downtown a cab driver (when did I finally get into a cab) is telling me how St. Lucia is only twenty-seven by fourteen miles so crime is not a huge thing around here. A hundred-sixty thousand people, most in Castries, and everyone knows everything about everyone. He explains how there were a handful of robberies two years ago but then the police took out the "five heads" and that pretty much took care of that. On an island so small with so few roads, there's really nowhere to hide.

I shake my head, laughing, saying, "A few guys were pulled over for speeding, I don't remember where. Guns and masks and duffel bags in the backseat, bank heist hobby kit, right? Anyway, the cops had to let them go. Legal bullshit, you know. Three weeks later they hit a bank and people died and I think they still got off on a technicality."

He shakes his head, "The cops out here, people fear them. But in a good way."

It was a weird conversation, but that's what you get when you ask where to buy a gun. He stops at the bank so I can get some cash out of the ATM, says he'll circle the block until he sees me then honk twice since most taxis look the same.

As I'm coming out of the bank a very tan white man approaches me with a Bible and says I seem like I have a heavy heart. He asks if he can pray for my foot to be healed. I grip the handle of the cane, but before I can say anything he waves an Asian girl over then an even younger white girl joins them and they start to mumble charismatically. Every Jesus, Lord and Hallelujah comes through in perfect American English. Missionaries. The man finally shouts Amen and now the locals are looking over and a few have stopped to listen as he claims healing and victory over my foot and says the warmth is coursing through my body and then asks me, loudly, how my foot feels, hallelujah, amen, et cetera.

I pull up my shorts so the fresh stitches peek out and say, "Good as new. But this still seems to be giving me trouble."

He just stares.

"Now heal my Mustang."

He takes a step back.

"And bring back my wife, asshole."

He trips over a local sitting at the curb.

"You know, pull a Lazarus."

He stuffs the religious tract back into his shirt pocket and walks off, but the other white girl is still speaking in tongues, holding out a hat with money in it.

The taxi honks twice.

★ ★ ★ ★ ★

Lights out, back in the butler suite with an empty bottle of Dewar's next to the bed, I can't get the faith healer out of my head. Or Sarah's auburn hair, or how often we argued about that car, the money and the time, and how I put a tarp over it until long after the wedding and would have sold it if only she'd asked me to. And how the storm ruined our honeymoon and every couple at the resort got a complimentary week's stay since the power was out for three days.

How we were sitting at a stop light on our way to the monthly Hot Rod Cruise in Escondido, not quite seven weeks ago, the way the door handle dug into my thigh when that BMW flipped end over end, its trunk slamming into Sarah's door, shoving us sideways until my door bent around the stop light.

Sarah was putting on her jacket. I remember that. No shoulder restraint, just lap belts and no headrests, and that newly replaced convertible top which offered no protection. But any car hit by a BMW doing sixty then flipping over a median and tumbling, trunk first, mid air, it just doesn't matter. I woke up a couple of hours later, a couple of hours too late. No goodbyes. Closed casket.

Three weeks after the funeral I turned the calendar on the

refrigerator to October and saw VACATION!!! in blue ink with red squiggles around it and everything began to sink in. How could I forget? The free week from our ruined honeymoon, plus the extra week we paid for. I couldn't bear calling to cancel, having to explain, so each time someone stopped by I'd ask if they would call for me but everyone said a break would be good, a couple of weeks in the sun or even in the hotel, the spa, just finding my center is what my brother said. I don't think they understood it was a couples-only resort. Making this point clear only prompted someone to suggest booking two tickets, then coming up with a story about changing the one. My mom said I ought to spend my time getting closer to Jesus, and whether I went on the trip or not they were only a half hour away. Suddenly I felt like getting on a plane.

★★★★★

Swim-up bar, alone, early, unsure of the day, something less than two weeks I hope. I'm avoiding Butler Burton when Georgie comes in through the back and unloads the empty glasses and then he's saying, "Mr. No Ice Baby," sort of like a line from a Vanilla Ice song. We high five. "Good Vibes, man." I've warmed up to Georgie.

I set down the empty glass and the bartender fills it back up without a word.

Out of my mouth comes, "Are you happy?" before I know what I'm saying.

"Look around, my friend," the bartender's voice, deeper than I expected, "Ocean and sky and lush mountains. Beautiful women, tan and shiny and drunk. You have this back home?"

"I live in L.A."

He nods, as if we came to an understanding.

Now with more resolve I turn to Georgie, "Are you happy?"

"I'm drunk."

The bartender laughs, then Georgie.

Now feeling really deep, really philosophical the way I get when I've had too much scotch, I ask a couple down the bar if they're happy but they turn to each other and swim away.

I get out of the pool and walk to my things, finish my scotch too fast and drop the glass on the chaise lounge. It bounces off the .44 or .45 beneath the towel; I can't remember which. The tumbler cracks on the no-slip concrete around the pool and with wavering resolve I head down to the beach and wade into the ocean, and the water stings, seeping in between the stitches, lightning shoots up from my knee, but I wade in deep enough to dip my head beneath the waves and I think about Choc Cemetery right next to the airport because I can't bear being buried next to Sarah, but when I come back up the sky is still blue and the waves are still crashing and everything is still here.

VON

CHRIS DEAL
WHERE THE WATER MET THE SKY

For the real Alvaro

Even with years and borders between them, Alvaro always strived to return to her. She was a daughter of the sea, her father a fisherman, as was his father and so on, back through the centuries. They went to the coast to celebrate their marriage, though they could afford little more than a room. She smiled at the way the land became the sea. They found a local who agreed to take them out, to show her what the earth looked like from the ocean, so she could feel what it is like to have only the depths beneath her feet. They went past the horizon, where there was ocean for a mirror of the vault of heaven. The weight of the sky crushed down upon his shoulders, the ocean eager to consume him whole. Alvaro's wife pretended not to see his tears.

Alvaro stood in line for ten minutes to pay his bill. Before the cellular phone, he would stand in line for the same time to purchase the calling cards. It was a ritual more than anything. He bought his calling cards from Josué, a tiny Ecuadorian man who ran the grocery store up the road from him. He paid his phone bill at a mall kiosk across from a stand that sold cups of elote and horchata. It was not so expensive any longer to call back to his home, to his wife and child, but as he gave the clerk his number and paid cash for his monthly allotment of minutes, Alvaro was aware of the growing pointlessness. He worked six days a week and wired money back to his family. He kept enough for his share of the rent and incidentals. To spend on himself was a sin. His clothes came secondhand and he slept on a living room floor. He had not driven since his last stay in the north. A friend had asked for a ride to the bus station. This was when he had gone to Florida for work. The car had been purchased for two thousand dollars in cash, and when the policeman tapped on his window Alvaro knew it was pointless. They put him in detention and he signed whatever papers they put in front of him before putting him on a bus with guards who dropped him off across the border, back home. This would be the first and last time he would return to the place of his birth. He was in that town for two days. Nothing but the clothes on his back, his wallet empty save for his Matrícula Consular and a sheet of paper with the names, addresses, and phone numbers of all the people he knew, wife and child, brothers and cousins. He had to call in favors he never wanted to call in to get enough money wired from his brother Jorge, who had permanently settled in the north, to get to his family's home in Guanajuato. His wife, Aida, would not answer her phone, nor would their son, Alejandro.

The clerk gave him his receipt and a fake smile. Alvaro considered a cup of elote but that would have cost him three dollars and those dollars were better suited for his son's pocket. He had come to the mall with Jorge and his family. They lived in a house within walking distance of the small apartment Alvaro rented with several others of his stripe. Their visits were regular, several times a week, and were always capped off with a request from Jorge for Alvaro to move into his family home, though Alvaro always said no, pride being enough to make a stupid decision. To inconvenience another soul was a sin. Jorge and his family came to the mall to prepare for the arrival of Chava, the third brother. Chava had found a coyote to bring him back north. He last called from El Paso two days before, where he was about to board a bus to bring him to the brother's chosen home in Illinois. He was due in that very night. Alvaro had made the trip twice before. The first time had been fine. He paid and they were men of honor. The second time had been different. It was a hot day when they met him for his last crossing. The coyotes Alvaro paid to take him north picked him up from beside his father's grave. He had not been there for the old man's passing, and could not say if he would be able to be buried in the same dirt as his family. The coyotes put him into a cargo trailer pulled behind a pickup truck. There was nowhere to sit except for the scorching floor. They drove for a day, picking up more crossers as they went until there were nine sweltering in the metallic heat. Each had given money for the privilege with the promise of more once they were safely across. The sweat that dripped from his nose evaporated before it hit the floor. They told Alvaro they would hand him over to some colleagues who would take him on the actual crossing. In the middle of the desert, they stopped the truck and pulled out their knives. A man, his skin burnt dark by age, resisted, and they used the blades on him. The rest acquiesced, and the men with knives left them standing under the noon sun, leaving one man with a gun to watch as they waited in the heat. The heavens stretched out above them like the maw of a god and Alvaro wept. Day turned to night and back again before a pin of light appeared on the horizon. They did not know on what side of the border they were on, all was desert and sky and it could have been people with guns meaning to send them back south or kill them trying. It was another truck, the colleagues to take them on the second leg of the journey. They had plastic milk containers of warm water and it would be three more days before the travelers were able to eat.

When he was a boy he was afraid of the sky. In daylight, it was an ocean suspended above, or Alvaro was hanging, ready to fall into the deep expanse at any moment like a spider dangling above a flame. Once, Alvaro took all his father's fishhooks and attached them to his shoes, so with each step he would be safe if the earth ever let go of its grasp. When Alvaro's father, Santos, found out, he made the boy bleed. Santos was a hard man, known in their village as a great worker and a strong fighter, but he was as pious as his namesake. He apologized to Alvaro, indirectly as was his way. He said that there was nothing to be feared in the sky, that as it was in the above so it is here below, that we came from up there and one day, if He wills, we would rise to the sky again. This did nothing to alleviate the boy's fear, of course. The sky of the day was one thing, but it was the night that moved him to tears, when the whole of the universe opened up, the vastness of it all revealing to him how little he mattered, how if there was a He up there, surely He couldn't be concerned with a runt of a boy in a small Guanajuato village. Alvaro's grandfather lived almost ninety years and even if he could come close to that lifetime, it would be nothing in the face of time. All traces of

Alvaro's blood would be wiped away with the rest of the chalk. It never went away, this fear, but he learned to protect against the fear. Walking through towns and cities and deserts with eyes cast downward, only seeing birds when they tried to steal his crumbs. Clouds became foreign, to say nothing of the stars. He lived on the earth with no thoughts of heaven. His eyes grew murky as time went by and it became harder for him to see. Years after the fishhooks, he met a young woman. She was beautiful, and she became his wife. After they went to the sea, they had a child and Alvaro knew what would have to be done. He paid the coyotes and they took him north.

Jorge found him sitting on a bench across from the kiosk. Alvaro's eyes had taken on a silver tint from the cataracts. Alvaro often found himself lost in his sight, trying to make sense of what used to be plainly shown to him. Jorge nudged his knee to wake him from the self-imposed stupor. Jorge and Paola, his wife, carried bags of clothes for Chava, some they hoped to give to Alvaro though they knew he would never accept them. He took the bags from Paola and they weaved through the crowd back to their car, Alvaro walking two steps behind them. Chava would need work, and that was something Alvaro could provide. His boss would need more workers out in the gardens. The storms would come soon and they would need to clean. The winter prior he worked eighteen-hour days to clear the snow away. When he finally slept his hand was tightly clawed as if he were still holding the shovel. Chava would not like it but he had debts to pay, he had children, Alvaro's nieces and nephews he had never met. It had been five years since he had kissed his own wife, shook his own son's hand.

The terminal was in Chicago. The bus would be there at just

past one in the morning. Alvaro would be back at work by seven. For a small moment he considered not going with Jorge to pick up their brother, but to show cowardice is a sin. They drove in silence punctuated by shared yawns. The interstates were clear out in the border towns, but even at such an hour Chicago's streets were a suicide run. Cars he would never dream of owning, cars that cost more than a lifetime of work, sped by like meteors in the night. Jorge lit a cigarette and cracked the window, as Paola had stayed at home with their children. He offered the pack to Alvaro, who accepted and mirrored his brother.

Chava was waiting for them outside the terminal, a backpack hanging from one shoulder, his clothes rumpled from the two-day trip. The whites of his eyes were a dark red. They embraced and exchanged their greetings. Alvaro had forgotten how much taller his brother had always been. Chava was asleep before they were back on the highway, waking as they pulled into Jorge's driveway. The three brothers sat in silence as the car cooled in the night, thinking to themselves how long it had been since so much family had been in one place. When an aunt died two years ago, Jorge, who was made legal during the amnesty, had flown home and seen sisters whose names he had forgotten. Alvaro found out about the death weeks later. She had been a favorite of his. Jorge asked his brothers to stay outside for a few minutes while he went in to check on his family, who had been asleep for hours. Chava and Alvaro stood in the awkward silence of the night, each stretching to break away the aches that were their burdens. Alvaro told Chava that he had a job waiting. Hard work, but good pay. Chava smiled, then his eyes went dark. He lit a cigarette and offered one to Alvaro, who declined. Chava asked, When was the last time you spoke to your wife, your family?

It had been longer than he wished. A month. The calls he made that he worked so long to afford went unanswered and unreturned. Despite the money he sent, his wife would have to work, and his son would be at school, and working as well. They were busy. When they sent Chava back south, he had gone to the town of their birth, where Alvaro had bought a home he never slept a night in. There is a man living with your wife, your son, Chava said, and Jorge heard this as he came back outside, three beers in his hands, spitting a low curse. Chava had not wanted to tell this to his brother, older but frailer than himself, and as he watched the light drain from Alvaro's eyes, he regretted it still, but a man needs to know such things.

The next day, Alvaro and Chava rode together to work, their manager having picked them up from Alvaro's apartment as he always did. He showed his brother the work and when they left that night, a day's worth of labor wearing on their backs, Alvaro knew he had worked his last day. When Chava went to sleep, he scribbled a quick note to his brother, leaving the apartment key and enough money to do him well for several weeks. Midnight came and, still weary, he started walking. He took Washington Street for several miles, through poverty and isolated blocks of splendor, past the train station and the dry docks, great boats bigger than homes tucked away from the coming cold. He walked through industrial blight, fields perfect for tending save the chemicals soaked through to the clay. He climbed a fence that blocked off the harbor for the night and went through the sand until he came to the dock, where he had to walk leaning forwards to brace himself against the wind. The lake was as big as the sea he had taken his wife to see so long ago. Part of him wanted to spit at the memory, but it would only blow back in his face. He had broken with his old life crossing to the north, now it was time to break with his current life.

In the desert there was nowhere to hide from the sky. It glared down at the world with hatred and hunger, but here there was more to fear. The very land was poison, picking them off slowly until there were two men. In the water it was worse. As above so it is below. He was a lone, small blur in the vastness of the world, creation looming large and uncaring around him. He kept rowing, further still, chasing the horizon, hands shaking from the cold and the fear, but he kept moving, because to stop would be a sin.

"One of my strengths in terms of the writing process is I usually tend to have a really clear idea of where I want things to start and how I want things to end. It's everything in the middle, that's the hard part most of the time."
—Booked #53 Interview with Michael Gonzalez

MICHAEL PAUL GONZALEZ
ONE SHOT (ONLY GOD KNOWS)

In less than two minutes, I will become the new Messiah. A martyr. A monster.

I'm perched on the edge of the roof at King/Drew Medical Center with hundreds of acolytes following my every move from the ground below. I'm hacking at the support cables for a 20-yard canvas banner that's just been hung on the hospital in protest. The damn thing is heavy, and it's blowing in the breeze, making slicing the ropes difficult. The sea of faces below me is distorted by that rarest of things in Los Angeles, a spring downpour. I can't tell if the roar I'm hearing is the rain, the traffic on the freeway, or their voices calling my name. Their eyes glint out at me, their mouths open, necks arched and straining to see me above them all, the whole thing is just so rapturous. What the hell am I doing?

This is our Faith, I tell them. This is our Hope, I shout above the gale. The last rope snaps and the wind takes the banner away. It's a huge replica of the little slips you get from the government-sanctioned death prediction machines. It bears an impossible message, a fate that no person could ever really receive: ONLY GOD KNOWS.

The crowd is frenzied now, arms raised, reaching, reaching. I turn as the banner continues to collapse, watching their eyes grow wider, wider. I splay my arms and point to the skies. I think only of my wife, Nadia, wondering if she'll take me back when this is all over. Security bursts through the door behind me. I tense my legs, and I leap.

★★★★★

When the machines first started telling people how they'd die, there were riots, rebellions, endless orgies in the streets. Someone knows how they're going to die, *you* try to tell them what they can and cannot do. The government stepped in, as they always do when something fun is created, and put the party down as quickly and quietly as possible. After that, we were over it in a couple of news cycles. Everything's regulated and well run now. Efficient, effective, trademarked.

A little cottage industry has taken off. Jewelers make platinum frames for necklaces, golden charm bracelets. Displaying your Fate™ is yet another part of crass cultural commercialism, which in itself is a sort of mystic religion in the United States. Sure, some people still don't want to show off their endings. The occasional embarrassing disease or sexually-related death certainly won't win you points at parties. For everyone else, death is a conversation starter. Status symbol. Another way to feel better about yourself through the misery of others.

Christians, Muslims, Jews, we believers have some serious problems on our hands. We'd always pondered the age old questions. When will I die? Where? How? The machines went a long way towards answering the first two questions, and pretty much solved the riddle of the third. How can we continue to profess faith in God when we can peek at the last page in our book?

When the government tried to enforce mandatory testing at birth, organized religion decided to push back–hard. The Vatican came down first: visiting the machines runs counter to the very idea of true faith. Anyone caught using the machine is excommunicated from the church. We all had to get ID cards and register with Mother Church, who links to government databases to ensure that her children remain pure of mind, pure of future.

Most countries in the Middle East banned the machines and placed strict travel restrictions on countries where the tests are legal. In the past, during the Haaj, Muslims traditionally threw pebbles at three black pillars in a ceremony known as the Stoning of the Devil. The ceremony now includes a symbolic treading over an effigy of the machines. Afterwards, you don't just shake the dust from your shoes, you burn them.

In the U.S., you either get your government-issued Fate™ and became part of "normal society," or you're the butt of the joke, the simple Hillbilly, the sheep following a myth. Some of us hide our faith, buying knockoff Fates™ from underground forgers (they call them Endingz or F8Z). We wear them with pride, pretending that we're like everyone else. "Yes, I'm going to be hit by a car." "Sure, I'll get a horrible case of cirrhosis someday, you betcha." I belong.

I was one of the shamed. I found a back-alley shop as quickly as I could and bought a F8Z that said PROSTATE CANCER. You can't tell it apart from the real thing. Wonderful pickup tool in the bars. I can't tell you how many times women read that slip, look me straight in the eye and call me lucky. The greater degree of predictability makes you a more ideal mate. The government issues forgery-proof Fates™ when it comes to certain things. As ambiguous as the machines are, there are the extremely rare times they spit out straightforward fortunes. If you know you'll die from old age or organ-specific cancer, you're a god among men.

At church, a different kind of movement started. People are getting an inscription on the flip side of their Endingz. Crucifixes, Stars of David, all of the religious symbols were replaced with forged Fates™ bearing the impossible legend: ONLY GOD KNOWS. I never saw myself as being strong enough to get involved in a movement. I believe in God, yes, but I can't carry the torch. I'm not the one to rally the troops. I'm the guy you can always count on to find the gray cloud for your silver lining, to help you pull defeat from the jaws of victory. The Underground tried to make me believe that I was capable of something better, something important for the future of humankind. They told me that this was my chance to make an impact on the world and leave it a better place.

Everything changes, and nothing changes.

Dear God,

Like so many things in the world, this disaster was set in motion for the love of a woman. I met my wife while attending church. She wasn't one of those "Burning for God" soldiers looking to change the world. We'd all pretty much given up on that concept. She was just the girl serving coffee in the back of the room, offering to froth it for you with a smile while the priest broke down the folding table that served as our altar and shoved it back into the storage closet. Church was now held in the basement (ironically located beneath a bar and grill that purchased and converted our former church). Anti-discrimination laws gave us the right to assemble, but with attendance dwindling, the church couldn't afford to hold on to all of its prime real estate.

We were all so scared. We felt completely left out. Everyone out there running around knowing the answer that would help them shape the rest of their lives; while we were in a moldy basement like unwanted stepchildren, staring out the windows at the sunny skies as if they were perched to fall on us at any minute. You'd think having the answer would make you nervous to step outside, but it's the not knowing that kills you.

★★★★★

"I can't do it anymore." That's Marty. He serves as our Deacon, our altar server, our usher. He's pushing sixty, and every year brings him more and more anxiety. We've been expecting him to crack. Some of us have an unofficial pool going, but we'd never say such a thing out loud. Looks like I'm about to lose five bucks. Father Patrick raises a hand to console Marty, but not too urgently. Why fight it?

"I have to know. This past week I've tripped twice. I went jogging and my heart wouldn't slow down for hours afterwards. I can't take it anymore. Bless me, Father?" Marty asks, one hand in his pocket pulling out his car keys.

"Until the moment you take the test, you're still one of us. You'll always be welcome here. But if you turn your back on your Faith–"

"How do we know these machines aren't divinely inspired? For fuck's sake, Father!" Marty recoils at his own profanity. It's an argument that many people try to make. But the Vatican III Council settled that matter long ago. We are to live life as we always have. Sickness means a visit to the doctor. If he can cure it, he will. If it's fatal, you'll find out the hard way.

"I have a polyp." His hands are on Father Patrick. Marty's eyes are covered by a sheen of water, his lower lip bouncing so hard

I think we might be having an earthquake. "They found a polyp. I'm waiting for test results. I could know in seconds. Seconds."

Father Patrick makes the sign of the cross on Marty's forehead. Marty's knees buckle and he staggers backwards towards the door, struggling to look at us as he leaves. He mutters apologies and begs forgiveness and those of us who can meet his eyes just give him a gentle nod. We know. We know.

The service, what's left of it, comes to a sloppy ending. Father Patrick approaches each of us in turn with the host, offers a closing prayer, and rushes to his desk at the back of the room. He removes his robe and grabs his coat. He hasn't taken his eyes off the floor. His face is red, angry, hopeless. He'll be back to go through this again next week, but I wonder how long he can hang on. I go to the table by the door for my traditional after-mass coffee. Nadia, usually ready with a cup for everyone, stands in the corner with a bag of coffee grounds shaking in her hand.

"Poor Marty, huh?" I ask.

"Are you doing anything after? Now?" she asks.

This is the first time she's asked me anything other than if I want sugar in my coffee. "I need to eat. A lot," she says. "Are you a good listener? Can we leave now? I need to leave. Now." Her fingers, still clutching the coffee pouch, run over the little tag on her necklace. Her nails trace the embossed letters over and over.

"Ever been to Pann's?" I ask.

★ ★ ★ ★ ★

We settle into a big horseshoe booth at Pann's Restaurant. This place has been making pitch-perfect comfort food since the 1950s. Quandaries of faith, for me, involve a hot plate of chicken and waffles. Nadia's staring down the barrel of the biggest piece of chocolate cake she's ever seen. We've been talking about local politics and the latest World Series, anything to keep our minds off the incidents of the day. Nadia takes a huge bite from the heart of her cake and watches the melting ice cream rush in to fill the void.

"Are you married?" she asks. "I mean, were you? Before it became illegal?"

"It's not illegal."

"You know what I mean." She chases a lump of chocolate ice cream around a chasm of fudgy icing in the middle of her plate. "I've been married twice."

"Really? You look so young. You can't be more than thirty-one."

"I'm twenty-six."

I've found in situations like this it's better to keep quiet until the woman starts talking again. I stuff a chicken wing in my mouth and make some appreciative grunts, suddenly fascinated by the way the syrup is coating my waffles.

"It's okay. I don't sleep. I know how I look. I mean … I know."

Now I have to finish chewing as quickly as possible to respond, steer her away from self-pity if I'm going to have a chance. It's not that I'm a letch or anything, but I haven't been on a nice date in a really long time. I pretty much swallow the whole top of the leg and grumble, "So your last marriage would have ended when you were, what, nineteen? How long has it been since they changed the laws?"

"My divorce just became final a month ago."

I sputter a bit and swallow some water. "So … you've been tested then?"

"Yeah. Yeah I took the test." This is a huge step for her to tell me. I could easily have her booted from the church. Why does she trust me with this?

"What's the result?"

She pulls the necklace from her shirt collar again and removes it, handing it across the table to me. Looking at the plate, I can see that the original Fate™ has been sandblasted from the jewelry, replaced with a crude engraving: *Only God Knows*. My heart sinks a bit. "Wait, you're a Born-Again?"

"God, no!" she laughs.

"I don't get it," I say. The Born-Again Christian movement took on a whole new meaning after the machines. People would blast their Fates™, erasing them and pledging their fate to God. They thought somewhere along the way, someone would pull it off, die in a non-prescribed manner, and the flaw of man-made technology would be exposed. They were wrong. And they quickly became a laughing stock among the layfolk and the Faithful alike. Hey, we all have to have our scapegoats. The entire movement died off within three years of the riots.

"He wanted his big dream wedding. I was only too happy to oblige. Obviously, I had to take the test to make everything legal. I never told him the results. I promised him I'd show him on our wedding night. If he loved me, he'd wait."

"So what happened?"

"I kept hedging. If he asked to see it, I'd just rip his clothes off and we'd start going at it. He'd always forget. Or at least, just let it go until the next day, week, month, whatever. It was a constant fight. So one night I showed it to him, and the next day he served me with papers."

She lets it go at that and returns to her cake. I can see her shoulders lifting slightly. This booth has become her confessional.

"So?" I ask. "What did it say?"

"You really want to know?"

"Yeah. This is intriguing. Kinda sexy. I feel like such a rebel right now."

"You men. Always after one thing." She holds her hand out for the necklace and I give it back to her.

"You know, this means we can't get married now," I say.

"We couldn't get married anyway, Churchy."

Well, she didn't freak out at the marriage joke. I'm doing okay here. I get up to pay the bill. "On that note."

She smiles a little and leans back in her seat. Her eyes dance over the geometric shapes in the restaurant. She's a completely different person. Glowing almost. I hand the cashier my credit card and try to decide my next move. Maybe she didn't need to talk about Marty after all. Something shook her up today. Was her day drawing near? Is she getting ready to die? I want to be her last happy days more than anything. That's as close to love at first sight as I suppose I'll ever get.

I saunter back to the table. "You wanna go count stars?"

"It's still daylight outside."

"Let's go."

★ ★ ★ ★ ★

We're outside of Grauman's Chinese Theater, putting our feet in the ancient footprints of silent movie stars, ducking requests for change from filthy knockoff spacemen and superheroes. I parked my car back at Sunset and Vine and we traveled the Walk of Fame to get here. Just my luck, she hates TV and only occasionally watches movies. She seems to be enjoying herself. She points to a bone-thin man wearing a Superman costume. "He kinda looks like my first husband."

"He was before the laws changed?"

"Yeah. He died on his way out of the office after receiving his Fate™. It said Suicide."

"Self-fulfilling prophecy."

"No, he didn't kill himself. Another man threw himself off the top of the building just as my husband was coming out. Ironically, the man lived, but Paul didn't make it."

"That's horrible!"

"Yeah. Wouldn't it be cool if it actually happened?" She smiles and nudges me in the ribs before running away to step on Jimmy Durante's noseprint.

The rest of the afternoon is pure magic. It turns out her first husband ran off to New York and she hadn't heard from him in years. After a lot of legal wrangling, she'd gotten out of the marriage. She met her second husband just as the riots started. They'd gotten stuck on a bus when the driver insisted that his Fate™ allowed him to drive to each stop at sixty miles an hour. He knew he'd die in a plane crash, and decided he had license to go crazy. After he wrapped the bus around the base of the Santa Monica Pier, Nadia and her man stumbled off into the future together. Luckily for me, things didn't work out.

We stop for dinner at an amazing Creole restaurant off Crenshaw. The subject of her nerves that morning never comes up. Neither does the true inscription on her Fate™. Somewhere between the Gumbo and the Shrimp Po'Boy sandwich, it's decided that I'll be going to her apartment to meet her puppy. Going to work tomorrow will not be an option. As long as she's alive, I'm living for her. If I can discover when she's checking out, I can plan our next date …

★★★★★

I wake up in a snap in a dark unfamiliar room. Halogen light slices across the carpet through venetian blinds. Our clothes are scattered around the room, and we're not facing the same direction in bed. I see Knuckles, her Rottweiler puppy, burrowed into my pantleg, his fuzzy bottom sticking out, legs splayed. The denim rises and falls with each of his little puppy snores. Nadia's arms are covering her head. Her brow is wrinkled in concentration, her left temple twitching. Each time her chest rises, the light catches the edge of her necklace. I swivel around slowly in the bed so as not to wake her. My face is inches from her chest. My eyes are adjusting to the minimal light. I know it's wrong to peek. I know if she wakes up now, it could spell the end of our relationship.

The Fate™ is real enough, evidenced by the remnant of the government holographic seal on the edge. If I'm seeing that, then the necklace is facing the wrong way. I reach a finger out to try to turn the necklace over. The early Fates™ were embossed from the rear. Regardless of what she blasted off the front, there should be a perfect negative impression of the word on the back. Nadia rolls away from me, then just as quickly changes direction and wraps herself around me. Her eyes crack open to narrow slits, deep black shining pools.

"Just ask," she whispers. "But not now. Please."

Her right hand snakes around the chain and lifts the necklace over her head. She tosses it and throws a perfect ringer around the puppy's tail. Knuckles gives one half-hearted wag and falls back asleep.

Four hours later, her alarm goes off and she's out of the bed like it's spring-loaded. She's not much for morning conversation. She's fully dressed before I even have my socks on. Her only words to me are about clothes and hurrying up. She throws a handful of dog food into a dish by the door and we're both out in the hallway in the bright light of day, staring at each other.

"Thanks," she says. "Thank you so much."

I manage to make a low guttural noise before she presses her mouth against mine, pinning me back against the door. Then she's off like a shot. I don't know her phone number, her last name. I barely know her address. I have to wait until Sunday to see her again, if she comes back to church at all.

★★★★★

Dear God,

A month of lonely Sundays with no coffee after service. Services are thirty minutes of talk, buzzing in my ears, up-down-up-hug-handshake-communion-prayer-time to go. Don't get me wrong. I spend at least an hour a week in prayerful meditation. But the absence of Nadia at church weighs too heavily on me. The empty space in the back of the room glows, pulses, screams. I can't focus on anything else. Father Patrick approaches me after mass near where the coffee should have been.

"Lost another one, did we?" he asks.

I shrug. "I'm not so sure. You heard anything about Marty?"

"I gotta go to the bakery over on Larchmont. You busy right now?"

My afternoon slate's clean, so I help Father Patrick clean up the church, and we head up the stairs.

"Sorry the table was so sticky. They had a leaky keg upstairs. Drained right into our storage closet."

"I thought the host smelled a little malty today."

"That was probably me. I was mopping that mess up for hours before you all arrived. The tabernacle stayed dry, praise God for small miracles." We open the doors at the top of the stairs and step into the blazing morning sunlight.

"Great smog day today. Look at that. Can't even see Mount Hollywood." Father Patrick is a little bulldog of a man, angrily trying to save a society that marginalizes his existence. His hairline is receding, his shoulders are constantly stooped, and his face is wrinkled. For all of that, he's still a welcoming presence. Once a month, we walk to the Village Bakery. Father Patrick gives me updates on the woes of the church, the decline of the city, and the end of civilization as we know it. I always leave feeling much better about my position in life.

"Have you talked to Nadia?" he asks.

"Not since Marty left."

"That's twice now you've mentioned him. I didn't think you two were so close."

"We weren't. Nobody could look him in the eye. I feel like he said what we were all thinking. So what are we doing every Sunday, Father?"

He falls silent for a moment as we cross Beverly and head for Larchmont. "Remembering. Always remembering. Out here, everyone thinks we're just a bunch of nostalgic fools pining for the old days. But they're the ones who've forgotten, and that's the easy way out. The easy answers aren't answers at all. Medical science has gotten better and better, but the public doesn't want cures. They want placebos. The less thinking they have to do, the better."

"So you think this is just a phase?"

"I think it's a step in a new direction. Things get shaken up, then they settle down. Nothing really changes. So you *remember*. That's what makes us special. We don't run from the past. We don't hide from the future. Right?"

I want to agree with him, I really do, but I stay silent.

"Look at it this way. Every Sunday, I present the Host. I say what Jesus said—this is my body. Not was my body. Not *represents* how my body used to be. It's present. It's alive. It's hard to get a hold of, even harder to wrap your mind around the concept. I know I haven't been able to do it. But I know that I'm getting there. Enough to know I don't need a silly machine to tell me how I'm going to die, because I don't care. I care about how I'm going to live."

He's done it again. My face breaks into a wide smile, and Father Patrick knows, without saying a word, the comfort he's brought me. He slaps me on the shoulder. "I'm buying." We turn into the little storefront and settle onto two stools, and we break bread together. I am satisfied.

★ ★ ★ ★ ★

The fifth Sunday, everything is different. I had a rough morning, and now it's evening mass. I never go to evening mass. Even before everything changed, they had the lowest attendance on Sunday nights. And now, I'm lucky if I'm not the only one in there. I'm circling the block to find a parking space, and someone waves at me from the corner. I slow down and she approaches my car. Nadia.

"Let's go to the observatory," she says.

I stare at her.

"Why didn't you give me your phone number?" she says.

She's kidding. She has to be kidding. I run through several witty ripostes in my mind, reject them all. I lean over and pop the door open for her and she scrambles in, bringing in the smell of chocolate and perfume.

"Just drive. I'll tell you as much as I can, and hopefully by the time we get to the observatory, you'll still feel like talking to me."

She fidgets with her hands for a while as we drive. She seems to have lost weight, and looks like she's given up on sleep. "You're going to kill me," she says.

"I thought we had something. I like you," I reply. "You can talk to me, you know? I won't–"

She thrusts a piece of folded paper into my hands. It looks old, well-worn and shiny. I try to open it at the first red light, but she covers my hand. "Wait until we get there."

Thirty minutes later, we're cresting the last hill in Griffith Park. I park on the street leading to the observatory so we can walk the last little part. Great view of the city when the smog isn't covering everything. "You can see the ocean today."

She looks out to the water, just a sliver of shining land, orange in the dying sunlight. I unfold the paper as she looks away. It's a rubbing done in pencil, a small rectangular shape with words surrounded by ghostly white lines. SHOT BY YOUR HUSBAND.

"Hooboy." It's the only word that comes to my mind, so I repeat it a few times. "Well. This isn't so bad, right?" If she'd have told me she was pregnant and kicked me in the balls, I'd probably be feeling less surprised right now. She turns around, tears in her eyes.

"I mean, we just don't get married," I try again.

"The machine is never wrong. I'm going to be murdered. Maybe not by you. But I get married and I get murdered."

Call me crazy, but I know this is one of those now or never moments. Sure, the Fate™ isn't looking so hot, but I'm a man in love. "I don't own a gun. I'll never own a gun. I swear. I'll put one on layaway, and then, when we're ninety years old, decrepit, miserable, falling apart, I'll shoot you. How's that?"

"Is this supposed to make me feel better?" She starts to walk up the path towards the observatory, arms crossed over her chest.

"Yes!" I follow her. "Besides, I don't even want to marry you. Yet."

"I can't see you anymore."

"No. You brought me up here so I could give you a reason to keep seeing me. If you wanted to break up, you would have done that by the church."

"You think you know so much–"

"I know you can't just run away from your fate."

"Now you believe in Fates?" Her eyes are wild, wide and shining. "That's a little un-Christian, don't you think?"

"What can I say? I'm a progressive guy."

She goes quiet again, and we walk in silence up the stairs to the roof of the observatory, around the towers to the overlook. Los Angeles spreads below us, evening lights starting to spark to life. She pulls her necklace from the front of her shirt and unhooks it, dangling the pendant between her fingers. She rears back and throws it over the edge. We watch it sail down, twisting ever so slightly before snagging in a bush next to a condom wrapper and a grocery sack. We're silent, the traffic below us like a dull roaring tide.

"How's Knuckles?" I ask.

She seizes me. I can't tell if she's trying to push me, hug me, or stop herself from falling down. Her fingers dig into my back and I feel her knees buckle against mine. I stoop and support her, stroking her hair, not knowing what comes next.

★★★★★

Dear God,

A month later and everything is pretty okay. We've been dating, not mentioning anything about getting serious. I'll skip over the petty little details of our lives together, because I have to tell you about the part where we fuck up and get married. I say that like it's a bad thing, but really it was the greatest thing that ever happened to either of us. Nadia, well, you know what happened to Nadia.

The Sunday after visiting the observatory, we're back in the basement church like nothing happened. Father Patrick is happy to see Nadia back in church, and since L.A. is what it is, there are no questions as to where she's been or why she was gone. The service is short and sweet, and I take confessional afterwards. Father Patrick offers to hear my confession on the way to the bakery, but I have to decline. I want to spend the afternoon with Nadia, so I ask if we can stay at church.

"I hate doing this here," Father Patrick grumbles. "Smells like beer and mothballs back there."

"Thank you, Father," I smile.

He gives me a curt nod as he shoves his way into the supply closet. He sets a small kneeler just outside the door. "If I hear one crack about me going into or coming out of this closet, you'll be saying Hail Mary until sunset." He picks up a sheet of lace, holding it between us. "Is this going to be a short one or a long one?" he asks.

"Indulge me," I say.

He grunts and uses two clothespins to hang the lace on the door. I can barely make out his shape as he leans back against the wall. "Batter up," he says.

"Forgive me Father for I have sinned," I begin. "It has been three weeks since my last confession."

"Three weeks? Have you been going to confession somewhere else?"

"All right, three months. What, was it Christmas?"

"At least. But I get the idea. Continue, my son."

"I'm in love, Father."

"Not a sin, last I heard."

"I know something about her. Something that ... I think I need to get tested, Father."

"Ah, not you too. You're my rock ..." He clears his throat. "Remember what I told you on our last walk? Living for the moment? Your love will be so much stronger without these need-less fears attached. You don't need the test, you've passed the test! God loves you and He'll give you what you need. Besides, I'm not here to preemptively absolve you of sin. What have you done lately that's bad?"

He's trying to catch me out here. He does this every time. I never feel like I've done anything that requires an apology to God. This may also be one of the reasons I feel my life has been so meaningless. I hear him drumming his fingers against his legs, jangling change in his pocket. After what feels like an eternity of soul-searching silence, he peeks his head around the edge of the curtain.

"You're a good kid. Your head's screwed on right. Don't worry so much, and stay on the narrow path." He takes down the curtain and folds it neatly. "And speaking of, I have a path to walk–straight to the donut shop. You sure you don't wanna come?"

I shake my head. He pulls a baseball cap from the top shelf and jams it on, closing the door behind him. "Thank you, son."

I nod. "Not getting too many people in confession lately?"

He looks me up and down. "You'll be okay. God reads your heart. If He sees what I'm seeing, you'll be fine."

With that, he's on his way. Nadia's near the door, kneeling before a tiny plaster Mary on a shelf. She finishes her prayer and stands. "Feel better?"

"Loads," I lie.

It's been eating at me for weeks. This oracular machine has never been known for giving spot-on predictions about life in general, but if my Fate™ said SELF-INFLICTED GUNSHOT WOUND, I could almost rejoice. A murder/suicide would be great. Maybe it's a hunting accident. I'm cleaning a gun, it goes off, hits her, I'm so filled with remorse I turn the gun on myself. Maybe it's just the fact that she knows and I don't. If my Fate™ says HEART ATTACK, maybe I die young, well before her, and it's only after she remarries that she's murdered. These are the thoughts that keep me up at night. I want to talk to her about it, but I don't want to upset her by bringing up the future.

I bring it up anyway. "I want to get tested." We're at the beach, and I'm ruining our relaxation.

"We're not getting married."

"Maybe I want to know for me."

"I think you want to know for me. It's a disappointing experience. You won't like it. You don't need it. Let's just be happy right now, okay?"

She stretches her hand across the towel to me, and I wrap her fingers in mine. "You happy?" she asks. "Because I'm happy."

Something dances right behind her eyes. It's not happiness. It's nerves, I think she's getting near her breaking point too. She wants to know. Are we getting married? Am I the guy who shoots her?

"Would you get angry if I got tested?"

"Yes. It's not who you are."

"I'm not sure if I know who I am. I might be the guy that shoots you."

"Only God Knows."

"Yeah …"

I can't commit to her until I commit to myself. I know this test is a one shot, all or nothing deal. There's no going back. Sort of like murder. Some commandments just shouldn't be broken. I tell myself that God would understand this. But I wonder if He's trying to get me to understand something else, something greater.

Two kids race along the water's edge, kites in tow. A boy and a girl, they don't look related. She's three steps behind him and catching up fast. He's too busy looking at her to see that he's drifting closer to the water. As soon as his foot hits the cold ocean, he jolts, dives to the side. Their kites tangle, a rapid tango in the air, a death spiral that sends them both into the water, soaked, bent and broken.

Nadia takes my hand. "We should get going."

"Wait," I say.

Coming down shore to help the kids out is a man we both know. Marty. He lifts up the boy, who's crying because the girl's affection turned to rage immediately after the crash. Nadia sees him too and shouts his name in spite of herself.

Marty looks at us and a broad grin breaks over his face. "Holy shit!" He sets the boy down and shoos him back towards the crashed kites. A titanic struggle ensues between the two kids, seeing who will get thrown into the watery abyss. In the moment, we don't care. It's Marty, and he's alive and well.

"How are you two doing?"

"Us? How about you?" I ask.

"Never better. Never better!"

"Did you … uh …"

"The test? Oh. Changed my life. Completely changed my outlook on everything."

Marty thrusts a small card into my hand. I unfold it. It's not his Fate™, but rather a business card for a testing center on Sepulveda. The address burns into my mind instantly, the 999 building. We always joke that it's the portal to the dark abyss. You have to travel upside-down to the roof and you're plunged into Satan's home. Never thought I'd have a reason to see it from the inside.

"If you're ever thinking about doing it, and I'm not pressuring you at all—wouldn't want to proselytize—that's the place to go!" Nadia's eyes track the card all the way into my pocket.

There's the silent command in her eyes: you're throwing that away when we leave.

Marty's obviously busy with the kids, and after some awkward small talk, we part ways and head back to the car. I give the card to Nadia and she throws it away before we've even gotten off the sand.

★ ★ ★ ★ ★

Ten o'clock the next morning, and I'm supposed to be at work, but I'm in a tiny corner office at the 999 building. There's not much here, three government-issue chairs. A window in the wall where a bored clerk sits. A small steel gray box at the front of the counter, just the right size to insert your hand. Your future in a metal nutshell.

I approach the counter and the clerk notices my necklace. "Only God Knows. You're one of them, huh?"

"Something like that."

"You lose your faith or something?"

"Something like that," I repeat. "Fell in love with a girl."

"Yikes."

"Yeah. Yikes. There's a question I need answered."

"You a good Christian?"

"I've been going to church in a dingy basement pretty much every week since the riots. Christ the Redeemer. That's not gonna change after today."

"Hey, you don't have to prove nothing to me. This ain't confession," he smirks. "Hand in the box, champ."

He opens the lid on the steel trap. There's an indentation for your index finger, a tiny hole under that where the needle comes through. I hold my breath and lay my hand inside. Thinking about this too much will just make it harder.

The instant my finger touches down, I feel the jab. I draw my hand back instinctively.

"Stings a little, don't it?" the clerk chuckles.

"Thanks for the warning."

"It'll all be over in a second."

I sit at a chair, absently pull a rosary from my pocket and start praying for forgiveness. Jesus, Mary, and Joseph. They'll understand this. Right? God will be okay with this, I tell myself. He knew I'd do this.

"All done," the clerk extends his hand over the counter. "Nice rosary. You might want to loosen up on it before you pop a bead."

I'm clenching it so tightly that there's a bloodless white cross indented in my palm. My little anti-stigmata. I take the piece of paper from the clerk. "So do I take this to an engraver for the official necklace or…"

"Read it out loud," he replies.

I unfold the paper. I laugh. This guy's some kind of prankster. "Only God Knows?"

"Hey, praying like that, you passed our test."

"Your … what?"

"Hold it up to the light."

I raise the paper up, and there, watermarked into the sheet, is the legend: *Fight for your Future!* with an address printed beneath.

"Memorize that. When you have it, slide the paper back to me. Next meeting's Tuesday night. Come alone, and bring snacks."

I check the address again and hand the paper back to him. He takes it and snaps the window shut in my face. Another client has arrived, and this is obviously not the kind of thing to discuss openly.

★★★★★

Tuesday night comes. I leave Nadia at home with a lame excuse about joining a company bowling league. The address is a tiny office building on Gower, a door tucked neatly between two shops in a strip mall. The door opens onto a well-lit stairway. I hear voices at the top.

"Come on up and close the door behind you."

Marty meets me at the door and my indoctrination begins. Long story short, after an initial test period to prove my worthiness, I'm inducted into a radical Christian underground movement to overthrow the machines. We're all guinea pigs. When you're indoctrinated, you get a Fate™ buddy. The test at the 999 building was only the beginning. The clerk takes the actual fate from the machine and seals it for the leader of the cell. The leader then goes on to assign someone else in the cell as your protector. The Guardian Angel Network. This guy or gal's sole mission is to help you die in a way other than what the machine predicted. You never get to find out what your real fate is until it catches up to you. So far, the machine is still batting a thousand. But if this experiment works, if the Underground can find a chink in the armor, expose the machine as being flawed, then we can shut the whole thing down.

Recently, we've started placing operatives into testing centers all over the city. They've been giving out false readings. Making people live pre-Fate™ lives, however unknowingly. The Machine might predict a stabbing for you, but we'll give you a slip that says DROWNING. The hope is that when one of these deaths occurs, someone connected will sue the government and the makers of the machine for such a grievous error. It could buy us months, even years, of machine-free living. And in that time, we could change society. Save the world.

★ ★ ★ ★ ★

Marty blows it for me a few weeks later by calling the house. She knows that I've been tested. Doesn't believe a word I say about the Underground, so I bring her to the next meeting. Foolish, yes. Blind trust. But she doesn't let me down. She jumps in whole-heartedly. The best part is our little inside joke, our way of side-stepping her fate. Marty introduces her as my wife. With any luck, the label will stick. A marriage without a marriage. I'm not really her husband, but as far as everyone else knows, we're June and Ward Cleaver. Catholics don't believe in government marriage anymore. Small church ceremonies are good enough for us now. We tell Father Patrick that it was a spur of the moment Vegas thing, we never meant to offend him. He's just happy we're together.

We spend the first month in the underground planting "Only God Knows" stickers at strategic points around town. Nadia even applies for a job at one of the major testing facilities, she'll be our mole. The underground is planning to forge work papers for her, but what they don't realize is that she's already got the perfect in. She's unmarried (on paper anyway), and fully tested with a fate that won't adversely affect her job performance.

She lands a job at one of the larger testing centers within a week. We celebrate by returning to Pann's for dessert. As soon as we're comfortably ensconced in our meals, I ask her how she feels about this whole project.

"I think it's the right thing to do. I don't feel right saying it's doing God's work, but it's as close as I'll ever get. I can't imagine how much happier my life could have been if I'd never known …"

She reaches out and touches my hand. She tells me that she's happier than she's ever been, but more afraid with each day. I try to comfort her, comfort myself against our knowledge of what's to come. By the time we're home, the whole conversation is forgotten. We're completely wrapped up in each other, making love in the living room. I caress her stomach and breasts, telling her that I'll keep her safe.

I rub her breasts again, and she laughs. I rub them again, paying more attention to the left one.

"Little fixated tonight, are we?"

I look up into her eyes. "Does this spot feel funny to you?"

★ ★ ★ ★ ★

Dear God,

Three of the worst months of my life later and everything has gone to hell. Nadia has breast cancer. Near her nipple, which ironically enough, is just the tip of the iceberg. When the doctors run further tests, they find evidence that the disease has gone malignant and systemic. Her ovaries are under attack. Her lymph nodes are decimated. Her spine, upon further tests, may also be harboring a surprise for her. I'm devastated. She's dying. I'm elated. She's a miracle. The Fates™ are wrong. She's going to die from cancer.

Medical science has made some major leaps, but none of them are keeping up with Nadia. Some of the hospital staff seem to think that she waited too long to get treated. Others insist that she should be showing signs of recovery, but her cancer is defying explanation, moving faster than anything they've ever seen. They get more aggressive with the chemo, and she looks more like a skeleton every day.

She doesn't want to beat the disease. It kills me to see her there in bed, her kerchief knotted just above where her eyebrows used to be. Her cheeks are sunken, her lips thinner, bags under her eyes. She's so beautiful. I don't want her to die. I don't know how to tell her. I know one thing for damn sure. I'm not buying a gun anytime soon. And she's not getting married to anyone else anytime soon. We say goodnight as we have every week since she got here.

"You're sure you didn't fake that test?"

"Positive," she answers. "You're supposed to shoot me. Don't."

"Say please," I smile.

"Pleeeeease," she rasps. When she swallows her throat clicks.

I kiss the back of her hand, just where the IV goes in, and tell her I love her.

"Tell the group."

"No. I don't want this to turn into a media circus."

"This isn't about what you want," she says. "Or what I want. I don't want to die. But I have to do this. God is trying to tell us something. The world has to watch this. Tell Father Patrick to unseal my true test."

"I'll see you tomorrow."

"Tell them!" she shouts, tensing her teeth as a wave of pain hits her.

I nod and walk out, hitting the lights on the way. I pull my rosary from my pocket and start reciting the Mysteries as the elevator comes to take me back down to earth.

★ ★ ★ ★ ★

The start of the next meeting, Father Patrick has good news for me.

"You're legally married now! We ran a fake test for you over at Lab 6 on Crenshaw, submitted all of your paperwork. You can go see her whenever you want. You'll be our eyes and ears at the time of God's visitation!"

The hospital would deny me access if it ever came out that we weren't legally married, so that matter is settled now. "That's great," I murmur. "Aren't you worried I'm going to shoot her?"

"I can read your heart, son. No need, right? Right?" He slugs me on the shoulder.

Father Patrick has really taken the bull by the horns with Nadia's case. He doesn't even know that she's been married before. He's had vigils going day and night outside the hospital, and while it's not out of control yet, it's starting to feel like they're putting up the big top over at the news channels.

The government quietly sends someone in to test Nadia every week on several different machines to verify that her fate is CANCER. There's never been a false positive, they say. I know from my last few visits that they're starting to eye me very suspiciously, which tells me they're getting the answer that they're supposed to have: SHOT BY YOUR HUSBAND.

They want to take her out of the hospital for further testing, but we refuse, and the church steps in to start a legal battle. The government has no reason to conduct further tests, they know what her Fate™ says, and they'll have to sit back and watch like the rest of us.

Through it all, Nadia tries to be brave. She's nothing now, a paper doll in a paper gown, pale green with raised veins. She jokes that she could get a senior discount at the movies. I only talk to her for about an hour a day now. It's all the time she can manage before she has to kick on the morphine. The cancer has shriveled her internal organs to nothing, but she's hanging on despite her best efforts.

I make my way to her room, greeted by two armed security guards. They frisk me, wand me, and have me step through a metal detector three times. Once they're satisfied I'm not packing heat, they let me through. I open the door, and Nadia's got a rubber swim cap on, big rubber flowers. Swim goggles rest over her eyes, and she's got flippers on her feet.

"Wanna go swimming?" she asks me.

"What's all this?"

"I asked the nurse for it. I've been watching the news, all of those idiot reporters giving monologues about how I'm trying to die with dignity. I'll show them. This is how I want them to wheel me out of this place."

A single tear rolls down her cheek, and her eyes close. I feel like it's taken all of her energy just to give me that. Her eyes still shut, she says, "I don't want this. I don't want to die. I don't want this fate; I don't want any of it. Stay here. Lie down next to me. It can't be much more than a day now."

I curl up next to her and we spend the afternoon talking about all of the crazy adventures we've had. I assure her Knuckles is fine, busily chewing his way through most of her apartment. Between sentences, she makes little whining noises in her throat, as if every heartbeat is torture. All I can do is hold her hand and pray. We say the Rosary together. On our tenth Hail Mary, we're interrupted by commotion in the hall. The guards are shouting. I'm on my feet, in between Nadia and the door. The door opens a crack and the sounds of shouting intensify. With a horrendous crash, a man slides through the door on his back, dressed in a tattered orderly uniform, a camera in his hand.

"Carlos Ruben reporting live from the hospital room of God's Miracle Cancer Lady, Nadia—" That's as far as he gets before guards and nurses hustle in and slam him to the floor with authority. He starts screaming about freedom of the press. The guards aren't hearing any of it. He grabs onto the shelves and drawers, fighting to stay in the room. He picks up medical supplies and throws them at the guards, grabs the nurses by the shoulders. He's shouting questions the whole time. "Nadia, how do you feel? Nadia tell us what it's like! Are you in pain? Are you happy with your cancer? Are you afraid of God?"

The guards have him by the hair and the waistband of his pants, hogtied and trussed. He's out the door, his questions still trailing down to us: Are you angry at God? Did you bring this on yourself? Does your husband own a gun?

Seconds later, more nurses are in the room, making sure everything's okay. It's not. Nadia is turning blue, her arms tremor against her sides. Her eyes grow wide, blinking as if she's seeing that bright light. Her back spasms and she starts to scream. The goggles slide from her face and the flippers kick off. I want to pull the swim cap off her head, but I stop myself. She calls my name, over and over. Reaches for me. I hold her hand, determined to be here for her until the end. The nurses and doctors work around me, check her vitals, give her shots. She bucks as the needles enter her skin.

I'm completely numb. One of the nurses tries to escort me from the room, and she gets me as far as the door. I grab the door frame. *I'm her husband, damn it*, I scream. I have to be here. I need to see this. She deserves to have me here. Cold steel saps the back of my head, and I drop to the floor.

★ ★ ★ ★ ★

Later, not sure how much later, I'm in a chair next to Nadia. She's perfectly still, eyes closed, lips slack. There's a knot on the back of my head. A doctor's face appears at the edge of my vision. She looks me in the eyes. "Security got a little overzealous. One guard late to the scene. He thought you were the scumbag from earlier. It's all over now."

"Nadia? Nadia!" I try to stand up, race to her, but the Doctor holds me down with a gentle hand.

"She's stable. All of the excitement was a little much for her."

I notice a slight rise and fall in her chest. She's breathing. I slump back, tears in my eyes. "I'm staying here."

"Hey, I wasn't going to ask you to leave. I've been through this once myself, maybe not on your scale. I'm on your side on this one. You were only out for a few minutes. A nurse will be here to clean up the mess in about ten minutes."

I nod and the doctor slides from the room. Nadia's alive. She's still here. The room looks like a grenade went off. Cabinets are torn open, pills and syringes are scattered across the floor. I start absentmindedly picking up the room, stuffing everything into my pockets; pills, paper, medicine, vials, it needs to be clean in here for her. As soon as the door clicks shut, Nadia's eyes snap open and focus on me. "Heyyyy," she slurs. "I feel like I'm drowning. Pressure. Pressure." She tries to motion to her chest.

We're alone, just me and the whistling pant of Nadia's breathing. "He's not coming," she croaks. "He's not coming for me. Help me, please!"

I wrap my hands around hers, and look into her eyes. Leaning forward I tell her to let go. Just let go.

"I breathe and it stabs me. I move and it slices. I can't be still. It won't let me be still."

I lie across her chest, feeling her arms beneath me, her fingers dancing under my stomach. Flicking at something in my pockets. I reach in and pull out my rosary, wrapped around pill packets, prescription slips, and two syringes. Epinephrine. Nadia sees it and her lower lip trembles. I try to stuff them back in my pocket, but Nadia seizes my wrist.

"My God …" she says. "It is you. He's been waiting on you …"

I grip the syringes tighter. It's a quick inject vial. Nothing to it. Pre-loaded. Snap the cap back and inject. Just give her a shot and end it.

"I love you," she says. Her eyes close and her mouth tightens. "Break my heart. Please."

"I can't do this," I say.

"Only God Knows. God always knows." She's said what she needs to say. I could try to walk away from this, try to let nature run its course, but I know it won't happen.

★ ★ ★ ★ ★

Dear God,

I'm climbing the stairwell to the roof. I've run these events through my head for You, just for You, to make sure we're okay. I think I've done what I'm supposed to do, Your modern unwitting Abraham. I finger the scalpel in my pocket, another remnant of the scuffle. Several floors below me, Nadia has checked out of the hospital. I can't say it was easy, or pretty, or quick, or painless. It was horrible. The most horrible thing I've ever done. She's with You now, I know that in my soul. You hold her tightly to Your heart. Free from pain, secure in the knowledge of Life, the Universe, and Everything. No more questions to answer. No more fear. No more Fates™. Just peace and quiet.

I take out my cell phone and dial Father Patrick. When he answers, I tell him I'm on the roof above the banner. They put it up just before I got to Nadia's room. The sight of it now makes me numb. I tell him it's over. He shouts the good news to the crowd. A cheer erupts, spontaneous Hallelujahs and songs of praise. No, I tell him. The machines won. They're right. We were wrong. We've been wrong about so many things. But he can't hear me. I spot him in the crowd and I wave to him. He waves back, gesticulating to the crowd, pointing me out. They begin to chant my name. I quickly kneel with the scalpel and saw through one of the ropes of the banner. The sky has grown dim and it begins to rain.

I hack at the last support cable. The damn banner is heavy, and it's blowing in the breeze, making slicing the ropes difficult. The sea of faces below me distorts under the sheets of rain. I can't tell if the roar I'm hearing is the rain, the traffic on the freeway, or their voices calling my name. Their eyes glint out at me, their mouths open, necks arched and straining to see me here above them all, the whole thing is just so rapturous.

This is our Faith, I tell them. This is our Hope, I shout above the gale. The last rope snaps and the wind takes the banner. ONLY GOD KNOWS. The words float above the faithful, and they'll never know just how right they are and how wrong they are.

Father Patrick consults with a doctor at the edge of the crowd. Police cars are approaching. The news spreads through the crowd like a virus. Nadia is dead. Dead by my hands.

They're frenzied now, arms raised, reaching, reaching. I turn as the banner continues to collapse, watching their eyes grow wider, wider. I splay my arms and point to the skies. I think only of Nadia. Security bursts through the door behind me. I tense my legs, and I leap.

It's amazing how slowly time seems to move. All of these details seem so sharp and clear now. These last few months of my life that, for me, have been my entire life. This has been my prayer. This moment was as close to true communion with You as I'll ever get. I'm sorry for everything I've done and failed to do.

The crowds below are so close, their arms upraised. Maybe to catch me. Maybe to pull me down. I've done everything I was meant to do. I close my eyes and let fate run its course.

I lift my eyes to the sky as the clouds show just the slightest break of blue above me.

Goodbye Nadia.

See you soon.

AFTERWORD
BY LIVIUS NEDIN

THERE IT IS. 25 distinct voices, all pulled from the multitude of authors who have been guests on our podcast.

We never expected to publish a book. We set out to talk about books because it sounded like fun. Meeting hundreds of new people, traveling the country to appear at events, and interviewing some of our favorite authors have tipped us over into a new realm of fun. We have been lucky enough to make connections and form friendships with writers and listeners all over the world. And now, with this book, we hope to connect with readers too.

A dedicated reader is a special kind of creature. Every medium of art has its fans, but the disciples of writing can take it to another level. You spend more time, offer more experiences, listen more closely to the experiences of others, and you hoard more content than most nonreaders. I've seen backlists of to-be-read books in the hundreds. Stacks lining the walls next to stuffed bookcases, and e-readers loaded with thousands of titles. And somehow you seem never to lose interest in talking about each one at length. It's that passion that has fueled our podcast, and we hope this collection sparks all the things that we admire about you.

We owe our success to you. As a special treat, we've put together a hidden episode of Booked. It's not accessible from our home page and you won't find it on iTunes. But hidden deep in the dark recesses of our website, just for you–reader–is an episode too crazy for nonreaders to handle.

Secret URL: www.bookedpodcast.com/von

Now, you can stop reading.

–Liv

ACKNOWLEDGMENTS

The Booked. Anthology team would like to thank the following:

ManArchy Masthead, Denise Brown, Todd Brown, Chantal Burns, Brayton Cameron, Mlaz Corbier, Chris Deal, Pete Goutis, Amanda Gowin, Gretchen Grajales, Mac Heller-Ogden, Gordon Highland, Anthony David Jacques, Michael Khayat, Jesse Lawrence, Cameron Pierce, Roger Sarao and Craig Wallwork.

–Robb Olson, Livius Nedin, Pela Via and Sean Ferguson

CONTRIBUTORS

TW BROWN is tucked away in the Pacific Northwest with his Border Collie and a very supportive wife who let him walk away from the daily grind to pursue his dream of being a writer. His Zomblog and *Dead* series have both managed to sneak into the Amazon Horror Best Seller's List.

CRAIG CLEVENGER is the author of two novels, *The Contortionist's Handbook* and *Dermaphoria*, and is currently at work on his third. He divides his time between San Francisco and the Mojave desert, though he much prefers the desert.

CHRIS DEAL is a North Carolinian in the Midwest. His debut collection of short fiction, *Cienfuegos*, was originally issued by Brown Paper Publishing and was republished by KUBOA Press. He has been in several anthologies, including *Warmed and Bound* and *You're Dead and I Killed You*.

JOSHUA ALAN DOETSCH was grown from an experimental pumpkin patch by Monsanto scientists in a top secret biotech project known only as "Agent Orange." He was genetically designed, honed, and perfected to do only two things: write stories and strangle baby otters. Please, please encourage his writing career at joshuadoetsch.com

CHRISTOPHER J DWYER is a writer from Boston, MA. His 2011 novel from the now-defunct Brown Paper Publishing, *When October Falls*, skirted the edges of noir and science fiction. His stories have appeared in numerous magazines and literary outlets. *Sixteen Small Deaths*, his new short fiction collection from Perfect Edge Books, will be released in mid-2013, and will feature stories spanning his nearly seven-year career as a writer. He can be reached through his official website, www.christopherjdwyer.com or via Twitter at @chrisjdwyer

SEAN P FERGUSON is a public servant. Please, send him money. He's been published at *Cellar Door*, *Colored Chalk*, *Nefarious Muse*, and in *Warmed and Bound: A Velvet Anthology*. He lives in New Jersey. Please, send him a lot of money.

MATTHEW C FUNK is a social media consultant, an editor of *Needle Magazine* and a staff writer for *Planet Fury*. Winner of the 2010 Spinetingler Award for Best Short Story on the Web, Funk has work featured at dozens of sites and in printed volumes, indexed on his web domain, matthewfunk.net

MICHAEL PAUL GONZALEZ lives and writes in Los Angeles. He is the editor at ThunderDomeMag.com, an online lit zine and small press. He is at work on his next novel as you read this. Seriously. He probably just rattled off a really amazing chapter, and some day you'll read it and think back to this moment, and exhale.

AMANDA GOWIN lives in the foothills of Appalachia with her husband and son. Her work has appeared in various anthologies and magazines online and in print. She is co-editor of *The Cipher Sisters* anthology and features author interviews at *Curiouser and Curiouser*. Information on her life and work can be found at lookatmissohio.wordpress.com. She has always written and always will.

NIKKI GUERLAIN lives in Portland, Oregon. She holds a B.S. in Fine Arts and a J.D. in B.S. She shares a birthday with Emily Dickinson and Meg White which means she rocks through dictionaries like you wouldn't believe. Her writing appears both online and in print. For more information, please go to nikkiguerlain.com

SETH HARWOOD is the proud father of a new baby girl. This spring, his novels *Young Junius*, *This Is Life* and *In Broad Daylight* will be released by Thomas & Mercer. Find more info at sethharwood.com

KEVIN LYNN HELMICK is the author of *Clovis Point*, *Sebastian Cross*, *Heartland Gothic*, and *Driving Alone*. Shorter works have appeared in *Pulp Metal Magazine*, *Noir at the Bar 2*, *Spinetingler* and *Manarchy Mag*. In the spring of 2012 Helmick signed with Blank Slate Press for the novella, *Driving Alone*, a dark, modernist, southern gothic.

GORDON HIGHLAND is the author of the novels *Flashover* and *Major Inversions*, with short stories in such publications/anthologies as *Noir at the Bar 2*, *Warmed and Bound*, *In Search of a City*, and *Solarcide*, among others. He lives in the Kansas City area, where he makes videos by day and music by night. Visit him at gordonhighland.com

ANTHONY DAVID JACQUES is an American author and freelance journalist. His fiction writing ranges from mainstream to transgressive, and has been published both online and in print. Currently living in the Caribbean, he teaches Gemology by day and still finds time to maintain his journalistic presence as a contributor and editor around the Internet.

DAVID JAMES KEATON'S fiction has appeared in over fifty publications. He won a Best Short Story on the Web Spinetingler Award for his contribution to *Crime Factory #8*, and his collection *Fish Bites Cop! Stories To Bash Authorities* (Comet Press) was released May 2013. He lived next to a crazy guy who swore he was in Three Dog Night, even though that would make it Four Dog Night.

NIK KORPON is the author of *Old Ghosts*, *By the Nails of the Warpriest*, *Stay God* and *Bar Scars: Stories*. His work has appeared in *Yellow Mama*, *Needle Magazine*, *Shotgun Honey*, *Beat to a Pulp* and a bunch more. He lives in Baltimore. Give him some danger, little stranger, at nikkorpon.com

BOB PASTORELLA lives in Southeast Texas. He's the author of *To Watch Is Madness*, and has been featured in *Warmed and Bound: A Velvet Anthology*, and *In Search of A City: Los Angeles in 1000 Words*. A staff writer for *ManArchy Magazine*, Bob has had short fiction featured in numerous publications and is currently writing a Horror/Crime novel.

CAMERON PIERCE is the Wonderland Book Award-winning author of eight books, most recently *Die You Doughnut Bastards* (Eraserhead Press, 2012), and the editor of three anthologies, including *The Best Bizarro Fiction of the Decade*. He is also the head editor of *Lazy Fascist Press*. He lives in Portland, Oregon, with his wife.

MARK RAPACZ is the author of the dime-store novel *Buffalo Bill in the Gallery of the Machines*. His short stories have appeared in a number of publications, including *Water~Stone Review*, *Southern Humanities Review*, and *Martian Lit*. In 2010 he received the Pushcart Prize's special mention distinction and recently was published in the 2012 edition of *Best American Nonrequired Reading*. He and his wife currently live in the Bay Area, where he works at Stanford University and continues to write stories.

CALEB J ROSS has been published widely. He is the author of *Charactered Pieces: stories, Stranger Will: a novel, I Didn't Mean to Be Kevin: a novel, Murmurs: Gathered Stories Vol. One*, and *As a Machine and Parts*. Visit: official page: www.calebjross.com, YouTube channel: calebjross.com/youtube, Twitter: calebjross.com/twitter, Facebook: calebjross.com/facebook, Google+: calebjross.com/google

AXEL TAIARI is a French writer, born in Paris in 1984. His writing has appeared in multiple magazines and anthologies, including *3:AM Magazine, 365tomorrows, Solarcide, No Colony*, and many more. His e-novelette *A Light To Starve By* spent a few weeks in Amazon's Kindle Best Sellers list. Read more at www.axeltaiari.com. You can also stalk him on Twitter, @axeltaiari

RICHARD THOMAS is the author of three books—*Transubstantiate, Herniated Roots*, and *Staring Into the Abyss*. He has published 75 stories, including placement in *Shivers VI* (Cemetery Dance), *PANK, Gargoyle, Weird Fiction Review, Pear Noir!*, and *Opium*. He also writes for *The Nervous Breakdown* and *LitReactor*. His agent is Paula Munier at TalcottNotch.

PAUL TREMBLAY is the author of two narcoleptic private detective novels *The Little Sleep* and *No Sleep Till Wonderland*, and the novel *Swallowing A Donkey's Eye*. He also wrote the short story collection *In the Mean Time*. His essays and short fiction have appeared in *The Los Angeles Times, Weird Tales, Clarkesworld*, and *Year's Best American Fantasy 3*. He is the co-editor of four anthologies including *Creatures: Thirty Years Of Monster Stories* (with John Langan). He is also on the board of directors for the Shirley Jackson Awards. www.paultremblay.net

FRED VENTURINI grew up in Patoka, Illinois, where he survived being lit on fire by a bully, a neck-breaking car accident, and being chewed up by a pit bull. His first novel, *The Samaritan*, was published by Blank Slate Press in 2010. His fiction has appeared in places like *River Styx*, *The Death Panel*, *Sick Things*, *Noir at the Bar 2*, *Johnny America*, and *Necrotic Tissue*. He lives in Southern Illinois with his wife, Krissy, and their new daughter, Noelle Marie.

CRAIG WALLWORK lives in West Yorkshire, England. He is the author of the short story collection *Quintessence of Dust* (KUBOA), and the novels *To Die Upon a Kiss* (Snubnose Press) and *The Sound of Loneliness* (Perfect Edge Books). His fiction has appeared in various anthologies, journals and magazines. He is the fiction editor at *Menacing Hedge Magazine*.

PUBLISHERS

PELA VIA is a writer and editor from the US West Coast. Editor in Chief of *ManArchy Magazine,* she edits for Perfect Edge Books, *Word Riot* and others, and in 2011 she compiled and edited the *Warmed and Bound* anthology. She has two sons and is married to a scientist.

ROBB OLSON is an avid reader, a sometimes writer, and an all-the-time co-host of Booked. He is also a contributing writer at *ManArchy Magazine.* When he's not editing audio and mooching wifi at a coffee shop, Robb is probably burying his nose in a book (at a coffee shop).

LIVIUS NEDIN is arguably the cynical member of the Booked team. He has tried his hand at writing and decided he's a far better critic than scribe. Between various TV shows, he manages to enjoy a wide variety of fiction but loves noir, the strange, and the original. Booked is his first podcast.

media

SPECIAL THANKS TO SEAN FERGUSON.
Sean is mentioned in nearly every episode of Booked. He has appeared as a guest reviewer on multiple occasions and was a great help in making this anthology a reality. Booked loves Sean probably a little more than we should. We have heard the words "restraining order" on more than one occasion, but we assume it means he wants to prevent us from getting too far away. That's how those work, right?

Listen to the podcast
at BookedPodcast.com

CPSIA information can be obtained at www.ICGtesting.com
Printed in the USA
LVOW08s1639101113

360699LV00003B/168/P